UNBRIDLED DREAMER

Hemingway and the Rise of Modern Literature

Volume 1

WYLIE GRAHAM MCLALLEN

OXFORD SOUTHERN

an imprint of Sunbury Press, Inc.
Mechanicsburg, PA USA

an imprint of Sunbury Press, Inc.
Mechanicsburg, PA USA

For information about special discounts for bulk purchases, please contact Sunbury Press Orders Dept. at (855) 338-8359 or orders@sunburypress.com.

To request one of our authors for speaking engagements or book signings, please contact Sunbury Press Publicity Dept. at publicity@sunburypress.com.

FIRST OXFORD SOUTHERN EDITION: April 2021

Set in Adobe Garamond | Interior design by Crystal Devine | Cover by Terry Kennedy | Edited by Jennifer Cappello.

Publisher's Cataloging-in-Publication Data
Names: McLallen, Wylie Graham, author.
Title: Unbridled dreamer / Wylie Graham McLallen.
Description: First trade paperback edition. | Mechanicsburg, PA : Oxford Southern, 2021.
Summary: The early years of Ernest Hemingway's career are covered, including his travels to Europe, in this first part of a two volume set.
Identifiers: ISBN : 978-1-62006-527-3 (softcover).
Subjects: BIOGRAPHY & AUTOBIOGRAPHY / Literary Figures | BIOGRAPHY & AUTO-BIOGRAPHY / Adventurers & Explorers | BIOGRAPHY & AUTOBIOGRAPHY / Rich & Famous.

Product of the United States of America
0 1 1 2 3 5 8 13 21 34 55

Continue the Enlightenment!

To Nickey Bayne McLallen

CONTENTS

ACKNOWLEDGMENTS

NO ONE really does anything by themselves; there are always other people involved in many ways. I would like to give thanks to the staff at the main branch of the Vancouver Public Library; they were always courteous and helpful, often searching for and finding obscure books in the stacks. I would like to thank Angela Hemingway, the widow of Jack Hemingway, who quickly and graciously granted me access to copyright material in the Hemingway Collection at the JFK Library in Boston, and also express my gratitude to Maryrose Grossman, an archivist of the Hemingway Collection at the JFK Library in Boston, who was courteous and interested and always quick to respond to my requests when we spoke on the phone. I give special thanks to Valerie Hemingway, who during the time I was conceiving this project, not yet even sure if I would do it, generously responded in detail to many emails I sent that were full of questions about Ernest Hemingway and the people he knew in Paris: in his last years, Valerie was a close assistant to Hemingway, an unforgettable man by all accounts. Don Stewart of McLeod's Books in downtown Vancouver was always helpful and encouraging, setting aside books crucial to my research and even providing for purchase an authentic copy of the *Transatlantic Review*, which published Hemingway's first stories. My older brother Lyman, a teacher whose love of literature is perhaps even keener than mine, also made contributions in his own special way. I thank Bill Ellis, an English professor at Simon Fraser University in Vancouver (and a true modern despite his love of nineteenth-century literature), who provided outstanding editing advice from time to time and whose friendship was always encouraging. There's the creative team of Sunbury Press: Terry Kennedy, Joe Walters, Crystal Devine, and Senior Editor Jennifer Cappello (who put many hours into the project): who care about their authors and help bring their books to life. And, lastly, but not least, to my family for their understanding and all the undisturbed hours of concentration.

A FOREWORD TO HEMINGWAY

THROUGH NEARLY all of his years as a young man in Paris, Ernest Hemingway was a fiction writer with a small audience of little reviews and limited print editions that published stories and books on a coterie basis. This changed in the fall of 1926 when Charles Scribner's Sons published *The Sun Also Rises* to great acclaim by the most discerning reviewers in America. The first few printings sold out quickly; the book was read by thousands and continued to sell through many more editions. Hemingway's writing style and the material of his stories were those of the "modern movement," and with the success of his novel, the modern movement took flight and changed the landscape of literature. He did not invent the modern movement, however; its literary threads can be traced to almost the year of his birth and were well in place by the time he reached Paris. But through the clear prose of his vivid storytelling, prose fashioned through the strict discipline of the greatest writers of the era, the modern influence became so pervasive that the brutal truths he learned to portray in his fiction stretched far enough to be a harbinger to the film art of the Coen Brothers and Martin Scorsese.

The magnitude of the change is comparable to what Elvis Presley would do in music almost thirty years later. Both men were young, intense, creative individuals, and a magnet to other people. As was modernism when Hemingway wrote his stories in Paris, Rock 'n' Roll was well in place when Elvis began recording songs in Memphis, its threads growing from different genres, and like that of the modern movement, were reactionary expressions to current forms of art and rigid social rules. And as Hemingway understood the modern movement and through its precepts was able to write "Indian Camp," "Soldier's Home," and "The Doctor and the Doctor's Wife," so, too, did Elvis understand the undercurrents of Rock 'n' Roll, and immerse himself deeply into it, and out came "Hound Dog," "Blue Suede Shoes," and "Don't Be Cruel"—again, not giving birth, but bursting forth from its roots and rocking the world with a new form of the art that had been incubating for years. Both men worked obsessively at their craft, and as Elvis would open a wide door for many people and ideas to pass through, so, too, did Hemingway with his writing.

Ernest Hemingway was born into a large family at the turn of the century in the small town of Oak Park, Illinois, hard-pressed by the boundaries of the gargantuan Midwestern metropolis, Chicago. His father was an obstetrician, and his mother taught music and was an ebullient, vivacious community leader. In summer, the family would take leave of Oak Park and Chicago to live in the near-wild countryside of northern Michigan at their cottage on Walloon Lake. These were undisturbed, peaceful times precious to the Hemingway family. Growing up, young Ernest's values were those of his parents and the conservative small-town community in which they lived: values of which he saw the seams, the hypocrisy of the bright public presentation versus the private reality that was often sordid. He drew away from these values as he edged into manhood, but never could he completely discard them, just as he could never completely discard his Victorian Age parents—whom he both loved and hated—nor could he discard the formal Protestant religion in which he and his siblings were raised. Dr. Hemingway was a serious, strict, and competent man, who drilled in his children the correct way of doing something; Grace, a brilliant and expansive person, brought out the artist in them. Ernest was not a prayerful person, nor very gentle, but was sensitive and searched for meaning in life—a life he almost lost when blown up in a trench on the Italian front in World War I.

It was in the autumn of 1917 when the life of Ernest Hemingway forever veered from boyhood. The Hemingways were an educated family and his parents wanted their eldest son to attend college, but he opted instead to work as a reporter for the *Kansas City Star*, where he immediately distinguished himself with his energy and grasp of the essentials of newspaper writing. But America had entered the war that was raging in Europe and the idea of such an adventure as war was one that Ernest could never turn down. He enlisted in the Red Cross as an ambulance driver and in the early summer of 1918 was assigned to the Allied front along the Dolomites in Northern Italy, where on a hot July night a canister, lobbed across the Piave River, exploded in the small dugout where Ernest was distributing chocolate. He was found barely alive and was lucky to have survived, and he knew it. When he returned home, after facing his own mortality and all he had seen in Europe, life in Oak Park was too restrictive and he could no longer live there. But he still had the summers in Michigan fishing for trout on wilderness streams. They were the most perfect part of his life, and at the age of twenty-one, when he returned from his last full summer in Michigan, he did not return to Oak Park but to Chicago to live with friends—and he wasn't satisfied there either.

Hemingway knew what he wanted to do: he wanted to marry, return to Europe, and concentrate on writing fiction. His mother once said that the best things he ever wrote were the essays, articles, and stories from when he was a student at Oak Park High, and they were excellent for a high school student. But as Hemingway grew into manhood and began his search for the right métier, it was when he briefly settled in Chicago in the fall of 1920 that he would find the right people to help guide him in his efforts. There he met the much older Sherwood Anderson, an innovative writer who was a leader in the modern movement. Anderson told him to go to Paris, that that was where a writer could write best. He would also find a beautiful older woman from St. Louis named Hadley Richardson who would capture his heart above all others. He would share his vision with this new and enticing woman and together they would plunge into his dream completely, crossing the Atlantic on an old steamer to France where they would live in cheap cold-water flats in Paris as he learned his craft in a Spartan meticulous effort. He would find his vocation in Paris under the tutelage of Gertrude Stein and Ezra Pound, shaping his own thinking and labor. And when Hemingway emerged from that labor, going further than he ever thought he would, he would change the world as only a few are ever able.

BOYHOOD

THEODORE ROOSEVELT did not remake the United States, but he gave the country a more vigorous and heroic concept of itself, which was a strong influence on American children, especially boys, born near the dawn of the twentieth century. This scholar, rancher, soldier, explorer, athlete, naturalist, and contemplative writer who was president in the early years of the century advocated "the strenuous life"[1] and believed that moral and physical courage were the underpinnings of a self-reliance so necessary, per Roosevelt, to the American character. He advised parents to "bring up their children not to shirk difficulties, but to meet them and overcome them,"[2] and encouraged in America's youth the need for "rougher, manlier virtues" and that "a coward who will take a blow without returning it is a contemptible creature."[3] After he was president, in the years before America entered the First World War, his exploits as a big game hunter in Africa, trekking across the Dark Continent with a large contingent from Mombasa into the Congo, were shown in newsreels at the movies on Saturday afternoons with the lions, leopards, water buffalo, and elephants he shot dead beside him as he stood or crouched in a determined pose.

Ernest Hemingway absorbed many of the president's ideas and interests. There is a picture of him as a boy of ten, standing with his large family and many of their friends by steps outside their house, dressed like Theodore Roosevelt on safari. Like Roosevelt, Hemingway became

---

1. Joshua David Hawley, *Theodore Roosevelt, Preacher of Righteousness*, 113.
2. Roosevelt, *The Strenuous Life*, 160.
3. Roosevelt, 282.

a force of concentrated energy nearly always seeking a center of activity and adventure. And like the president, too, he was contemplative and would reinvent himself throughout his life, wearing the mask of masculinity, sometimes naturally, at other times with difficult effort. He read illustrated articles by the president that appeared in *National Geographic* and *Century* magazines and devoured the books Roosevelt wrote about history, nature, and hunting. But, in time, he did not particularly like the effusive way they were written and eventually concluded he could do better. This boy would grow up to become one of the foremost writers America has ever produced and change the landscape of literature and prose by writing his stories and memories in a tight, clear, declarative style that he mostly developed as a young man in Paris—though the process had started soon after his birth.

Ernest Miller Hemingway did not come from a family of professional writers. Though his father was a doctor and his mother taught music, all in his family, especially his mother, could write very well, and reading and writing were strongly encouraged throughout his childhood and adolescence. He was born and raised in Oak Park, Illinois, an affluent village just west of Chicago, at the turn of the twentieth century. Like most small towns in America then, the streets were unpaved and lit by gas lamps. Hemingway's father, an obstetrician, made his rounds in a horse and buggy. Oak Park was described as "the place where saloons end and the churches begin,"[4] and was deliberately insulated from the gross goliath industrialized city, where just a few miles away teeming multitudes with hardly pronounceable names, mostly from Eastern Europe, lived and labored in such a ghastly poor environment that upon reading *The Jungle*, Upton Sinclair's novel about the meatpacking plants by the stockyards, President Roosevelt was shocked into initiating legislation to provide more sanitary working conditions throughout the country. Oak Park, with its vocal preachers and wealthy gentry, would have none of that crime and poverty: they would let the world in, but only on their own proper terms.

---

4. Leicester Hemingway, *My Brother: Ernest Hemingway*, 21.

Both grandfathers were Union veterans of the Civil War who had become prosperous businessmen in Chicago and settled beyond it into a quiet neighborhood of trees and lawns and large houses in Oak Park and raised families living across the street from each other on North Oak Park Avenue. Ernest's mother and father, Grace Hall and Clarence Edmonds Hemingway, knew each other almost from childhood, graduating from Oak Park High School almost together, Clarence in the class of 1889 and Grace the following year. Both had kind of a wanderlust and ambitiously left to pursue individual careers before returning to Oak Park to marry and move in with Grace's widowed father, Ernest Hall, and raise a large family of their own.

Ed Hemingway was a tall, handsome, physically robust man with dark brown hair and eyes so extraordinarily far-sighted that he could observe and identify individual animals on a distant hillside. He had a sharp, beaked nose, wore a dark full beard, and loved to hunt and fish. As a youth, he once spent three months with Sioux Indians in South Dakota absorbing nature lore and gaining an admiration for their ways. While a medical student, he signed on as a cook one summer with a government surveying party in the Great Smoky Mountains of North Carolina and astonished his fellows with a blackberry pie sweetened with wild honey, having rolled the crust on a pegged log with an empty beer bottle and baked by a campfire next to a pot of squirrel stew. He loved the outdoors and would make it a part of his children's lives too. After obtaining his medical degree from Rush Medical College, he spent a year in Scotland as an intern at the University of Edinburgh and wrote to Grace, who also traveled overseas, about his experiences.

Grace branched away from the norm of the village. A beautiful, assertive, large, buxom young woman with blue eyes, fair skin, and a fine contralto voice, she could never fit into any assumed situation or designated position. She studied music, and after her mother died, went to New York to sing opera, even appearing on the stage of Madison Square Garden. However, her eyes were acutely sensitive to light, and the glare of footlights was too much to bear. She soon went abroad with her father and traveled through Europe, returning to the Midwest village of Oak Park to marry the young, competent doctor in the fall of 1896. Ed Hemingway longed to be a medical missionary like his brother Willoughby, but Grace, who had longed to be on the world's great stages, would not have it, and they stayed in Oak Park and raised their family in a particular manner.

The large Queen Anne house of Ernest Hall had an awning porch that wrapped around the front and a round turret with a cupola. On the top floor of the turret the doctor kept his coins and stamps and arrowheads and all his wildlife specimens, stuffed or preserved in bottles, collected on shelves. The first children were born in a front bedroom: Marcelline in January 1898; then Ernest on July 21, 1899, a hot, bright summer day, with his mother writing, "the robins sang their sweetest songs to welcome the little stranger into this beautiful world."[5] The son was a sturdy little boy who loved picture books and nursery rhymes; his voice was noticeably masculine from the first sounds he uttered. "When asked what he is afraid of," wrote Grace, "he shouts out *fraid a nothing* with great gusto,"[6] and he liked to play at being a soldier, even memorizing parts of Tennyson's "Charge of the Light Brigade." As a baby, Grace dressed Ernie in dresses like his older sister, Marcelline (not too unusual at the time), and let his hair grow long. Another daughter, Ursula, was born in 1902; then in November 1904 came Madelaine, whom they called "Sunny" after a character on a cereal box. Ernest remembered the birth of Sunny: riding in the carriage with his father that morning, he was disappointed because he had wanted a brother.

When Grandfather Hall died in 1905, Grace used her inheritance to buy the corner property a few blocks north on Kenilworth Avenue and build a new home, which she designed in collaboration with an architect. It was a large gray rectangular stucco house with an extended porch on the narrow end facing the street and gabled windows projecting from the slanting roof of the third floor. There were eight bedrooms and a huge music room with a fifteen-foot ceiling and a balcony. Grace used the music room to give voice lessons and recitals to the children of Oak Park;

---

5. Grace Hall Hemingway, scrapbooks.
6. GHH, scrapbooks. / "fraid" [sic].

it was much bigger than the two rooms the doctor used as his office on the first floor. Two more children would be born to the family: Carol at the cottage on Walloon Lake in Michigan in the summer of 1911, and Leicester in a bedroom at the home on Kenilworth in 1915. Nearly all the children's names were from Grace's side of the family. Ernest was named after his grandfather Hall and a great-grandfather named Miller.

The parents gave the Hemingway children special gifts. They learned about music and arts from their mother, and from their father, knowledge of animals and nature and exact methods of doing things. Grace was extravagant and gifted; all the children grew up with the sound of her lovely voice. The doctor was firm and serious, more constrained, and sometimes used a razor strop to enforce the rules. Keeping her independence, Grace was active in town affairs, particularly cultural events and women's suffrage; women voted on local issues in Oak Park long before the rest of the nation, and Grace's voice was one of the strongest heard. She also ran the choir at the Third Congregational Church. The music lessons she gave to children of the village, including her own, created an income sometimes greater than that of Dr. Hemingway, who, in addition to obstetrics, had a good general practice. The doctor was an excellent cook who liked to clean and buy groceries and can his own food. His wife did not bother with housework; young live-in German women were hired for that work. The Hemingways were not wealthy, as many families in Oak Park were, but were well thought of in the village as a family of integrity.

In the late summer in the weeks after Ernest's birth, the family made their first long journey to the wilderness of the northern woods of Michigan where the doctor had bought property from a farmer named Bacon and built a cottage on the north shore of Walloon Lake. They took the train into Chicago and boarded a steamer at the pier on Lake Michigan, traveling more than a full day all the way up to Harbor Springs on Little Traverse Bay where they boarded a train south along the curving tracks by the bay to Petoskey, then took a small branch line to the foot of the lake and rowed to their property. Every year thereafter they would travel to northern Michigan to spend the summer. Dr. Hemingway was meticulous in leading the preparations, packing into trunks and boxes for transport sugar, flour, tents, utensils, and all the clothing and blankets the family would need.

Grace named their cottage Windemere after a lake in her ancestral England. The cabin was built facing southwest across the shimmering water near the bottom of a grassy hill and had a large living room with a huge fireplace, two small bedrooms, a tiny kitchen with a wood stove and hand pump for water, and an outhouse among pines up the slope. There was a stretch of sandy beach where the water was shallow and driftwood and logs that broke from a sawmill boom collected along the shore. The driftwood was cleared and burned for fuel, and sometimes the doctor hired Dick Boulton and Billy Tabeshaw, muscular Ojibway Indians who lived in the woods nearby, to cut up the logs for firewood. The family swam and bathed and washed their clothes in the blue water. Across the lake were low green hills and, in the evening, pastel sunsets.

The summers were special times for the Hemingways. The northern woods of Michigan were a place of water and wood and feasts and fishing where they all relaxed, and beyond the necessary chores, did what they wanted to do. Far away from the village of Oak Park and the great modern city of Chicago where life quickened at an accelerating pace, they lived like pioneers growing their own vegetables, catching fish, and roasting pigs on a spit across an open fire. The only roads were sandy swaths over the low hills. Lake neighbors quickly became precious friends. The children called the old farmer who had sold them their land, and still owned all the land behind them, "Grandpa Bacon," and he provided them with fresh milk and eggs and treated them like they were his own. Walloon was where the doctor's perception asserted itself: he liked the cool country and primitive life and often gave his services at no charge to people around the lake, including the Indians. Even Grace was enchanted, composing a waltz called "Lovely Walloona" which was a hit within the family, and shared the domestic chores of cooking and cleaning and washing clothes in the lake with her husband. Under the watchful eye of the doctor, the children learned to fish and swim, and, in time, clean and fire a gun. They helped with the maintenance and cleaning of the cottage and grounds, raking the beach in the morning and getting the milk and chickens from Grandpa Bacon.

They soon bought more property across the lake, forty acres on a sloping hill renamed Longfield Farm, where Ed, who loved manual labor, planted orchards and vegetable patches; the children would come and play and work here, too. At Longfield, as a young boy, Ernest became friends with an older boy named Wesley Dilworth, whose family lived two miles across the ridge on Lake Charlevoix at Horton Bay, which was a cluster of buildings and houses with a small Methodist church. Wesley's mother, Liz, whom the Hemingway children called Aunty Beth, owned a chicken-dinner restaurant called Pinehurst Cottage, which overlooked the lake; his father, Jim, was a blacksmith. During clear summer days, the bay was blue and breezy and the hillside was cool and shady and smelled of pine needles and sandy loam; ore barges traveled the water, and sometimes the wind would blow hard from Lake Michigan. Horton Bay became almost as familiar to Ernest as Windemere and Walloon Lake.

Ernest and his father were close these years. They would camp and hunt in the woods and spend whole days fishing together. The lake had trout, pike, perch, and bass, and they would go off in the boat to fish or troll around the old sawmill pilings. The doctor was strict and exact in his instructions, teaching Ernest how to tie wet and dry flies, to bait a hook and cast a fly, to use an ax and build a shelter of hemlock boughs, to make fires and prepare game and fish for the frying pan. The closeness with his father and nature continued in Oak Park, where his father had founded the local branch of the Agassiz Club, a boys' group dedicated to the study of nature. On Saturdays in the spring, Ernest tromped the banks of the nearby Des Plaines River with the older boys and Dr. Hemingway, gathering specimens of frogs and salamanders and identifying birds and plants by their Latin names—and, like Roosevelt, learning the rudiments of taxidermy. The doctor with his great eyesight and reflexes was a marvelous wing shot and taught his son to be so too. When Ernest turned twelve, his grandfather gave him a 20-gauge shotgun and, in the fall, he and his father went on a hunting trip together down to the farms of Ed's older sister, Aunt Nettie, and brother-in-law, Uncle Frank

Hines, in southern Illinois, where they shot quail and small game among wheat and corn fields near the Indiana and Kentucky borders.

But Ed Hemingway was a nervous man and sometimes absurdly strict, even by the standards of Oak Park at the time. He was always busy, and any idleness or procrastination among his children made him snap with sharp words and harsh scolding. His children never had any money; the doctor had been raised with frugality and gave them pennies for an allowance. In the summers they could supplement their meager allowance with small payments for picking fruits and vegetables at Longfield Farm. One summer when Ernest was older, a friend visited from Oak Park and they pitched a tent at Longfield, tended and harvested the garden, and took the motorboat and peddled the potatoes, beans, carrots, peas, and rutabagas to the cottages and small hotels around the lake. During the school year, their father forbade any recreation on Sundays; church attendance was mandatory, and punishments could be swift and hard: first, there was the razor strop and then the child had to kneel and ask forgiveness from God. The doctor was not abusive in punishment, but always it was there.

Ed Hemingway was predisposed to emotional stress, suffering from anxiety and depression, which worsened through the years. As time went on, Dr. Hemingway became more detached, spending more time working and less time at the lake in the summer. Even the Agassiz Club was dropped, and the close relationship he had with his oldest son began to evaporate. As the father dropped away, the son could only look back in longing and remember when it had been so good between them. Ernest Hemingway, years later as an adult in the story, "Fathers and Sons," would write,

> Like all men with a faculty that surpasses human requirements, his father was very nervous. Then, too, he was sentimental, and, like most sentimental people, he was both cruel and abused . . . when Nick was a boy . . . he was very grateful to him for two things: fishing and shooting . . . Nick had loved him very much and for a long time.[7]

---

7. Ernest Hemingway, *The Complete Short Stories*, 370.

If the father's detachment created a void, the mother was more than ready to fill it. Grace Hemingway was creative and fanciful, consuming the air around her. She dressed lavishly in long gowns and big hats with ostrich feathers, laughed a great laughter that shook her enormous breasts, and took notice of everyone around her as everyone around her took notice of her. She was not so strict as the doctor but prodded her children into creativity by having them sing in her church choir, where Ernest could hardly carry a tune; and practice music, as Ernest played the cello but never progressed past sawing; and sent them to the Chicago Opera, which Ernest enjoyed, and the Art Institute to look at the paintings, which he came to love. She could be overbearing; when Ernest was assigned to read Jack London's *Call of the Wild* at Oak Park High, she went before the school board and complained that such a book should not be read by Christian gentlemen. As Grace grew older, she put on weight, wore glasses, and tied her whitening hair above her head.

There would be conflict between Ernest and his mother. Ernest would blame his father's declining influence in the family upon his mother's expansive personality. This was not true. Twice the doctor took off from work to go down to New Orleans alone; the second time followed a course he took in obstetrics in New York. These were nervous breakdowns, which the mother dealt with discreetly. Grace did not want people in Oak Park to know about her husband's nervous condition and wrote him,

> Do you want me to let the local press know about this vacation? Don't you think it perhaps wise to let them keep the first idea in their minds that you are taking 'post-grad' work in New York? . . . Try to forget about us while you are on board ship and rest the worry place in your brain. Just make a business of eating and sleeping and forgetting.[8]

When Marcelline and Ernest entered high school together (Marcelline had been held back a year so that she and Ernest could go through

---

8. GHH to CEH, Oct. 17, 1908, Research Center, Texas University.

school together), each parent did their best. It was an exciting time. The streets had been paved, the doctor now had a Ford Model T, and electricity coursed through the town. Oak Park and River Forest High School, a palatial brick structure several blocks south on Scoville Avenue, was an easy morning and afternoon walk along sidewalks through elm-shaded streets. When they began high school, walking the streets together, Marcelline was taller than Ernest by almost a head, and he was sensitive about his lack of height. They were both good students, having been disciplined to do their work at home, and each did well from the start. Ernest often excelled in studies and began reading a lot more, borrowing books from the Scoville Institute, the public library a few blocks away. He liked reading best of all and read books by Horatio Alger, Rudyard Kipling, and Stuart Edward White, who wrote stories of the American West and explorations to Hudson Bay. In the summer, Ernest devoured the stories in the bound volumes of *St. Nicholas* and *Harper's* magazines his parents kept at the lake, reading Richard Harding Davis and Stephen Crane. His imagination was active: after reading Bram Stoker's *Dracula*, he howled in the night with nightmares.

Between his freshman and sophomore years, Ernest began to grow: reaching almost six feet, he became large, had big feet, and looked older than he was. He loved sports and developed strong competitive instincts, taking up boxing and football. Ernest boxed neighborhood boys using his mother's music room as an arena, which was all right unless the matches degenerated into fights, and he played a clumsy lineman on the football team, his father on occasion accompanying the boys on road trips. But his real facility was intellectual: this was where his intense curiosity came most into play, and he would read, listen astutely, and absorb ideas, methods, and conduct very well. His teachers took an interest, and he began to write in earnest, showing a good grasp of syntax and displaying an acute proclivity for catching and phrasing the slang of the street. Much like his mother, he loved to be noticed in public performance, and his public performances were in print. The short fiction he wrote began appearing in the *Tabula*, the literary magazine of Oak Park High. He also wrote remarkable imitations of Ring Lardner in the pages of the school's weekly newspaper, the *Trapeze*.

Some of his stories in the *Tabula* were quite good for juvenilia, and the themes would be revisited in his mature fiction. "A Matter of Color" is a humorous tale about a fixed boxing match between a black man and a white man that goes awry because the Swede hiding behind the curtain on one side of the ring is color blind and knocks out the wrong man. "Mister Armstrong," said the Swede at the end, "I bane color blind."[9] Another story called "The Judgement of Manitou," set in the northern woods, is about an Indian named Pierre who, mistakenly believing his partner stole his wallet, sets a trap along a trail, and, when he discovers the thief was a squirrel, rushes back to rescue his partner but finds wolves have already killed him; in shock, he steps into a bear trap and reaches for his rifle to save the wolves the trouble of killing him too.

In the summers as he grew older, Ernest began to show more independence from the rest of his family. In June of 1915, he and Lew Clarahan packed up early and noisily took the steamer up Lake Michigan and disembarked at Frankfort on a hundred-mile hike to Windemere—fishing, talking, singing, and shouting, and eating trout and canned beans along the way—to take down the shutters and clean the outhouse and prepare the cottage for summer occupancy. They then pitched their tent at Longfield Farm, where Ernest looked after the garden and prepared chickens for the oven when needed by his mother. This was the summer Ernest impulsively shot a blue heron and lied when the game warden approached him, saying someone had given it to him, and then fled to Windemere where he told his mother the truth, and rowing a boat across the lake to Longfield, went into hiding. When game wardens came to the cottage looking for him, Grace, a formidable woman who could turn fierce, met them at the door, scolded them, and ran them off the property. The game wardens stayed away; Ernest paid the fine at his father's discretion. Hemingway would brag about trouble with the law, but, in fact, in a personal way, such encounters frightened him. He liked to stay beyond the law and would often create his own domains.

---

9. *Tabula*, April 1916, Oak Park High School.

He and Lew made the same trip the following year, but this time they set out earlier, were better equipped, and took a longer, more leisurely route. They walked along railroad tracks, camped by stream banks, and fished with rods, pulling up trout from the waters. Taking a train to Kalkaska, from there they hiked to a river where they fished a pool below a small power plant, and while Lew slept, Ernest fished through the night and kept adding trout to the pile in a basket. Back in town, they ate dinner in a lumberjack joint. Lew then departed, catching a southbound train for Chicago, and Ernest went on alone to the "rough burg" of Mancelona, where he waited in the depot for the train to Petoskey, spending the time watching an Indian girl and talking to a lumberjack. Something about the scene moved him and he made notes thinking somehow there might be a story here.

From Petoskey he hiked to Horton Bay, where he stayed with the Dilworths, fished in the creek, and came to better know a brother and sister named Bill and Katy Smith from St. Louis, Missouri, who spent their summers with their aunt, Mrs. Charles, who had a farm nearby. Katy and Bill were older than Ernest, Bill was 21 and Katy was 25, but he liked them very much, especially the sister, who was a slim, attractive, outspoken girl with arresting green eyes. Katy would tell Ernest that his fingernails were dirty, which, in fact, they often were. When his family arrived in July, he asserted his independence even more, pitching a tent in the yard behind Windemere, setting up a camp at Murphy's Point up the coast of the lake, and spending more time at Horton Bay with the Smiths. He began to conceal his emotions from his parents and may have had a fling with the daughter of the half-Indian Dick Boulton, a pretty girl named Prudy. Ernest's younger sisters adored him and vied for his affections, but he and Marcelline, who was looking and acting more like their mother, began drifting apart.

In his senior year at Oak Park High, he played on the varsity football team. He was still very awkward; his feet so big no shoes would fit him, a cobbler put cleats on an old pair of his high-laced shoes. The season went well enough, and, at Ed Hemingway's urging, the coach awarded Ernest a large OP to wear on his sweater. Reading and writing were a lot easier than sports, and young Hemingway became more aware of his talent. His themes were always read aloud in class, and another short story appeared in the *Tabula*; this one, called "Sepi Jingan," was an eponymous tale of a dog belonging to a young Ojibway Indian that ferociously defends his master against an evil killer. Hemingway wrote prolifically for the *Trapeze*, working on an old typewriter in his third-floor bedroom cranking out stories every week. He still used Ring Lardner as a model and could be very funny, (about a swim meet he wrote, "since you have went and ast me to write a story about the swimming meet I will do it because if I didn't you might fire mee off the paper and then I would want to sling the stuff that Perkins the new air line pilot is named after I would have to go and be a military lecturer or something"[10]) but could not quite get underneath the wry vernacular of the master's style. At commencement, he was selected as Class Prophet. Across the ocean a great war was being fought, but in his speech in June 1917, Ernest sidestepped the fact that America had just entered and predicted all classmates would become rich and successful. The valedictorian, a boy named Edward Wagenknecht, was more prophetic, telling the assembly, "America has entered the war and we must enter it with her. The day has come when no nation and no individual can entertain the monastic concept of life."[11]

Upon their graduation, Ernest and Marcelline, who also spoke at commencement, were both given the opportunity to further their formal education. Marcelline opted to attend Oberlin College, where their father and all his siblings had gone. But Ernest, imagining a more strenuous life, wanted something else. His father was against him going to war, and he was too nearsighted to pass the physical anyway. But Dr. Hemingway, always looking out for his children, wrote his brother, Tyler Hemingway, a businessman in Kansas City, about securing a job for Ernest on the *Kansas City Star*. There could be a job there, word came back, but it would not be available until the fall. This was fine with Ernest because summers in Michigan meant so much to him that he dreamed about the fishing and the smell of the pines during the rest of the year. So, he put

10. *Trapeze*, February 1917, Oak Park High School. / "ast" [*sic*], "mee" [*sic*].
11. Senior Tabula, June 1917, Oak Park High School, Valedictorian speech.

off his decision and traveled up to Michigan with his father and mother and baby brother Leicester, this time in the doctor's Model T, plowing through the mudholes of the primitive roads and camping along the way, and, all the sisters soon arriving, spent the summer with his family at the cottage and farm on Walloon Lake, working and fishing and talking to others and deciding to take the job on the newspaper. And when October came and young Ernest Hemingway left Oak Park for Kansas City, the boy inside of him left home for good.

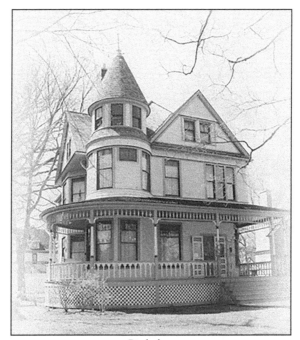

Birthplace

Grace and the doctor with Marcelline and Ernest at Windemere

600 Kenilworth Avenue

Ernie at Walloon

Hoboing to Michigan

High school graduation

The Hemingway family

OF NEWSPAPERS, WAR, AND ROMANCE

IN A story called "Crossing the Mississippi," published posthumously, Hemingway wrote about seeing the great river for the first time:

> The river seemed to move solidly downstream, not to flow but
> to move like a solid, shifting lake, swirling a little where the
> abutments of the bridge jutted out. Mark Twain, Huck Finn,
> Tom Sawyer and LaSalle crowded each other in Nick's mind as he
> looked up the flat, brown plain of slow-moving water. Anyhow
> I've seen the Mississippi, he thought happily to himself.[1]

It was the middle of October 1917: The United States was at war in Europe, the White Sox were playing the New York Giants in the World Series, and Ernest Hemingway had left for Kansas City to take a job as a cub reporter for the *Kansas City Star*. In the morning of the day of his departure, Dr. Hemingway, accompanying Ernest to the old Union Station on the corner of Madison and Canal in Chicago, was emotional at their parting. Late in the afternoon, near Quincy, the train moved into a siding just before the railroad bridge. When it started again a news hawker came swaying down the aisle announcing the White Sox had won the last game of the series. It was a good omen. Young Ernest, elated, sat back reading the *Saturday Evening Post* and glanced out the window at the broad breadth of the Mississippi River.

---

1. Ernest Hemingway, *The Nick Adams Stories*, 13.

In Kansas City, Uncle Tyler met him at Union Station and drove him to a tall Victorian house on Warwick Avenue, a neighborhood of lawns and shade trees much like the streets of Oak Park that Ernest had just left. On the following day, he accompanied his nephew downtown to the Star Building, a large brick building occupying almost an entire city block. Stepping off the elevator onto the second floor, a large open room full of desks and typewriters and noise and people, Tyler Hemingway introduced his nephew to Henry Haskell, an old school chum and graduate of Harvard, who was the chief editorial writer for the *Star*. Haskell passed Ernest onto George Longan, the city editor, who offered him a reporter's job at $15 a week and introduced him to Pete Wellington, the assistant city editor, who showed him an empty desk where Ernest, sitting down with a broad grin on his face, commenced his career as a professional writer. There was much to learn, and starting by reading the newspaper itself, he would absorb very much very quickly.

Kansas City was a growing, sprawling municipality of 300,000. The railroads had brought wealth and continued economic expansion to the city, which, geographically near the center of the country, contained both eastern and western attitudes, and the *Star* was reflective of this vitality and growth, and disparity, too. The editors encouraged its reporters to concentrate on the craft of writing—they had to practically memorize the *Star* Copy Style, a long sheet of rules dedicated to clear, concise writing—and yet write with a creative freedom unhampered by anything except the truth as they saw it happening. Pete Wellington in particular, with his thoroughness and love of language, instilled in the young reporters gathered around him a belief in themselves and even a sense of greatness of purpose. The result was loyalty among the staff and pride for what they did, and for their city, which made the *Star* one of the best newspapers in the country.

Some of the brawling, violent post-Civil War frontier character of Kansas City was still retained in the cheap hotels and barrooms along the dark avenues in the region rife with crime that ran from Union Station down to the stockyards by the Missouri River. This part of Kansas City was rougher than anything the young cub reporter had known in Chicago, and he reveled in its unsavory qualities; though Ernest Hemingway had good parents and a wholesome, peaceful childhood, he was fascinated by the dark, gritty parts of life. Covering fires and crimes and the comings and goings of people, his beats included the 15th Street police station, Union Station, and the General Hospital, which was up on a long hill from the train station. He did not at all mind the footwork and later wrote, "I hit it lucky, because people there liked to see young guys get out and deliver. . . . I used to go out with the ambulances, covering the big hospital. It was just police reporting. But it gave me a chance to learn what the help thought, as well as how they did their jobs."[2]

Soon after arriving, Ernest moved into a boarding house down the street from his uncle and lived there through most of the fall. Many at the newspaper saw him as a large, exuberant boy. Like many Midwestern-ers, there was a w-sound when he pronounced his l's, and he sometimes appeared at the office wearing a buffalo plaid hunting shirt. The editors had difficulty knowing his whereabouts. "When we would put in a call for him at the hospital," remembered Pete Wellington, "we would learn that he had gone out on an ambulance call. He seemed to always want to be wherever the action was."[3] But all were impressed by his enthusi-asm and energy, and under Wellington's supervision, young Hemingway learned to write short declarative sentences, avoid overused adjectives, and develop an interesting narrative style as he applied the precepts of the *Star* Copy Style to the reports he made on his beat. Though he had no byline and the short paragraphs he wrote were mostly items of local color, he took on the air of an older, more experienced man who knew all the inside facts. But he was sensitive, too, once writing a story about a prostitute outside a dancehall weeping because the soldier she loved was inside dancing gaily with the socially acceptable girls.

War news consumed most of the front page of the *Star*'s morning and afternoon editions and much of the space inside. The paper published a series of long dispatches from the French and Italian fronts; first-person accounts full of close observations of the war with attention to detail

---

2. Leicester Hemingway, *My Brother: Ernest Hemingway*, 45.
3. Carlos Baker, *Ernest Hemingway: A Life Story*, 49.

written by a local minister and civic leader named Burris A. Jenkins. "On the Champagne front," Jenkins wrote in one story,

> [W]e stood talking, a group of us, in the offices of a half-destroyed factory upon a hill. The Boche lines were a few kilometers away. We had just been looking down upon them. . . . We had been talking with the manager of the factory about his difficulty in keeping employees. No wonder. Shells come there every day; he pointed out the spot where a man had been killed a few days before in the courtyard.[4]

Jenkins also noted that though the land was covered with shell fragments, the Champagne countryside was still producing grapes. Hemingway may have met Jenkins, for during his first week at the *Star* Jenkins was in town giving a series of lectures about action on the three fronts and his encounters with British, French, American, and Italian soldiers, and Ernest may have attended these lectures at the end of his day in the newsroom.

On October 24, 1917, the *Star*, running the headline "Striking in Italy," told the ominous news of Austro-Hungarian forces, reinforced by German units, breaking the Italian lines in a mountain valley near Caporetto and forcing the disastrous retreat of the Italian army onto the plains north of the Adriatic, where on the tenth of November they were finally able to establish a position along the Piave River and hold it. No doubt Ernest read these reports, fueling his desire to join the action. He soon joined the Missouri Home Guard, was given a woolen uniform and overcoat, and practiced drills and maneuvers. He wrote to his sister Marcelline, "I couldn't face anybody after the war and not have been in it."[5] In December, he moved into a house on Agnes Street to share a room with Carl Edgar, an older friend living and working in Kansas City whom he knew through Bill and Katy Smith from Michigan. They got on well, though Carl complained that Ernest always wanted to talk about

---

4. Burris Jenkins, *Kansas City Star*, October 20, 1917.
5. EH to MHS, Nov. 6, 1917, *The Letters of Ernest Hemingway, Vol. 1.*

"the romance of newspaper work"[6] late into the night when it would have been better for them to sleep.

Ernest was active and engaging at the newspaper and made friends quickly. "He was a big good-natured boy with a ready smile," remembered Pete Wellington, "and he developed a friendship with all those on staff with whom he came in contact."[7] He looked around, asked questions, and listened; used the resources of the paper, particularly the library room; and sometimes spent the night in the pressroom at the Muehlebach Hotel downtown on 12th Street after working late, too tired to make the trip back to Agnes Street. By his own later admission, he was "constantly talking to older writers on the staff about how they got their stories and how they wrote them."[8] His reporting skills improved, and in March 1918, he helped break a story at the hospital about politicians and members of the health board grafting $27,000 from hospital funds.

One of the men at the paper who impressed him the most was an older renegade reporter named Lionel Calhoun Moise, a large, tough man who liked to drink and brawl and who never stayed at any one newspaper for any long length of time. Yet, like Hemingway, Moise could be quiet and observant, and, as Hemingway later remembered, was:

> a great rewrite man. He could carry four stories in his head and go to the telephone and take a fifth and then write all five at full speed to catch an edition. There would be something alive about each one. He was always the highest paid man on every paper he worked on. If any other man was getting more money he either demanded a raise or quit. He never spoke to the other reporters unless he had been drinking. He was tall and thick and had long arms and big hands.[9]

The two men observed each other at a distance. "I saw very little of him because we worked in a different part of town,"[10] wrote Hemingway,

6. Charles Fenton, *The Apprenticeship of Ernest Hemingway*, 36.
7. Fenton, 36.
8. Baker, *Ernest Hemingway: A Life Story*, 49.
9. Baker, *Ernest Hemingway: A Life Story*, 49.
10. EH to Fenton, July 29, 1952, *Ernest Hemingway, Selected Letters*, 774.

who, though he admired Lionel Moise and, too, liked the seedy dives and burlesque theatres along 12th Street the older man frequented, did not care much for his pervasive violence nor how he wasted his prodigious talent. Years later when Ernest was famous and it was suggested that Moise was the most prominent influence on the younger man's journalistic style, the older man objected and wrote, "Like all real writers, he owes his well-deserved eminence not to any 'influence' but to his ability to select from a host of influences—part of that little thing called genius."[11]

It was the younger reporters at the *Star* to whom Ernest drew closest, and some of these friendships were lasting. Charley Hopkins, an assignment editor who always needed a reporter handy, liked him immediately. Ernest called him "Hoopkins," or sometimes "the Hooper," and often covered his extra assignments. Charley was impressed by his abilities and, so Hemingway reported to a high school English teacher, assured him, "Don't let anyone ever say that you were 'taught' writing. It was born in you."[12] Much of Hemingway's innate shyness and diffidence, something he was good at hiding, began to evaporate, too, as for the first time living away from any supervision he began to assert himself more freely—and sometimes aggressively. When a teamster bullied his stocky little friend Leo Fitzpatrick in a cafeteria one night, Ernest threw a haymaker that on the follow-through broke a glass pane on a showcase of cigars. This made Hemingway a kind of hero in the office. Though his behavior was sometimes loud, he was always polite and still struck some of the other fellows as basically shy. As was his penchant, he often gave nicknames but did so with a twinkle in his eye.

His closest friend in Kansas City was a local fellow named Ted Brumback, whose father was a prominent Jackson County judge who had gotten Ted a job on the newspaper soon after Ernest had arrived. When they first met—Ernest importantly handing a story to a copyboy, then quickly welcoming him aboard in a hail-fellow-well-met fashion—he thought Ernest was a seasoned reporter. Ted, who had lost an eye in a golfing accident and could not enlist in the regular service, had driven ambulances

---

11. Fenton, *The Apprenticeship of Ernest Hemingway*, 41.
12. Fenton, 47.

in France as part of the American Field Services and told romantic tales of Europe. Ernest, who had poor eyesight, thought this was a great way to get into the war. By Christmas, he, Ted, and another young reporter named Wilson Hicks made a pact to apply to the Red Cross as ambulance drivers. On Ted's advice, they would wait until the spring when the rain had stopped in Europe and the roads were no longer quagmires. By the end of April, they gave their notice to the newspaper. On a Saturday night before they left, Hemingway invited Brumback to spend the night at his attic apartment. Ernest had a jug of red wine and began reading Browning aloud. Ted dropped off to sleep but awoke at four to hear Ernest still reading and looking very fresh. The next day at work he was as vigorous as ever. It seemed to Ted that Hemingway's boundless energy was a sign of incipient genius, and later he would write, "When the rest of us mortals have finished our work . . . [his] genius was only starting."[13]

Grace and the doctor, pleased with their son and the decisions he had made, and relieved that he would enter the war as a noncombatant, wrote him encouraging letters. "I am proud of you and your success," wrote his father. "Both mother and I loved you devotedly."[14] Ernest would briefly return to Oak Park, but first, before leaving for the war, he wanted some good fishing in Michigan and encouraged his friends from Kansas City to join him. After receiving his final paycheck at the *Kansas City Star*, he boarded the train to Chicago along with Charles Hopkins, Carl Edgar, and Bill Smith, who had been visiting in Kansas City, and arrived in Oak Park early in May. They spent a night with his family in the large house on Kenilworth and left the next day for Horton Bay. Dr. Hemingway agreed to forward the orders from the Red Cross and in a few days sent a telegram to Northern Michigan where Ernest, fishing with his friends near Horton Bay, tromped out of the woods and returned to Chicago where he quickly caught an eastbound train to New York City, Ted Brumback joining him a few days later.

In New York City, the Red Cross put them in the Earle Hotel by Washington Square, and as soldiers about to embark on a war across

---

13. Baker, *Ernest Hemingway: A Life Story*, 52.
14. CEH to EH, April 17, 1918, Hemingway Collection, Kennedy Library.

the seas, he and Brumback, making new friends among their compa-
triots, were entertained in the evenings and chauffeured around during
the day. They went along Riverside Drive from the Harlem River, past
Grant's Tomb to the Upper Bay in view of the Statue of Liberty, to the
Battery and the top of the Woolworth Building, and saw quite a bit of
the city. They passed their physicals—a doctor recommended eyeglasses
for Hemingway, which he ignored—were inoculated against typhoid
and smallpox and given uniforms and equipment, which included a
trunk. Then they spent time in classrooms, becoming indoctrinated
about war conditions and driving and maintaining ambulances. Ernest
embellished his uniform by using money his father had given him to
purchase an expensive pair of cordovan leather boots, which he wore
up and down Broadway. He also embellished his life a bit, writing Dale
Wilson at the *Kansas City Star* that he was having an affair with Mae
Marsh, an actress he had seen in *The Birth of a Nation*, and had bought
her an engagement ring, "but for God's sake don't let it get out amongst
the gang and in the sheet."[15]

When President and Mrs. Wilson came to New York to launch the
city's Red Cross War Fund Drive, Ernest Hemingway was among the
75,000 men and women who paraded down Fifth Avenue in fine sunny
weather on Saturday, May 18, to salute the occasion. Then on the morning of the twenty-third, when an old French Line ship named the *Chicago*
slipped out of the harbor bound for Bordeaux, Hemingway and his fellow soon-to-be ambulance drivers were on board as she steamed south
of the usual sea lanes to avoid German U-boats. The weather was bright
and warm, and the sea was placid and blue the first two days, reminding
Ernest of Walloon Lake. On the third day they ran into a storm, and
the *Chicago* pitched and rolled and swung in wide circles; the dining
rooms emptied and the rails were lined with retching men. When the
sea calmed, he stood on the deck at night watching the phosphorescence
trailing like brands from a campfire. When the ship docked in Bordeaux,
the boys ate a good dinner with wine and hurried onto the night train

---

15. EH to Dale Wilson, May 19, 1918, *The Letters of Ernest Hemingway, Vol. 1.*

to Paris; arriving the next morning, they were quartered in a small hotel near the Madeleine Church.

It was his first time in Europe, and though it was important to see and do as much as possible, in any new place, wherever he was, Ernest Hemingway was never a tourist: like his father, he needed to know and understand things and was robust and physically active (which makes his writing, a sedentary act, all the more impressive); and like his mother, he had a strong, expressive, domineering personality. Paris was under bombardment from a huge long-range siege gun placed seventy-five miles away behind the German lines. The shells came down irregularly with a great noise, frightening the population and tearing apart streets and buildings. Ernest grabbed a taxi and, along with Ted Brumback, pursued the noise of shell bursts through the streets: as they approached their small hotel, one of the huge projectiles came very close and hit the façade of the Madeleine Church, knocking off some of the stone, and that was enough of that. Gathering his companions together—along with Brumback, there was now Howie Jenkins from Chicago and Bill Horne, a graduate of Princeton—they saw Napoleon's tomb, the Arc D' Triomphe, the Tuileries, and other sights of Paris as they waited a few days for a contingent of men to arrive from London and then boarded a train to Italy, moving through the Alps in boxcars, dangling their feet, enthralled by the magnificent mountainous scenery. "Having a wonderful time!" wrote Ernest on a postcard to the *Kansas City Star*.

When they arrived in Milan, Ernest's first real taste of war came quickly as a large munitions factory exploded in the Lombard countryside outside of town. It was afternoon, and when they heard the explosion, Hemingway and others were rushed in trucks along poplar-shaded roads to the scene of destruction to gather the bodies. A fellow volunteer named Milford Baker wrote,

> In the barbed wire fence enclosing the grounds and 300 yards
> from the factory were hung pieces of meat, chunks of heads,
> arms, legs, back, hair and whole torsos. We grabbed a stretcher
> and started to pick up the fragments. The first thing we saw was

the body of a woman, legs gone, head gone, intestines strung out.
Hemmie and I nearly passed out cold, but gritted our teeth and
laid the thing on the stretcher.[16]

Gathering the dead as such, nearly all of whom were women, was
gruesome, shocking work. The fellows talked it over together to give it
perspective and remained ready to go to the front to do the work of driving ambulances. The experience left a deep impression on Hemingway
and would surface years later in a grim story he sardonically wrote, called
"A Natural History of the Dead."

On the plain north of Venice, the Italian front had bogged down into
trench warfare. Then, in the late spring of 1918, an Austro-Hungarian
advance was beaten back in the Battle of the Piave River, and a new line of
defense was established on the west side of the river, which ran south from
the mountains to the Adriatic Sea. Hemingway and his comrades were
posted to Section Four of the American Red Cross ambulance unit in the
village of Schio in the foothills of the Dolomites about four miles from
the front. They were quartered with the officers in a large room lined with
cots on the second floor of an abandoned wool factory that had a paved
courtyard with sheds for the ambulances. For three weeks in June, much
of it during but away from the battle, Ernest Hemingway drove a large,
heavy Fiat Ambulance, gears grinding along high sharp narrow turns up
and down Mount Pasubio, to pick up the wounded and sick at medical
receiving stations to transport them safely to nearby hospitals.

The young American volunteers called their post "The Schio Country Club" because their building was bare and smelled of sheep, but the
farmland and mountain scenery were beautiful and their time off was
spent pleasurably playing baseball and swimming, visiting men in other
units, and eating in the mess hall with the Italian officers where waiters
served spaghetti, rabbit stew, and as much good red wine as one could
drink. There was a good tavern in town where they sometimes drank beer
in the evenings under the spreading vines of wisteria, and the section

16. James R. Mellow, *Hemingway: A Life Without Consequences*, 57.

published a sheet called *Ciao*, to which Ernest contributed one of his Ring Lardner imitations, writing in the form of a letter, "Well Al we are here in this old Italy and now that I am here I am not going to leave it . . ."[17] But he soon became dissatisfied and restless, telling Brumback, "There's nothing here but scenery and too damn much of that. I'm going to get out of this ambulance section and see if I can't find out where the war is."[18]

The opportunity came quickly. When the Austrian offensive failed in the mountains, the work there lessened and men were needed to run emergency canteens set up behind the trenches along the Piave River. When the call came for volunteers from Section Four, Ernest, Howie Jenkins, Bill Horne, and a few others quickly stepped forward. These canteens served as a place for off-duty soldiers to rest, and provided tables, writing material, phonographs and records, and counters that dispensed coffee, soup, cigarettes, and candy. Sometimes, too, after hours, the volunteers would carry cigarettes, chocolate, and postcards to the men on the lines. At the end of June, the volunteers from Section Four were driven to Mestre, a railhead north of Venice, and placed under the command of Jim Gamble, a Yale Graduate from Pennsylvania, who was the inspector of rolling canteens with the honorary rank of captain. Gamble gave his new charges a night pass to Mestre, where, in a brothel named the Villa Rosa, when a prostitute approached Ernest, he became extremely shy and blushed and probably did not go upstairs. The next morning, they were driven to their stations along the Piave front.

Ernest was dropped off at Fossalta, a much-battered village beneath a grassy dike along a sharp bend in the river. The Austrians had advanced upon this plain of the river valley, and during the day across the river the opposing armies exchanged small-arms fire; at night this would often intensify and bursting shells would light up the sky. Ernest's billet was a farmhouse outside of town. At first, there was little to do; canteen supplies had not arrived, and it was hot and full of mosquitoes. Yet he could now glory in proximity to the war: seeing close-up the effects of battle as

---

17. Baker, *Ernest Hemingway: A Life Story*, 59.
18. Baker, 60.

dead were strewn along the road, trees barkless and defoliated, and hearing gunfire and blasts. He took his meals with officers of the Italian 69th and 70th infantry regiments of the Brigate Ancona, and, in the company of men at war, became friends with a young priest named Don Giuseppe Bianchi, a chaplain from Florence who wore a dark-red velvet cross above the left pocket of his tunic.

On the Fourth of July, riding a bicycle up the road to San Pedro Novella, he visited Bill Horne and Warren Pease, spending the night in a rundown building where racks of silkworms fed on mulberry leaves. Pease fell asleep, but Bill and Ernest, listening to the droppings of silkworms as they munched on the mulberry leaves, talked through the night. They confessed their feelings of loneliness and spoke about plans for the future. Bill was bored with the inactivity and soon returned to Schio to drive ambulances, but Ernest stayed on as supplies began to arrive. In the evenings, he loaded his haversack and delivered cigarettes, chocolates, and postcards to soldiers in the trenches nearby. The night of the seventh of July was very warm and moonless as he put on his helmet and haversack, rode his bicycle along the road to the front lines, and ducked into the trenches, keeping low. Soon after midnight, he had moved up beside the river to a forward listening post, a hole in the ground with two other men. The noise of battle began with booming cannons and the crack of rifles. From the far side of the river, they heard a "cough," then a "chuh, chuh, chuh, chuh,"[19] as an Austrian projectile hurtled across, and, descending like a coming freight train into the very confined space where they stood, exploded upon contact.

"There was a flash," Hemingway later wrote, "as when a blast-furnace door is swung open, and a roar that started white and went red and on and on in a rushing wind. I tried to breathe, but my breath would not come and I felt myself rush bodily out of myself. Then I floated, and instead of going on I felt myself slide back. I breathed."[20] His legs were nearly shattered, embedded with over 200 metal fragments, but his life was spared. Upon explosion, of the two men between him and the bomb,

---

19. Hemingway, *A Farewell to Arms*, 54.
20. Hemingway, *A Farewell to Arms*, 54.

one was dead, the other hardly alive. It is not known if Hemingway was carried out of the trench or if he carried the other wounded man out, but he made it out and lost consciousness. Through the rest of the long night, in and out of consciousness at a dressing station, immobile and in pain, his legs felt as if he had been stung by a thousand hornets. Surrounded by so many dead and dying, there were probably moments when he felt like he wanted to die too. Near dawn, an ambulance took him to a field hospital where he was given morphine and a tetanus shot and surgeons removed some of the bigger fragments from his legs. Jim Gamble came to see him there, crouching by his side, speaking to him kindly, and continued to visit when he was moved farther behind the lines to Treviso, where the doctors watched the patient carefully for infection and gangrene.

A few days later, his legs swathed in bandages, Ernest was on a hospital train pulling slowly away for Milan. Jim Gamble accompanied him on this trip, as he and Ernest had become good friends. Jim's concern for Ernest was true: only a month before, another American Red Cross volunteer under his command had been killed during a bombardment and he wanted Ernest to stay alive. Gamble was thirty-six years old and came from a wealthy family in Pennsylvania. He could knowledgeably speak of many things, and Ernest was glad to listen. Jim spoke about his grandfather, who was a lawyer and judge, and of his family's large summer estate in the Allegheny Mountains, and he spoke of artists like Giotto, whom he admired for his powerful simplicity. He brought Ernest gifts—mosquito netting, brandy, and English newspapers—and listened with delight when Ernest told tales about summers in northern Michigan and confessed that he hoped to be a good writer one day.

When the train pulled into Milan on the morning of July 17, Gamble arranged for transportation to the American Red Cross Hospital, and then he said goodbye and departed to his command on the Lower Piave. The journey from battlefield to hospital had been long and hard. In the months ahead, as the young wounded volunteer began to heal, Ernest realized that under such slaughter as he had experienced, courage is an irrelevant concept. The real courage needed would be to face life again, and in this, he found help from others and from within himself, and he would again have prevailing luck. For in the romantic setting of wartime Milan, he would meet a girl and fall in love, desire and feeling would return to him again, and even after the love that heals the wounds would break away, the wounds would still be healed.

The American Red Cross Hospital was in the heart of the great city of Milan. It was inside a huge stone mansion on a corner of a narrow street by a narrow winding lane connecting to the Piazza Belgioioso (it was in one of the palaces rising along this piazza where the novelist Alessandro Manzoni had once lived) and just a block from La Teatro alla Scala, which was visible from the hospital entrance. Across the street from La Scala was the huge Galleria Vittorio Emanuele, and beyond that, farther along narrow streets, the Piazza Del Duomo and the great marble Cathedral of Milan with its pinnacles and flying buttresses, of which centuries ago Leonardo Da Vinci had once worked on its design. Into this treasured setting the wounded Hemingway was carried by orderlies, carted onto an elevator, taken to the top floor, and placed in a private room with a small balcony. The rooms of the ward were dim and cool, interconnected, and had high ceilings. When he arrived, there were eighteen nurses and only four patients; not many Americans had yet been wounded in Italy. Four days later, on July 21, he turned nineteen as the hospital began to swell with visitors and other wounded and stricken soldiers.

In addition to the surface wounds, some of them deep, shell fragments were embedded in Ernest's foot and knee (he may have been hit by machine-gun fire before reaching safety), and the surgeon planned to remove them before the end of July. Ernest adjusted to the tedium of convalescence. Ted Brumback visited just as Ernest had woken up, and at his request, Ted wrote a cheerful letter to his parents in Oak Park, describing the accident and their son's brave conduct; Ernest himself added a postscript, "I am all O.K. and include much love . . . Lots of love, Ernie . . . Dont worry, Pop!"[21] One day, the Pathé news service arrived at the hospital and filmed Ernest in uniform in a wheelchair with a blanket across his knees. This became part of a newsreel shown in theatres across

---

21. EH to parents, July 14, 1918, *The Letters of Ernest Hemingway, Vol.1.* / "Dont" [sic].

the United States. Marcelline saw it in Chicago and returned with the whole family the next day. His injuries were serious. After surgery to remove fragments from his right foot and knee, the leg was put in a cast and all he could really do was lie in bed. But his treatment was excellent, as many there were concerned about his and the other patients' welfare, and his wounds were healing nicely. Among the staff was a tall, thin-waisted nurse from Washington, DC named Agnes von Kurowsky, who had light blue eyes and dark brown hair.

Agnes von Kurowsky had gone to nursing school at Bellevue Hospital in New York City and was engaged to a doctor when she sailed for Europe in June 1918, but all the handsome, gregarious soldiers on the boat quickly distracted her attention and the engagement was more or less off by the time she arrived in Milan. She was pretty and kind, bright and bubbly, had a healing touch, and all the men and the other nurses liked her. So did some of the visitors. Not at all shy, she accepted a date with a friendly rakish blond Italian captain named Enrico Serena, who often dropped in at the hospital, and, among the others, befriended Ernest, calling him "baby." Though it was against Red Cross regulations to go off with a man unchaperoned, Agnes let Captain Serena take her to a private dining room with piano and couch, where she nervously begged off his seductive behavior saying she had to report for night duty at the hospital. Agnes was twenty-six years old, liked to work the night shift, and soon took a special liking to Ernest. By the middle of August, Ernest, bravely recovering from his wounds, had fallen in love with this nurturing beauty, who was careful and conscientious.

In the long confinement of recovery in the romantic setting of wartime Milan, Ernest shed the outward remains of his boyhood and became manly and effervescent, smiling a warm, brilliant smile, even when lying in bed or standing on crutches, and was both attracted and attractive to the nurses. Elsie MacDonald, an older, motherly nurse from Scotland who accompanied him to his surgeries, bantered with him in a joking, scolding manner and was well aware of his feelings for Nurse Kurowsky. He was ebullient as he gloried in the grace of his behavior under the ordeal of fire and long recuperation, and to the other men in the hospital he was an admired, irrepressible brother and comrade-in-arms who told stories and greeted all comers. He dismissed any talk of possible amputation, insisting on having the fragments extracted "no matter how long it took and how great the pain." He drank a lot of cognac and was hardly concerned when the nurse-in-charge found all the empty bottles stashed in the armoire of his room. People brought him gifts, Americans and other soldiers, and sat in his room and listened to him talk. It was like he had a certain power over others, and knew it, and yet remained unspoiled. "You know how he was," remembered Agnes years later, "men loved him."[22]

Agnes often came into his room at night when the ward had settled down and sat on his bed or in a chair next to him. Ernest let himself go. They kissed and held hands; maybe they did more than that even though he was injured and in a cast and there was little time to be alone together. By September, their feelings were strong. As Ernest got better the cast was removed and he was able to get around on a cane. Out on the town together as part of a group of nurses and with other patients on the mend—he in a uniform with a Sam Browne belt (which he was not entitled to wear), she wearing the cape and high white hat that were the official uniform of Red Cross nurses—they went to the horse races at San Siro, placed bets, and drank champagne. Alone together, they probably walked through the high arcade of the shops of the Galleria, had dinner at Biffi's (for Ernest had money to spend), and strolled around the Piazza of the Cathedral. Agnes had some concern about the difference in their age, but Ernest did not. He wanted to marry her. Agnes did not feel that way, though she didn't say so, but she kept his picture in the pocket of her uniform and missed him when they were apart. By the end of September, Ernest felt strong enough, and sure enough about Agnes, to spend a week's leave away at the Gran Hotel Stresa on Lago Maggiore, where he met a ninety-nine-year-old Italian count with charming manners named Giuseppe Greppi, a prominent politician of an old Lombard family, who kept buying rounds of champagne as they talked and played billiards.

22. Mary Dearborn, *Ernest Hemingway*, 69.

In letters to his parents and folks back home in Oak Park, Hemingway embellished his reputation and let people think that in the aftermath of the explosion he had carried a man out of the ditch to safety. He had, in fact, been awarded the Silver Medal of Military Valor by the Italian government; but, in all probability when the large bomb exploded, the shock of the impact of the blast and the injury to his legs (he was knocked down and his legs felt like he was wearing boots filled with warm water) made him too incapacitated to move. He also claimed he was a second lieutenant and fought with the Arditis, a crack unit of Italian soldiers, and wore the Sam Browne belt, a wide leather belt supported by a diagonal strap across the chest over the right shoulder, as part of his uniform, though only officers in the United States Army were entitled to do so, and, in fact, he was just a Red Cross volunteer ambulance driver. He did receive a letter from Reverend William Barton, the minister of the First Congressional Church his family attended in Oak Park, where at meetings, by request, Dr. Hemingway read aloud from his son's letters. Though the reverend was a personal friend, biographer, and kinsman of Clara Barton, the founder of the American Red Cross, this was not something Ernest was impressed enough by to use to impress others.

Ernest liked the sartorial splendor of the military uniform and had a British style tunic of olive-drab whipcord specially fitted by the Milanese tailor Spagnolini that he wore on his return to the hospital after his leave at the end of September. Seeing him like this, Agnes thought he cut a romantic, handsome figure. But he quickly plunged into depression, the worst since his wounding, when informed she was being sent to Florence to help with an outbreak of influenza. He wondered if she hadn't volunteered. They had a long talk before she left. He saw her off at the train station and wanted her to write every day. She was quite busy but wrote back when she could. "If you were only here," she wrote, "I'd dash in and make you up about now, and you'd smile at me and hold out your brawny arms."[23]

In the middle of October, the weather clear and fine, Ernest felt lonely and blue without Agnes. Letters came from his family, and he wrote back. To his father he wrote, "there are no heroes in this war. . . . all the heroes are dead. . . . Dying is a very simple thing. I've looked at death and really I know. . . . And," using his imagination, "how much better to die in all the happy period of undisillusioned youth, to go out in a blaze of light, than to have your body worn out and old and illusions shattered."[24]

The war was still going on. Ernest decided he was well enough to get back to it and returned, limping to the front on his cane. The Italians were about to make a final offensive against the Austrians when Ernest reunited with Bill Horne and Emmett Shaw in a village near Bassano. There he saw regiments of Arditi, tough, swaggering shock troops dressed in their distinctive gray uniforms with black tasseled caps; they would take the mountains in the coming battle and slaughter many Austrians. When night came, he watched the Italian guns light up the mountains like lightning in a thunderstorm. But when the advance started, he was stricken with jaundice and returned to his hospital bed in Milan, hardly moving. His eyes were yellow, and he felt like his gonads had been hit with a rifle butt. He soon got well, but Agnes remained in Florence. Though sad without the woman so much in his heart, he still went out on the town and met a British officer named Chink Dorman-Smith. It was early November, the Italians had been victorious in their final campaign against Austria, and the war was quickly coming to an end.

Chink Dorman-Smith was a professional soldier, a graduate of the Royal Military College at Sandhurst, who had been fighting since the Battle of Mons in 1914. Under heavy fire at Railway Wood near Ypres, through multiple wounds from shrapnel and bullets, he organized the withdrawal of the survivors of his regiments and for this action was awarded the Military Cross. He had been posted to the Italian front and was in Milan as the commandant of British troops when he met Ernest Hemingway in an officer's lounge on the day the armistice was signed between Italy and Austria-Hungary, ending the fighting in Italy. Chink was twenty-three, tall and thin, had a calm manner, and in a

---

24. EH to parents, Oct. 18, 1918, *The Letters of Ernest Hemingway, Vol. 1.*

clipped British accent told war stories, one about putting up a "priceless" barricade from a wrought-iron fence, which absorbed Ernest's interest entirely. The two men got on very well. Ernest felt much better to know such a man as Chink, who reminded him of the stoic soldiers in Kipling's war stories, and insinuated that his own wounds he had received while fighting with the Arditi in the mountains. Chink may have seen through this but still seemed to sense that his new young friend felt unsettled about his wounds and combat experience and quoted Shakespeare, "By my troth, I care not; a man can die but once; we owe God a death . . . and let it go which way it will, he that dies this year is quit for the next."[25] Ernest liked it so much he asked Chink to write it down.

On the day the Armistice was signed, November 11, 1918, ending World War I, Agnes returned to Milan and was together again with Ernest. But she soon left again, this time to Treviso to minister to American doughboys, who, stricken with influenza, filled the wards of a hospital. Ernest still wanted to marry her and settle down and have children. She held out hope in the letters she wrote when she could spare the time from her duties. "I sometimes wish we could marry over here, but since that is so foolish I must try & not think about it."[26] When he wrote that Jim Gamble had offered to pay his expenses for a year of travel in Europe, she clearly tried to discourage it. "How nice the trip to Madeira sounds—but I'm afraid you'd never want to go & be somebody worth while . . . I'd hate to see somebody like you minus ambition, dear lad."[27] Jim Gamble had continued visiting Ernest in the hospital, and Agnes knew they were good friends, but, though she didn't say so to Ernest, she thought Gamble might be a homosexual in love with her fine young man. "My idea was to get him home to the United States," she claimed many years later, "because he was very fascinating to older men. . . . I told him he'd never be anything but a bum if he sponged off someone else."[28] He evidently listened to her because, his wounds healing, in a few weeks he would book passage back to the United States.

---

25. William Shakespeare, *Henry IV, Part II*, Act 3, Scene 2.
26. Mellow, *Hemingway: A Life Without Consequences*, 82.
27. Mellow, 82.
28. Mellow, 82.

While Agnes was away, he attended opera at La Scala, wrote to his mother and father, and drank and ate good dinners with Chink. He also began to write prose again. On Red Cross stationery, he sketched out a tale about a fellow named Nick from Petoskey, Michigan, who has lost both his legs and an arm in combat and lies in a hospital bed in Italy contemplating suicide. But outside the window the crowds are cheering, the peace having been won, and he reads the citation from the Italian government listing his brave deeds in battle and changes his mind. "I had a rendezvous with death," the fellow says. "But death broke the date and now it's all over. God double crossed me."[29] The story was never published, but the heroic feats of the wounded soldier were based on a new friend, an Italian soldier named Nick Nerone, who had fought at Caporetto and Vittoria Veneto.

Agnes was very busy but wrote to him from Treviso. "Every now and then [I] jump because I think I see a familiar stalwart figure in a good-looking English uniform & overseas cap and cane." Ernest wanted to see her. He made the trip, hitching rides, and arrived at her hospital on the morning of December 9 in full uniform with stripes and medals, limping on his cane. To the recuperating doughboys sprawled on their bunks smoking, he looked ridiculous and they laughed. Ernest Hemingway never took criticism well and perhaps that was why he was loud and assertive when Agnes introduced him to the other nurses. She scolded him afterward for being "so brutally outspoken," but reflected in a letter, "perfect people are not nearly so loveable, and of course you have some very fine qualities also."[30] He promised her during this trip that he would return home to the United States.

His time in Italy was growing short, and when Jim Gamble invited him to Taormina, Sicily, it gave him the opportunity to see more of the country. He took a train south to Naples and beyond and spent a pleasant week with Jim in this beautiful Mediterranean fishing village on the east coast of Sicily with the smoking top of Mount Etna rising in the near distance and the moon upon the sea. They lived in a house in separate

29. Peter Griffin, *Along with Youth*, 95.
30. Baker, *Ernest Hemingway: A Life Story*, 75.

studios. Jim had a cook to prepare their meals and introduced Ernest to a pair of English artists and another gentleman nonagenarian, the Duke of Bronte, who claimed to be a descendant of Admiral Nelson. Upon his return to Milan, Ernest told Chink Dorman-Smith a concocted story about seeing nothing of Sicily "except a bedroom window because his hostess in the first small hotel he stopped in had hidden his clothes and kept him to herself for a week."[31] Chink was getting used to Ernest's tales and seemed to like him all the more.

The surviving letters of Agnes von Kurowsky indicate that she and Ernest Hemingway saw each other again before he departed Italy. In his last week they may have met in Padua, and, while traveling to Milan together on a train, quarreled about her decision to remain in Italy after he had gone: there were so many Americans still sick and wounded, she told him, and there was too much work to do as a nurse. Apparently, too, they were together again on the last day of the year. Then he left Milan for Genoa, where on January 4, 1919, he embarked across the ocean on a steamship back to the United States of America. In her letters, she addressed him as "Dear boy"[32] and hinted that maybe in a year or two they might be married. Her affection for him was genuine. She wrote, "Now Ernie I'm looking to you to do big things."[33] But when he stepped on the boat to America, he would never see Agnes again. There was, however, another life waiting for him; though it was a difficult course to pursue, he was on the right track to find it. And in time, too, when he was ready, he would return in his mind to the Italian front, the hospital in Milan, and a tall, beautiful nurse, and write an eternal story.

---

31. Mellow, *Hemingway: A Life Without Consequences*, 84.
32. Mellow, 86.
33. Mellow, 86.

Kansas City Star building

Ernest on the Italian front

Italian trench along Piave

Agnes with Ernest

Milan Cathedral

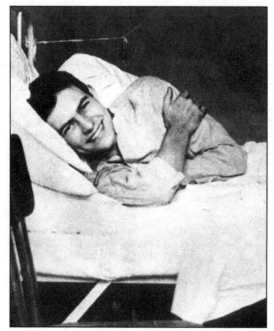

Ernie recuperating in bed

At the racetrack in Milan

HOME FROM THE WAR

IN THE New York harbor on the morning of January 21, 1919, a cool, fair day, the *Giuseppe Verdi* steamed slowly up the Upper Bay in the wake of other giant transports carrying soldiers arriving home, to a pier at Jersey City on the Hudson. Crowded with navy pilots and ground crewmen from the Adriatic, young Ernest Hemingway watched from the rails as the ship docked into the berth west of Manhattan, holding himself back as the others walked down the gangplank into the waiting multitude, seeing the reporters from the city's newspapers picking the ones who seemed most interesting, the ones with the most medals, for on-the-spot interviews. Ernest was not a soldier, nor had he been one, but he had been severely wounded on the Italian Front, almost killed, and on this day, he wore the uniform of an American soldier, specially fitted by Spagnolini in Milan, along with a Sam Browne belt worn by officers, cordovan leather boots purchased the previous spring in New York, and an Italian officer's cape with silk lining and a silver clasp.

He walked down the ramp carefully with his cane to help support his wounded knee and was quickly spotted by a young writer from the *New York Sun*, who duly reported the 227 shrapnel wounds endured by this tall decorated American emerging back onto his homeland. Ernest knew how to get attention and took credit for the heroics reported in the story in the following day's paper: "The first wounded American from the Italian Front arrived yesterday . . . with probably more scars than any other man . . . who defied the shrapnel of the Central Powers . . . being more than six feet tall and of ample beam . . . he is Ernest M. Hemingway . . . hailing from Oak Park, Illinois . . . a shell from a trench mortar burst over his head . . . he crumpled up and two Italian stretcher bearers started over the parapet with him."[1] But he would change the story of his wounding in the coming months and years; had already done so in letters home to his parents and in light conversation among the soldiers on the transport, to whose tales he had been listening and, in turn, letting them believe that he had fought with the Arditi troops at Mount Grappa.

Bill Horne, his Red Cross compatriot in Italy, was also on the dock to greet Ernest, and after the *New York Sun* reporter was finished, no doubt wishing him well, they crossed the Hudson and had lunch at the Plaza Hotel where Bill's pretty girlfriend, awaiting, could hardly take her eyes off the large, handsome, would-be soldier just off the boat, enthusiastically asking him many questions. Ernest was only nineteen yet had been in a war overseas, seen men and women die, and putting himself in the path of danger, very narrowly avoided his own death. In the hospital in Milan, he had fallen in love with a beautiful American Red Cross nurse eight years older, whom he still thought he would marry, and had taken up with a crowd of experienced older men and absorbed their tales. Ernest was a good listener and began creating some tales of his own.

After spending a few days with Bill, Hemingway boarded a morning train at Grand Central Station to take him home to Oak Park, to his parents who thought the world was properly strict and Victorian, a way that Ernest had learned was not how he saw it nor wanted to live; with him, he pulled along a part of the other world, the one of war and Europe, which he had not really left behind. He had keepsakes, some from the war, packed with his trunks to show the folks back home, and stepped stiffly off the train that very evening, a snowy night, at the very place, the LaSalle Street station, from where he had started the long, eventful journey only seven months before. He was met by his father and older sister. Upon seeing his son returning, the father teared up and offered his help up the stairs, which the son promptly, though kindly, refused. And Marcelline, waiting at the top of the broad stairs, at the sight of her brother in uniform limping with a cane, cried and hugged him too.

---

1. *New York Sun*, January 22, 1919.

That night, the house on North Kenilworth was ablaze with light as family and neighbors celebrated Hemingway's return. Even the youngest children, Carol and Leicester, were allowed to stay up to greet their heroic big brother, already knowing the quotes from the story in the article in the *New York Sun* that had also appeared in a Chicago paper. Ernest raised Leicester up on his shoulders and then did the same for Carol. It was a joyous occasion, but on the days that followed, the joy diminished as the large, wounded young Hemingway was not the same as before. He spent his mornings in the big iron bed in his third-floor room. His legs still aching, he would get out of bed before noon, dress in his uniform with his cape and his brown polished high cordovan boots, and come downstairs rather cheerfully, have lunch with his family, then, taking his cane, walk around town, going to his old school or to the library where he checked out many books.

Not all at once, but sure enough, Ernest was finding Oak Park different from the years of his boyhood. No longer a small town with more horses than cars where everyone knew each other, it had become modern and almost a small city. The change had been happening all along; he had not much noticed it before. But now he had returned from a foreign war and he had changed too. After seeing the great cathedral in Milan, the First Congregational Church no longer looked to be so big and important. The newspaper recommended veterans take permanent leave of their uniforms and find work. Dr. Hemingway and Grace thought so too. But Ernest had seen much more of the world and wanted something beyond the life now surrounding him. : Leicester remembered climbing the stairs to see his big brother, the walls of Ernest's room covered with maps and pictures of Europe. During those first months home, in part because he did not want to revert to the boy who had grown up on the manicured lawns of the prairie town, he never left the house out of uniform.

When people gossiped, Marcelline came to his defense. At a matinee in a Chicago theater, she overheard two women in the row behind her. "Why does that boy have to flaunt that fancy uniform? Why doesn't he stop trying to be a hero and put on civilian clothes," said one as Marcelline listened, breathless. "Why doesn't he get a job? He likes having the

girls moon over him! That's why Ernest Hemingway wears his uniform."
Marcelline turned around to face two teachers she knew from Oak Park
High and angrily proclaimed,

> "He has to wear that uniform all the time. Pieces of metal keep
> coming out of his legs. Sometimes he has to wear dressings over
> the places that are festered. Do you know that those high boots
> give his sore legs support? Most people don't know it, but Ernie
> has a lot of pain. He can't get a job yet, as you suggested, because
> he isn't able to stand on his feet more than a few hours at a time.
> I should think teachers like you would be more understanding."[2]

Afterward, the teachers apologized, and when Marcy told her mother,
Grace became angry, too, but warned her not to let Ernest know what the
teachers had said because it would hurt him deeply.

As winter turned to spring, Ernest, continuing to wear his uniform,
had trouble getting along with his parents and avoided them as much as
possible. At home in the room upstairs he read books about the war he
had just helped fight, wrote to Agnes von Kurowsky, and carefully read
the cautioning letters Agnes wrote back to him. Grace wanted him to do
more than he was doing, and Dr. Hemingway, as good as he was, often
worried unnecessarily, especially about money. The doctor worked hard
and well but seemed to have a poor image of himself, and his mood would
unpredictably shift from gentle to angry. The children were beginning to
notice it more; his wife, Grace, had known for a long time. Actually,
Ernest was working very hard, turning his room into a kind of garret,
spending time using a pencil to write short stories he wanted to sell, but
it was not the kind of toil most people thought of as work, especially his
parents. However, there soon developed opportunities to speak publicly
about the war, a role he very much liked, when an interview about his
experience on the Italian front was published in the *Oak Parker*.

Embellishing his actual wartime experience, claiming he had fought
with the Italian army, he made speeches throughout the town. The ones

---

2. Marcelline Hemingway Sanford, *At the Hemingways*, 191.

he made in the assembly before all the students at Oak Park High—graphically explaining the mortar burst, along with the claim of carrying a wounded soldier out of the trench, showing an Austrian helmet and a revolver and displaying the tattered pants he had worn—were enormously popular. It did not bother him that other veterans who had been in Italy knew the truth of his service: that he had not really fought at the front, nor been an officer, nor served with the Italian Army. The perception that he wanted to create was what was important to young Ernest Hemingway. He had been at the front and he had been wounded; he had seen men die and knew the sound of a mortar coming into a trench; he had listened to veterans who had fought the battles; he read books in the libraries about the war to better understand what had happened; and he had fallen in love with a beautiful nurse, a woman now ready to let him go, and so he decided he could be whatever he wanted to be and even make things up, for the uniform he wore around town was neither the uniform of a Red Cross driver, nor that of an officer in the American Expeditionary Forces, but something put together by Hemingway himself. For him, the real reality was to be a teller of stories; everything else was supplemental.

He did not yet write from actual experience, nor did he yet employ in his fiction the concise, clear sentences he had been taught to write at the *Kansas City Star*. He wanted to be a commercial success (perhaps like Edgar Rice Burroughs, who was also living in Oak Park and knew tremendous success with his Tarzan stories), and the stories he began writing in his Oak Park home were a myriad of words beginning with a labyrinth of story possibilities. For example, from "The Mercenaries":

> If you are honestly curious about pearl fishing conditions in
> the Marquesas, the possibility of employment on the projected
> Trans Gobi Desert Railway, or the potentialities of any of the
> hot tamale republics, go to the Café Cambrinus on Wabash
> Avenue, Chicago. There at the rear of the dining room where the
> neo-bohemians struggle nightly with their spaghetti and ravioli
> is a small smoke-filled room that is a clearinghouse for the camp
> followers of fortune. When you enter the room, and you will

have no more chance than the zoological entrant in the famous camel-needle's eye gymkana of entering the room unless you are approved by Cambrinus, there will be a sudden silence.[3]

Fashioning his stories from the ones he read in popular magazines, Hemingway penned fantastic themes, characters, and settings, mostly about war and mostly imagined from what he had read or heard, and he sent them off to famous magazines like *The Saturday Evening Post* and *The Red Book Magazine*, and they were all quickly rejected. This did not discourage him. He was sure of himself and felt an urgency to get out and do things. And although he knew he would write about the war someday, he did not think about writing great literature. When the time came that he did write great literature, and in the process completely dissect and reconstruct his prose to do so, the closest he would ever come to writing about Oak Park and his family is the story "Soldier's Home," which, set in a small town in Oklahoma, is about this time spent upon returning from the war in Italy.

His right leg still had shrapnel and pain, and he hobbled around town with a cane wearing his uniform with the great cape and boots and cap (interestingly, at this time a young William Faulkner in Oxford, Mississippi, was also wearing a uniform around town, that of the Royal Canadian Air Force, in addition to affecting an English accent, though the war was over for him too), going to the Scoville Library to read about the war, study it, and absorb what had really happened. He also hobbled down the street to the high school to meet Ursula at the end of the school day. Ursula was his favorite sister, and they were close; sometimes, to comfort him, she even slept with him in his room at night, often, at his request, leaving the light on. Marcelline was not living at home, but when she returned she would visit Ernest in his third-floor hideaway. He gave her a drink from a bear-shaped bottle of Kummel brought home from Italy and told her, "Taste everything, sis. . . . Sometimes I think we only half live over here. The Italians live all the way."[4]

---

3. Peter Griffin, *Along with Youth*, 104. / "gymkana" [*sic*].
4. M. Hemingway Stanford, *At the Hemingways*, 184.

Other women were attracted to him too. When two young school-girls made him a valentine, placing it at the front door and running away, he found them and took them into his mother's music room and showed them souvenirs of the war carefully arranged on the small podium next to the piano. To a pretty girl named Kathryn Longwell, he read one of the stories emerging from the room upstairs.

Ernest was ebullient, publicly and privately telling his story of the war so well that Italian-Americans in Chicago heard about him and, to the delight of Ernest and his sisters, twice came to the house with cooks and musicians and hampers of food and held parties in his honor in his mother's large music room with lots of food and drink and loud singing that disquieted the neighborhood, especially Dr. Hemingway who prohibited them thereafter. Marcelline later wrote, "Ernest was remarkably uncomplaining" and "was careful not to shock the sensitivities of our Victorian-trained parents," but that, "it must have been something like being put in a box with the cover nailed down to come home to conventional, suburban Oak Park living, after his own vivid experiences."[5] He was not really deeply discouraged when he received the letter from Agnes von Kurowsky telling him that she had fallen in love with an older Italian officer and that though she cared about him deeply their affair had really been only "a boy and girl" fling. He had wanted to marry her, but young people, if they let themselves, recover quickly.

However, he wanted to get away from Oak Park, and when a summer friend, Bill Smith from St. Louis, stopped to see him on his way to Michigan, they took the rail into the city and went out on the town. Ernest's imagination was rampant, especially when lubricated by spirits, something forbidden by his father and mother, and he told a tale to Bill about a hardened Arditi soldier demonstrating the use of the short sword by killing an Austrian prisoner with a stab to the heart through the hollow in the left shoulder blade. Returning from Chicago they encountered Kathryn Longwell on the train. They were still talking about the war, and she asked about the girls in Paris. Ernest had only spent two days in Paris, and that chasing long-range shells hitting the city, but wine at dinner

---

5. M. Hemingway Stanford, 184.

made him vivid and imaginative and he was still talking about Paris girls when they got off the train at Oak Park.

Ernest had been giving much thought to the lakes and woods of the northern country, and when Bill left for Michigan he went along, carrying the cache of stories he had written, returning to country unspoiled by the war and Europe, to the fishing and camping and summer friends. His mother would be there, too, although he would not have to see her much; but his father would stay behind in Oak Park, ostensibly to work and relax and calm his nerves away from the large family. Ernest had been a good son, but now there were problems. He did not want to go to college, though this is what his parents wanted, nor did he want a conventional job. He wanted no consequences and, needing to break away, would become recalcitrant to his parents, first to his mother and then to his father. As the summer of 1919 approached, the dilemma had no real end in sight. Upon this first trip back to Northern Michigan following his wartime trauma, though Ernest may not have known it, he was leaving his family and Oak Park for good, returning for only a few brief, unsatisfying stays in the years ahead, and setting out on his own.

He and Bill went to Bill's aunt's small farm near Horton Bay. Ernest helped with some of the gardening and took his meals with Liz and Jim Dilworth at Pinehurst Cottage by the waters of the bay that jutted up from Lake Charlevoix. His leg still bothered him, and bits of fragments continued to emerge, but the sight and fight of the rainbow trout in the lake were thrilling, and for a time, this was enough. Leicester remembered,

> Ernest savored the delights of roaming afoot through the woods.
> He loved the smells of pine needles and newmown hay, the
> fresh caught trout when laid in ferns, and the sound of cow bells
> carrying far on the calm evening air. [That summer] he was like
> an animal that has traveled far and returned to the place where he
> was raised, finding reassurance that things were as he remembered
> them and that this was truly the place.[6]

6. Leicester Hemingway, *My Brother: Ernest Hemingway*, 60.

When his mother and sisters came up in June, he helped unpack the crates of summer goods.

This was the summer Grace Hall Hemingway, over the objections of her husband, built the small cottage across the lake from Windemere on the hill at Longfield Farm and embattled the family because of it. During the spring, the doctor had been so adamantly against the extra expense, even though he was debt-free and Grace paid for it with her own money, that he wrote the contractor saying he would not be responsible for his wife's debts. In Michigan, Grace wrote her husband a letter, too, saying how for years she had felt "shut in by the hills and lake, no view, no where to go, acting the part of the family drudge, standing at sink and cook stove until the agony in my spinal nerves forced me to lie down and then turn up again and at it, day in and day out."[7] Through the summer, each parent continued to defend their position: the doctor worrying about money, and Grace needing "quiet and peace" and "communion with God" and to pursue her artistic development. And in the end, as almost always, Grace had her way. The cottage was built, and she moved in with her two youngest children, Carol and Leicester, and with Ruth Arnold, a young woman who was like a surrogate daughter. The older children could hear their mother's piano across the waters of the lake and could even see the new cottage in the distance. Whenever Mother wanted to return, she would hang out a towel or sheet, or ring a bell, and someone would cross the lake in the motorized launch and bring her back to Windemere.

The summer saw much shifting within the Hemingway family. Grace was taking a more independent, ever more dominant position. The doctor, even as he stayed in Oak Park, away from his family conflicts, was working very hard and his nerves were getting worse. Ernest was back from war, mostly well, but seemed off on a different course. The three older girls had grown into attractive young women, attracting young men; Marcelline had her first serious beau, and Ursula, filling out and beautiful, flirted with several boys. Grace understood this but naturally

---

7. GHH to CEH, spring 1919, Research Center, Texas University.

had concerns. She was getting older and suffered from arthritis and needed a man, like the doctor had once been, to help with the work of the cottage. At the lake, even though she spent most of her time with Ruth Arnold at her newly constructed cabin on Longfield, she wanted Ernest to help more with chores and the upkeep of Windemere.

There was always much work to do: painting and repairing the dock and buildings, washing, digging holes to bury garbage, clearing debris, and raking the sand on the beach. But Ernest seemed insensitive to his mother's age and ailments, and when he did appear, he would usually come with other fellows and they would eat lunch or dinner and then leave. He did a little of the work, but hardly enough, spending most of his time away from Windemere in the company of his summer friends around Horton Bay, where he smoked Russian cigarettes and drank whiskey and beer and took a keen interest in some of the girls, especially Katy Smith, Bill's very attractive older sister who found Ernest attractive too. To his mother, he was often contentious and seemed to loaf and have no goals. Grace complained about this in letters to her husband, but she understood, too, telling Marcelline, "Ernest is very like me . . . when he gets through this period . . . of fighting himself and everybody else, and turns his energy towards something positive, he will be a fine man."[8]

Ernest did have goals and thought about the future. He had some money from speaking engagements and insurance payments on his wounded knee, for which he wore a tight elastic brace. But he needed to relax and heal from the war, and with the assembled crowd of summer people in northern Michigan, he felt there could be no better company. That summer he and Bill Smith assembled others whom Ernest knew and liked and who liked to fish, some from high school, some from Kansas City, and some from the Schio Country Club, and traveled to secluded rivers and lakes in the region and camped and fished as freely and happily as American Indians before the Europeans. Throughout his life, Ernest would assemble close friends to go off on far and challenging adventures. He needed to go beyond comfortable boundaries, even when

8. M. Hemingway Sanford, *At the Hemingways*, 198.

he was writing. And the stories he was writing at this time, stashing them in his cache once they reached a certain point in composition, probably to go back to later, were not yet beyond the comfortable boundary and into the new territory he would find in the coming years. His last good country, a special place in his mind, before he set out to work on however he would develop as a writer and a man, was there in northern Michigan, and having had a good taste of the trout from the lake by Horton Bay, he would go farther off on his first real fishing trip in two years.

In June, as he worked with Bill at Mrs. Charles's farm, spending the sunny days spraying the apple trees and planting a garden and taking big trout out of the lake, which thrilled him, unexpectedly he received a letter from Agnes telling him she had broken with her lover, whose family were wealthy nobility and would not accept her as his bride. He felt sympathetic, but that was all; it was over between them. By early July, his legs were strong enough to go with Bill into the Pine Barrens, the wild dry country southeast of Horton Bay, an area oft given to wildfires that kept the canopy open where, for seven days, seeing no one or nothing but the pines and the streams and deer and partridge, once even startling a bear, they camped at a different spot each night and pulled in trout by the dozen with wet flies on a hook. Returning home triumphantly along the dusty roads in Bill's old car, they smelled of the field and stream and sported incipient beards. Beyond writing, this was the element Hemingway loved the most, and he quickly planned another trip.

In August, Fever Jenkins and Larry Burnett, two men who had been in Italy with Ernest as ambulance drivers, joined them and they went back to the Pine Barrens and fished the Black River, catching many trout while wading in the stream. They camped in tents along the bank. At night, the moon came out and they smoked and drank while Ernest did much of the cooking, rolling the trout filets in cornmeal and frying them in a pan over the heat of a campfire. After a week or so, they drove back home over the soft, loamy roads in the touring car Larry borrowed from his father, and, like boys, they shot out some streetlights as they passed through Boyne City and were stopped by a cop on a motorcycle outside of town, who, glancing upon these rough-bearded young characters, especially the large one named Ernest, decided to let them go. These trips were therapeutic to Ernest Hemingway; later in Paris, when he was much more developed in his craft, he would write about them truly. There would be one more fishing trip before the summer ended; this time further afield, to the Big and Little Fox Rivers beyond a hamlet called Seney in the Upper Peninsula. He took the train but was not alone; with him were Al Walker and a friend from high school named Jock Pentecost. In seven days of casting, they pulled about two hundred trout from the waters. "I lost one on the Little Fox below an old damn," wrote Ernest to Howie Jenkins, "that was the biggest trout I've ever seen."[9]

At the end of the summer, the three oldest Hemingway daughters returned to Oak Park. The doctor came up to help close down the cabin and was alone with Grace and the two smallest children, and for a few days there were no arguments or letters or concerns, and the summer, which had started so rough between them, ended as peacefully as the lapping water on the quiet shore. Ernest had deliberately stayed away from conflict within the family during the summer of 1919. He had not wanted any entanglements, especially with his mother, to ruin the path of reconciliation he needed to find in the summer adventures in the great northern wilderness of Michigan with his boon companions. Now that the summer was over and he was finding himself again, he wanted to extend it further and stayed on around Horton Bay in September, helping the Dilworths with their potato harvest.

He was close to the Dilworths. Liz had a jolly face, and Jim, the village blacksmith, was short, dark, and had a big mustache. Sometimes he supplied Ernest and Bill Smith with hard cider to drink while fishing Horton Creek. Ernest would sit on the porch of Pinehurst Cottage after dinner, looking out on the waters of Lake Charlevoix, smoking the Russian cigarettes he bought from a store on Wabash Avenue in Chicago while waiting for his girlfriends, young waitresses at Liz Dilworth's restaurant, to get off from work. A sandy lane led past the Dilworths' cottage to a wood plank dock on the bay at Lake Charlevoix. Apparently,

9. EH to HJ, Aug. 31, 1919, *The Letters of Ernest Hemingway, Vol. 1.*

one evening he may have become intimate with one of the cottage wait-resses in a mutual seduction on the dock down the sandy lane that led to the water, and, if so, it was probably his first time. He was writing but still not creating from his own experiences: "Up in Michigan," a sensitive tale about a harsh seduction on the dock of a lake, which he would begin to write two years later, would be the first of his stories where he would really do so.

When the water became too cold to fish, he rented a room in a board-ing house in Petoskey, the town just north of Walloon Lake. He would write in the mornings on a typewriter borrowed from Bill Smith and eat meals at a diner on Howard Street that had a long counter and a shelf with a wicker flap opening to the kitchen where a Negro worked as the cook. On many days he would gather friends, one of whom was Marjorie Bump, a cute high school senior whom he sometimes met after school, and read to them stories he had written for the popular market to try to make some money. There was a craft to these stories; he worked hard on them, imitating others' styles and experimenting with narrator's point of view. Many were about crime and criminals (Ernest read about organized crime in the Chicago newspapers and from this knew about gangsters Johnny Torrio and Al Capone) and exotic places, not things he really yet truly knew about, and though the stories were precious to him and remained a part of his self-valuable cache, none would ever be published.

However, a true divergence toward something else did happen that fall when he and Bill Smith thought to profile people they knew in Hor-ton Bay. Bill sketched a local farmer, and then Hemingway wrote out sev-eral sketches of his own, which he sent to Bill in St. Louis. Calling them "Cross Roads," they were concise vignettes, each a paragraph or two, shrewdly revealing the foibles and thoughts of people, real and imagined, in and around a village like Horton Bay, and were unlike anything he had yet done. One was about a beautiful girl named Pauline who "was like an Easter Lily coming up straight and lithe and beautiful out of a dung heap"[10] and was frightened of intimacy; another was of a lumberman

---

10. Michael Reynolds, *The Young Hemingway*, 95.

who had once boxed Stanley Ketchel, his heroics now forgotten; and there was one about an Ojibway Indian named Billy Gilbert returning from the war still wearing the kilt of his Scottish regiment and discovering that his wife had sold their small property and left him to marry someone else. Bill Smith, who, like his older sister and brother, Katy and Kenley, had a strong literary interest, liked these vignettes very much and, perceptively, recommended to Ernest that he use more dialogue to reveal character.

Though it seemed to be an inadvertent exercise done for the fun of it, Hemingway was tapping into a popular genre appearing in mainstream magazines; short sketches of people in small towns were then on the center stage of American Literature as publications such as *Spoon River Anthology* by Edgar Lee Masters and Sherwood Anderson's *Winesburg, Ohio* were hitting the market. The *Saturday Evening Post* was running a series called "Anthology of Another Town," a collection of small-town characters whose dull lives were punctuated by a singularly remarkable experience, which the nostalgic American public, many of whom were themselves only a generation removed from the farms, enjoyed very much. These sketches of Hemingway's would not be forgotten, but the young writer was not yet ready to develop upon this and kept writing artificial stories for the popular market. Still, "Cross Roads" was skillfully written, using an undertone of irony and sympathy, and the sketches were an intonation of the extraordinary writer he would become.

In December, he was invited to speak about his war experience to the Ladies Aid Society in the Petoskey Public Library. He donned his Italian cape with the silver clasp and his highly polished boots and gave a fine talk without the racy anecdotes he told to the fellows. One of the members present was a rich lady named Harriet Connable, who lived in Toronto where her husband was chairman of the Canadian division of Woolworth's five-and-dime stores. As were most older people, Mrs. Connable was impressed by Ernest. The Connables' home was a huge mansion on Lyndhurst Avenue, and they offered Ernest the job of looking after their handicapped son, Ralph, who would remain in Toronto while they spent the winter months in Palm Beach. It was an easy job, and Ernest took it; all he had to do was accompany Ralph to concerts and sporting events at night.

In Toronto, the Connable family found him polite, manly, and sensitive. (His friend from Petoskey, Dutch Pailthorp, who was also in Toronto and sometimes accompanied Ernest and Ralph Connable to boxing matches, noticed that Ernest acted tough in public but that "inside Hemmy was as soft as a meringue pie."[11]) They liked him very much and gave him the run of their huge house. In fact, at Ernest's request, Mr. Connable introduced him to Arthur Donaldson, who was the chief of advertising for the *Toronto Star*. At the Toronto Star Building, sometimes, during the day, Ernest took to hanging around two veteran reporters, Greg Clark and Jimmy Frise, who were impressed enough by his credentials with the *Kansas City Star* to take him to meet the editor, J. H. Cranston, who, letting him write human interest stories, discovered "Hemingway could write in good, plain Anglo-Saxon, and had a certain much prized gift of humor,"[12] and soon gave him a by-line and raised his pay to a penny a word.

Ernest clipped his articles and sent them to his father. The doctor, who, encouraging his son's efforts in fiction but not putting too much credence into it as a career, kept the clippings and was pleased that his son was a journalist again. Ernest, however, saw journalism only as a means of supporting a true literary vocation. The jobs in Toronto, one quite easy, the other quite natural, stretched through the spring. Even though John Bone, the managing editor, liked him and hinted there might be a future for him at the *Star*, Ernest was more committed to one last good summer in Michigan fishing along the wild rivers in the Pine Barrens and relaxing in the company of the summer people at Horton Bay. And so, in May, he left Toronto, not for the last time, taking the train to Oak Park. Along the way, gathering information by talking to other passengers, he cobbled together a story about rum-running from Canada into the United States and sold it to the *Star* for eleven dollars, which covered his train fare home.

---

11. Carlos Baker, *Ernest Hemingway: A Life Story*, 93.
12. Charles Fenton, *The Apprenticeship of Ernest Hemingway*, 81.

The home on Kenilworth Avenue was no longer a happy place for young Ernest Hemingway. It did not help that he stayed out late and kept his room a mess. He was a son who did not want to be in the orbit of his parents, especially that of his mother, whom he so much resembled in temperament. His brother Leicester later wrote about Ernest, "Strict parental restraint was behind him, though mother and father had not completely faced that fact," and about their parents, "Our parents ran their lives and those of their children on the basis of the Victorian morality in which they had been brought up. There were rules which could not be broken, and expectations which absolutely had to be met."[13] In Oak Park that spring, Ernest's mother and father wanted him close and had plans for his life. The doctor, reticent, his emotional health continuing to decline, best communicated to his son through letters where he still often sounded like the wonderful father he had once been and expressed the hope that they might even one day practice medicine together. But the mother was the strong, ever-looming presence who, for the most part, had usurped real authority within the family. Almost demanding, Grace wanted her son to go to college. But Ernest, whose path was not as vague as Grace may have thought, would not make such a commitment. When he expressed a desire to ship out to the Far East as a stoker on a steamship with Ted Brumback, harsh words were exchanged and the distance kept growing between them. Older children will often rebel against their parents in some way, and Ernest would rebel most strongly against his mother; it would be a storm that happened at Windemere in the summer.

He remained in Oak Park long enough to march with the honor guard on Memorial Day to dedicate the war memorial; his own name, Ernest M. Hemingway, was among the several hundred on the bronze tablet. When Ted Brumback came through town in his car, Ernest packed up and left with him for another summer in Michigan—his last, and a final reprieve from the hard decisions of adulthood, which he knew must come even without his parents telling him. A few days after arriving

---

13. L. Hemingway, *My Brother: Ernest Hemingway*, 60–62.

in Horton Bay, he received a letter from his father, who wrote, "think more of what others have done for you and try to be charitable and kind and gentle . . . soften your temper and never threaten your mother and father. We have both tried many trying years of your life to help you . . . I want you to represent all that is good and noble and brave . . . and fear God and respect women."[14]

Ernest had a shrewd, intimate knowledge of his good and brilliant parents, yet it was incomplete; nor did the parents fully understand their brilliant son. For he was of an era of brutal, rapid change, and he had placed himself on the frontline of the war just fought—a war much bigger and not like any before. Its purpose of saving the world for democracy, once vigorously believed, was now in question and seemed to be falling away into the hands of grasping politicians as revolutions broke out and economies kept falling and President Wilson's plans for permanent peace were as fragile as his own incapacitating health. Ernest would never be political, but he would come to have an understanding of politics better than either parent. He was contemptuous of his mother and father at this time, and a break was coming; but never could he really discard them, and much of what they taught him remained with him throughout his life.

For Ernest, there were girls again that summer in Michigan: Katy Smith, older and pretty and keenly intelligent; and Marjorie Bump, the waitress from Petoskey, a few years younger, cute, and somewhat in love with him: and there was fishing and reading, swimming off the dock at Pinehurst, and a good group of fellows with whom to enjoy it. At the cottage of Mrs. Charles, Bill and Katy Smith's aunt, he worked cheerfully in the apple orchard and was kind and charming and confident and smiling, bringing fresh trout to the dinner table and telling tall tales with a fine sense of humor. But at Windemere, there was an ongoing row with his mother, and he showed a different side to his personality. His friends that summer thought the fault was all with Grace, but not so with those in his family.

---

14. CEH to EH, June 4, 1920, Hemingway Collection, JFK Library.

Grace was almost fifty, her arthritis hurt more each year, she was overweight, and not in such good health, certainly not enough to do the required labor to keep cottage life going smoothly, and really needed a man like her son Ernest around to help. From Oak Park, the doctor wrote to advise her "to take a day off, you are working too hard my darling."[15] But she was too devoted to shirk her summer responsibility and, after working all day washing and lifting and cooking and cleaning, would be so achingly tired in the evenings that all she could do was sit at the table, hardly able to bring a cup of coffee to her lips. Ursula and Sunny wouldn't help much, and Ernest, spending little time at Windemere, worked begrudgingly, often just lounging around, demanding meals, and cussing and smoking and making no secret of his drinking and gambling, openly disregarding the morality Grace and the doctor had so stringently taught. Angry words spilled between the two, and he was the one who pushed it.

Dr. Hemingway wrote Ernest, asking him to leave the family cottage at Walloon Lake, to not be a sponge. But it was the mother who was finding Ernest impossible: their angry disagreements were between two strong-willed people, neither ever really backing off. After one of his insults, she brought up that he had been back eighteen months and was still not working. The father wrote to the mother, "I think Ernest is trying to irritate us in some way," and, "Keep up your courage, my darling." And Grace wrote back, "I got supper for him when he came home at 9 o'clock last night and sat down with him for I had had none, and he insulted me every minute; said 'all I read is moron literature,' . . . and asked me if I read the *Atlantic Monthly* just so someone would see me doing it."[16]

The son was after a break with his parents, and he would get it. He and his father had been drifting apart for years. Gone was the close relationship they had when Ernest was a boy. This puzzled Ernest and hurt, too, because he needed a close relationship with a man like his father. But the fact that the father's emotions were weakening, and had been since

15. CEH to GHH, June 25, 1920, Research Center, Texas University.
16. James R. Mellow, *Hemingway: A Life Without Consequences*, 119.

Ernest was a small boy, and the vacuum left by the increasingly emotionally distraught father was being filled by the strong performing will of the mother, was something Ernest could hardly accept. Dr. Hemingway came up to the lake in the middle of the summer to be there for his son's twenty-first birthday, but the bickering and disagreements drove him away and back to Oak Park from where he sent his son a check for five dollars on his birthday with a request that he attend to some chores by helping Mr. Warren on Longfield farm with the hay—a request which Ernest ignored. Ernest did not seem at all bothered by his parents' emotions and kept fishing with his friends and spending more time with Katy Smith, who had accepted him on an equal level.

Finally, after an incident, Grace became frustrated and took the time to compose an extraordinary, beautifully written, cautionary letter comparing a mother's love to a bank account from which her son had severely overdrawn. She handed it to him after dinner one night, and, along with his friend Ted Brumback, he was banished from Windemere until further notice. If Ernest looked for sympathy from his father, he did not find it; the doctor was decidedly on the side of his wife. The incident that caused his banishment was a late-night picnic in July. Well after midnight, Ernest and Ted and Ursula and Sunny, along with the Loomis girls staying at the next cottage, rowed across the lake and built a fire and cooked hot dogs and had a good time. They were caught, Grace and a furious Mrs. Loomis waiting with lanterns along the shore, and though it was a harmless picnic, the mothers saw it as bending the rules, and that Ernest (it was not his idea, but he had just turned twenty-one and so was an adult) was a bad influence for having gone along, incurring the strict wrath of his mother. So, she wrote and gave him the letter telling him to "stop trying to graft a living off anybody and everybody . . . trading on your handsome face to fool gullible little girls, and neglecting your duties to God and your Savior Jesus Christ"[17] and banished him. He moved out of Windemere, having finally forced the break with his mother.

---

17. GHH to EH, July 24, 1920, Research Center, Texas University.

The rift would heal—they were mother and son—but Ernest had asserted his independence and spent the rest of the summer (for a while feeling hurt, or at least acting the part, while staying in a shabby boarding house in Boyne City and grieving about his dilemma to Grace Quinlan, another one of his young girlfriends) and into the early fall away from his mother on the farm of Mrs. Charles, helping to pull the ripe apples off the trees of her orchard and going off on fishing trips with friends. In some way, it was bound to have hurt the doctor and Grace that Ernest would be so kind and work so willingly at Mrs. Charles's farm just down the road from Longfield while he was so disagreeable and neglectful to them. When October came and the long summer was over, Walloon Lake would be in his past. Although he would carry it with him forever, and from the memories write some of the most memorable fiction ever written, he would not return there ever again as before, even though his mother bequeathed him the cottage. Years later, when Ursula wrote and reminded him of all the good summers there, he replied that Walloon remained the clearest part of his life, and for that reason he could never go back.

The long summer ended with the fall. The apples were all picked in the Charles's orchard, and the summer people had departed to other places. Ernest had made a break with Michigan and his childhood, and he was about to break away even further. He rode as far as Chicago with Mrs. Charles and Bill Smith, along the way keeping up a nice banter, talking about maybe working for the *Kansas City Star*, which was really not much of a possibility. The only real, clear idea he had about his future was that he had his satchel of stories and was determined to write more fiction. He had not yet succeeded in the way he was writing fiction, he had not yet even had a story published, though he had tried very hard. Still, he was certain. He knew he could not live with his parents in Oak Park, nor did they want him to be there. But as he pulled into Chicago and was given a room for free in the apartment of Katy and Bill's older brother Y. K. (Kenley) Smith, he felt something would happen. And it did. For in the fall of 1920, Ernest Hemingway met a girl from St. Louis named Hadley Richardson, and his life began to dazzle.

First Congressional Church, Oak Park, Illinois

Scoville library

Soldier's home

Italian Party

Trout fishing

Grace cottage at Longfield

Windemere from beach

The Summer People

Bill Smith and Ernest in Petoskey

Ernie with satchel of stories

THE CHICAGO YEARS

THE GREAT Midwestern city that Ernest Hemingway returned to in the fall of 1920 had recently spawned a renaissance of arts and letters so remarkable that H. L. Mencken called Chicago "the Literary Capital of the United States."[1] The young aspiring writer did not yet know this part of his city. He had grown up in the undisturbed Gentile enclave of Oak Park and knew Chicago's ballparks and railroad stations, and through his parents, its museums and opera house, but not the community into which he landed that had helped spawn this lasting diaspora—though he would soon learn much about it through some of its most active and prominent participants. Within another year, this new knowledge, and a young woman with whom he fell in love, would help lift him well beyond what he and his bride had come to see, in a personal sense, as the restraints of the American Midwest.

On his way down from Michigan he knew there was a lot more to Chicago than the museums and ballparks he had visited throughout boyhood. He also knew that the world beyond was an even bigger place, for in Italy he had taken part in the "War to end all Wars," had almost been killed there, and spent months recuperating in an old palace in Milan surrounded by even more unforgettable buildings and monuments representing centuries of cultural achievements by some of the world's greatest artists, while tended to by a beautiful nurse with whom, of course, he had fallen in love. In Chicago, a room was promised with his friend Bill Horne, where he could stay until a job came through, and until

---

1. H. L. Mencken, "The Literary Capital of the United States," 1920.

Bill Horne had his apartment, Ernest could stay with Y. K. Smith, who lived with his wife, Doodles, in a big apartment that was like a hive for people keenly interested in the life around them. These people were all older than Ernest, but that was fine because he was always around people years older than himself. Katy Smith was living nearby, rooming with Edith Foley, a journalist with whom Katy, who had a degree from the University of Missouri, was working on a writing project, and there was a man named Don Wright living with Y. K. who worked in advertising.

Yeremya Kenley Smith was the older brother of Kate and Bill. Their mother had died when they were young, and their brilliant father, a mathematics professor at Tulane University who veered into philosophy and literature and wrote books disputing the existence of Christ, had left them to be raised in St. Louis under the guardianship of their mother's sister, Mrs. Joseph Charles. The apartment Y. K. rented was in a gray stone house at the northeast corner of Rush Street and Chicago Avenue, one block west of the old Water Tower in the heart of Chicago's cultural bohemia. It was close to the lake and Lincoln Park and just blocks from where Harriet Monroe had founded *Poetry*, a magazine that revealed to the public the poems of Carl Sandberg and Vachel Lindsay and for which Ezra Pound scouted for talent in Europe. These points of interest would matter to Hemingway, but he was not so much seeking them out as just trying to find nesting among friends until he found a job and could settle into more writing.

Y. K. had graduated from Harvard years before and was interested in religion and philosophy. He had met Doodles in a sanitarium where they were both suffering from tuberculosis. They lived together in a loosely arranged marriage. In the fading splendor of the residential streets on the near "North Side," their apartment was like an open salon with people coming and going, the rooms alive with talk about books and plays and scandals and art; some of them, like Ernest, would from time to time take up temporary residence. On any evening, while the gramophone played the syncopated rhythms of the new Jazz music, Y. K. pontificated upon Marxism and Nietzsche. He worked at the Critchfield advertising agency and very much liked the engaging young man from Oak Park who was such a good friend of his brother and sister.

For the gang that gathered around Y. K., Chicago was an exciting place. Speakeasies and nightclubs were thriving. The recently passed Volstead Act that brought on Prohibition was no problem at all since the Irish and Italian gangs led by mobsters like Bugs Moran and Al Capone were there to provide any kind and all amounts of liquor. The wine flowed freely, and libations were aplenty with restaurants reflecting neighborhood ethnicity catering to nearly all tastes late into the night. The apartment on 100 North Chicago Avenue was large with several rooms; it had been subleased from the wealthy Aldis family, who were noted benefactors of the late Chicago Renaissance. When Ernest first arrived in late October, hardly before putting his duffel bag down, he was met by Katy Smith who told him there was an old friend of hers upstairs whom she wanted him to meet and be nice to. Ernest was always nice to girls; he had learned this growing up with his sisters under the watchful care of a strong, creative mother and devout father; and in an eager, bounding manner, he climbed the stairs to meet this new girl.

He came upon a tall, statuesque woman with beautiful auburn hair, shy of all the attention that would not cease. She reminded him very much of an earlier crush in Kansas City: Mae Marsh, the star actress in silent movies. Ernest later told his brother, Leicester, that he knew then she would be his wife; though, at first, Hadley was not quite so sure. Convention did not apply to this young crowd of mostly men who had so suddenly surrounded her. Amid the smoke and conversations, she could hardly keep up with or understand them. They were exuberant and fast-moving, openly foolish, calling each other by strange-sounding nicknames: Katy was "Butstein," her brother Bill was "Boid," Bill Horne was "Horney," and Edith Foley was called "Fedith." They spoke actively about fishing, writing, artists, lakes, and were further creative in their use of words, referring to money as "seeds," food as "eatage," cigarettes were "pills," and death was "mortage"; and their leader, the one they called "Wemedge,"[2] was the tall, dashing Ernest Hemingway, who had entered the room with Katy's brother Bill, wearing his black Italian officer's cape

2. Carlos Baker, *Ernest Hemingway: A Life Story*, 101.

draped across his broad shoulders. Before the end of the night, Hadley found herself downstairs playing on Doodles's piano with Ernest leaning toward her.

Though gregarious and popular, that night he focused his attention upon this new girl. Hadley wore a new blue serge dress that went just below the knee; "I had a lot of confidence in that dress,"[3] she recalled. Usually unsure about her appearance, her beauty almost lost to her because of years of tragedy and misunderstanding, there was a calm, intelligent grace within the fairness of her statuesque figure. More than anything else, she wanted life and love and was ready for sexual adventure. A feeling sprang up for this "hulky, bulky, something masculine" younger man who kept standing around before her. "He was very handsome,"[4] she thought, and as love often happens, they fell for each other quickly. He was a good friend of her good friend, Katy Smith, with whom Hadley had grown up in St. Louis and who, after the recent death of her mother, had understandingly invited her to Chicago for an extended stay. She was glad to get away from St. Louis, which had never been a good place for her.

Elizabeth Hadley Richardson had deep American roots with ancestors at the settling of the Massachusetts Bay Colony in 1630. Her family also had money. Her grandfather, James Richardson Sr., established the largest pharmaceutical firm west of the Mississippi, the Richardson Drug Company, and her maternal grandfather, Edward Wyman, was a prominent educator who founded Wyman Hall on Market Street. Hadley's mother and father grew up in the same small, restrictive circle of the wealthy upper class of St. Louis. Her parents were at odds from the time they met and were never a good match to enjoy the bliss of domestic life. Much of what Hadley had experienced in family life was strikingly similar to what Ernest knew, but there was a lot less stability and her experiences were more extreme and happened earlier.

Her mother, Florence Richardson, was a gifted musician and a strong, overbearing woman, much like Grace Hemingway, and the father, James Richardson Jr., suffered from depression. They built a red brick

---

3. Hadley Mowrer, Alice Sokoloff tapes, Hemingway Collection, JFK Library.
4. Baker, *Ernest Hemingway: A Life Story*, 101.

mansion in the fashionable West End of St. Louis, its most exclusive part, away from the gross teeming inner city, and had six children. Their life together began to disintegrate when two of the children, both sons, died in childhood. Thereafter, the father descended into debt and the mother, who took a leading role in the local women's suffrage movement, was given over to an abhorrence of men and sex; rumors put forth by a grandchild hint that Florence may have been sexually abused by an uncle during childhood. In a household dominated by a mother who believed in theosophy and spirits of the dead, the daughters were taught that sex was not pleasurable and should only be done to bring children into the world—a strong contrast to the frank discussions about sex and some of the pleasurable ways to practice it that Hadley and Ernest would write and talk about during their year of courtship. Hadley was the youngest of the six children, born on November 9, 1891. With a sound inner being, she remained afloat like a sturdy ship in the stormy seas of her early life.

Her father, given an enormous income but lacking interest in business, found little warmth at home with Florence's severe attitudes and domineering nature, and offset his misery by drinking and gambling and carousing with friends. Yet, despite their strong differences, they were good parents. James was a devoted if distant father, and neither would demean the other to the children. Music was the center of their lives, and two Steinway grand pianos stood in the yellow music room; even James the father would often sing along in his rich baritone voice as Florence played lovely melodies on one of the pianos. There was an older sister named Dorothea, whom Hadley loved and looked much like, and James; an older brother much like her father except more gentle and kind; and another sister, also named Florence, called "Fonnie."

Hadley and Fonnie were beautiful children born two years apart, and like their mother and older sister, were sent to the Mary Institute, a prestigious girls' school founded by William Greenleaf Eliot, the grandfather of the poet T. S. Eliot, who, while Hadley attended, was a child living with his parents next door to the school. The founder's philosophy was that girls should be as rigorously educated as boys, even if they weren't expected to use it. Hadley was a kind and thoughtful girl and as musically gifted as her mother, but it was Fonnie whom their mother favored because she was submissive to her harsh ideas—ideas to which Hadley was not so receptive. When Florence took her daughters out of Sunday school because she couldn't reconcile Christianity with her new passion for theosophy—a faddish creed mixing science, philosophy, and religion that never appealed to Hadley—Hadley missed the healthy, social aspects of going to church. If the mother could not influence or control her youngest child one way, then she would always try to find another.

When Hadley was six, she leaned out of the window to talk to a handyman and fell from the second-floor balcony, hurt her back, and couldn't walk for several months. She recovered well and was actually fine, but her mother forced her to believe that the fall had made her frail and wouldn't allow her to swim or do anything too strenuous. Florence's control over the father was not as complete: they would fight, and he would drink more and go off with his friends. Her father's behavior probably wounded the family more than her mother's austerity and sexual repression. Neglecting the Richardson Drug Company, James put his money on risky commodity ventures and nearly lost it all. His drinking increased, and he avoided people and went into debt. Very early one winter morning in 1905, with all in the house asleep except for his married daughter, Dorothea, he put a revolver to his head and pulled the trigger.

Florence was more shattered than anyone. Determined to recoup some of the family's lost fortune, she sold her dead husband's stocks and their large home and bought a smaller house on Cates Avenue in a middle-class neighborhood within the city. No longer living among the elite, she threw herself into suffrage and civic activities. It was during this time that she helped found the St. Louis Symphony Orchestra and committed herself to the movement for women's rights. Fonnie had grown into a lovely blue-eyed girl with a pretty face and slim, graceful figure, and demonstrating a fine speaking ability, became a star on the suffragist circuit. According to Hadley, her mother and sister never developed the militant tactics of some of their colleagues, but "they both hated men"[5]

---

5. Mowrer, Sokoloff tapes, Hemingway Collection, JFK Library.

and blamed sex for the subjugation of women. Humorless and unyielding in their interests, they reinforced these traits in each other.

Hadley felt that her feminism and her independent spirit threatened them and that they wanted to break her will. "My mother and sister loved me," she recalled, "but they were also out to get me."[6] Her isolation from them deepened. Florence, still treating Hadley like an invalid, kept her home so often for supposed illnesses that she lost a school year. Also, unlike Fonnie, who threw herself into parties and dances and made her debut, Hadley was gangly and insecure during adolescence. Music remained the center of her life and gave her a needed release. Their mother soon introduced Fonnie to a history professor at Washington University named Roland Usher, and they married and lived with their children on the main floor of the house on Cates Avenue with Hadley and Florence living above them.

Hadley was sullen and withdrawn at home, but outside the house, she was friendly and easygoing. She had a cool, almost sophisticated manner at the Mary Institute and seemed more mature. "Hadley was smart," remembered a classmate. "She seemed to have grown up sooner than the rest of us."[7] In the spring of 1911, she graduated from the Mary Institute and decided to attend Bryn Mawr College, just outside of Philadelphia. She was looking forward to getting away, but terror always seemed to strike during her formative years. The family spent that summer on Ipswich Island near Gloucester, Massachusetts, living in a gray shingle house near a picturesque lighthouse surrounded by high shifting dunes overlooking the water. Life was slow and relaxed. Hadley spent her days reading on the beach, paddling about the bay in a rowboat, and helping to take care of Fonnie's baby. Then one day in August she answered the telephone to hear from her brother-in-law that her beloved sister Dorothea, eight months pregnant, had been terribly burned in a brush fire, her baby girl delivered stillborn. The family waited desperately, the mother returning to St. Louis to be with her oldest daughter. When

---

6. Mowrer, Sokoloff tapes, Hemingway Collection, JFK Library.
7. Gioia Diliberto, *Hadley*, 17.

Dorothea died eight days later, the family was inconsolable. It was with a heart heavy with grief that Hadley left for Bryn Mawr.

At Bryn Mawr, a close friend named Edna Rapallo sensed the seriousness of her depression and invited her to Windsor, Vermont, which was across the river from an artist's colony. Constance Rapallo, Edna's mother, also sensed her neediness and was kind and intimate. Hadley had fun on these vacations, her friendship with Edna and her mother was very close and healing, but when she wrote home telling her mother how Constance often embraced her, Florence suspected the Rapallos of being lesbians and accused Hadley of having lesbian longings. This shattered her friendship with the Rapallos and further ruined her confidence. Still stricken by Dorothea's death, and with the high spirits of the other girls at Bryn Mawr underscoring her deepening depression, she was nearing emotional collapse. "I was just eaten up alive and exhausted,"[8] she later told a friend. She did poorly on her exams, withdrew from Bryn Mawr, and returned to the house on Cates Avenue.

Hadley and her mother constantly argued, and with no real separation between them upstairs and Fonnie and her family downstairs, she had no place to escape, grew more depressed, and had trouble sleeping. With the break from the Rapallos still tormenting her daughter, Florence became concerned; she knew that children of suicides are especially prone to killing themselves and regretted ever mentioning lesbian longings. Hadley said of her mother, "She was afraid a bad moment would come and I'd think I was too queer to live."[9] But there was no lesbianism in Hadley: she was deeply traditionally feminine and lit up whenever a handsome man entered the room. Music became even more the great outlet of her life. Her niece, Fonchen, playing in the backyard, listening to the sad tones of Chopin and Rachmaninoff wafting out of the music room and through the trees, would later say, "I remember hearing her playing as though her heart would break."[10]

---

8. Mowrer, Sokoloff tapes, Hemingway Collection, JFK Library.
9. Hadley to EH, January 7, 1921, Hemingway Collection, JFK Library.
10. Diliberto, *Hadley*, 26.

The years were difficult for Florence too. Having lost three children and her husband to tragic deaths, she had become sad and exhausted and spent her days on the couch by the window of her parlor. Still trying to run things, however, she continued to make Hadley's life miserable. Concerned about her daughter's isolations, Florence encouraged her to invite people over but would watch everything closely whenever a man did visit. Her insistent presence made one beau so uncomfortable that he never returned. "I could have loved that boy," remembered Hadley. She also thought that her mother sensed the effect she was having and tried to change "but she just couldn't. She had a domineering nature, and I was the main chick at home."[11]

Fonnie began showing signs of being mentally unbalanced. People thought she was tense and fearful and often heard her shouting at her children in a loud, piercing voice. She seemed to suffer from delusions, once telling her brother-in-law that she had been a princess in ancient Egypt. In her lucid moments, she still worked passionately for social causes, often speaking at black political meetings on behalf of improving conditions for Negroes. But her marriage was becoming a disaster, too, as she and her mother grilled Roland for neglecting his family for work. Hadley took Roland's side in the arguments. In turn, Roland saw how Florence and Fonnie crushed Hadley's spirit, and he urged her to leave home. When she did talk about getting a job in another city, her mother, vehemently against it, would explode in anger.

Despite all the friction and factions, Florence had restored much of the family fortune, and with her daughters, continued to entertain a widely varying array of visitors: scholars from Washington University, women suffragists, and Negro political leaders. Hadley was adored by her nieces and nephews, attending their plays at school and home, and became a surrogate mother to Dorothea's sons. During the First World War, she worked in the basement of the St. Louis library sorting out books to be sent to soldiers overseas, which gave her a feeling of independence. For years, Florence had suffered from diabetes, and then in 1920, she learned

---

11. Mowrer, Sokoloff tapes, Hemingway Collection, JFK Library.

she had Bright's disease, a failure of the kidneys. Hadley devoted herself to caring for her dying mother, staying up almost every night from June to August "rubbing, pleading, cajoling, and pitying."[12] It was exhausting, and yet it eased her own depression; and as her mother faded, Hadley sprung more to life. People had always liked "Hash," as she was often called by friends, and she hired a nurse and started going out again on dates and to parties. Then on the night of August 19, as Hadley sat in a wooden chair next to the bed holding her mother's hand and wiping her face with alcohol, Florence gasped and stopped breathing. It was a few minutes after midnight. Downstairs, the Usher family slept undisturbed.

Austere and sexually repressed, Florence Richardson was a bluestocking who became one of St. Louis's leading suffragists and promoters of culture. A plaque on behalf of her suffrage work still stands in the city's Forest Park. At her funeral service the Episcopal minister, Dr. Putney, told Hadley that her mother "had done more than any one person in St. Louis for cultural and spiritual progress."[13] Hadley was proud, for, in spite of their differences and troubled relationship, she had loved her mother. Yet she couldn't help feeling emotionally released. At twenty-eight, she was a very attractive woman, and after years of a struggling, subdued existence was ready to live. She wanted to find someone who "hit my soul's center"[14]; she was ready to really fall in love.

Ernest was looking for someone special too. As a young man who had broken away from his parents, but not from the family values he had grown up with in Oak Park, that someone special he was looking for would be someone he would want to marry. He had wanted to marry Agnes von Kurowsky, but she had not wanted him, and he was now wiser. It would not be Katy Smith, although there was something between them—and more than just a strong love of literature—and it would not be the young girls he had been courting in Michigan and Toronto who were writing him letters of love and to whom he was writing letters too. When he met Hadley, he felt he had found the right one. Admiring her

12. Baker, *Ernest Hemingway: A Life Story*, 100.
13. Diliberto, *Hadley*, 35.
14. Diliberto, 35.

as a drinking companion, he wrote to Bill Smith that, "Hash is a good scout . . . and a splendid hand with the grog."[15] During the weeks she spent in Chicago that fall, they were together nearly all the time, even going up on the roof of the building with no one but themselves.

The "hulky, bulky, something masculine" whom Hadley came to know in Chicago was extremely ambitious and played his cards carefully but did not choose the path of a conventional career. He had a love of literature that precluded any course of action except that of a writer, and though he did not quite know it then, he had to be a writer of fine literature; he really didn't know what that was yet either, though it was something he would soon discover. When he returned from Northern Michigan that fateful autumn, he still thought of himself as breaking into the popular market by selling his stories to the *Saturday Evening Post*, and although he was quite imaginative and absorbed the air and the thoughts of people around him, what lay beyond that he could not yet imagine. Ernest knew that Chicago was a center of art and commerce where both good and bad things happened; Henry Louis Mencken called it a "gargantuan and inordinate abattoir," and indeed it was an enticing place.

The theaters and restaurants on the broad, bustling avenues of Chicago created an exciting atmosphere. It was the age of silent movies, Charlie Chaplin, and the new music of Jazz springing up in the streets. Jazz was Negro music with sexual origins that became part of Hemingway's soul and would appear in his fiction and remain in his life—and Chicago was the beating heart of this new music. Jazz, with King Oliver (soon to introduce to the world a protégé named Louis Armstrong) composing new music and playing with his band in the clubs in the south end of town, was taking hold in the dives and halls, and gaining a place in the imagination alongside the great opera house, which had already been there for a while. It was a city with many parts and much reportage. The world funneled in and out through its railroads and barges and slaughterhouses. Anything could happen in Chicago. Ernest had his best and most dear friends there, his family close by, and he had met and was

---

15. EH to BS, Oct. 25, 1921, *The Letters of Ernest Hemingway, Vol. 1.*

smitten by a woman with whom he was falling in love. But he would not stay, nor would he ever write about Chicago, as he and Hadley would plan to leave the Midwest and America for reasons of their own that came together so well and nicely.

For a woman turning twenty-nine, never having really been in a relationship with a man, and seemingly on the verge of becoming the spinster aunt of her sisters' children, Hadley was open and true to the responses of love. Sometimes she went out with Katy and Y. K. One night, they took her to meet Sherwood Anderson, whose book *Winesburg, Ohio* had been published the previous year. Still, she spent most of her time with Ernest, in the evenings going to parties and movies and dancing and drinking wine. People could tell they were falling in love. He told her all about his writing and how much it meant to him; sometimes, when he rushed into her room to show her what he had just written, she didn't quite know how to respond. "It wasn't the kind of writing that I had adored like Henry James, but I got very into it," she remembered. "He was absolutely sure of what he wanted to do."[16]

When Ernest took her to the train station at the end of this first visit, she had made up her mind that she wanted to marry him, but his mood had shifted a bit and he was no longer so sure. He was in love with her but was not yet ready to drop some of the other girls, one of whom was Katy Smith. But Hadley was like a butterfly breaking from the cocoon and knew how to spread her wings and fly, because, for someone of little experience—unless you consider all the books she read, music she played, and hard thought she had given to life—she played the boy-girl game very well. Back in St. Louis, she overcame all the obstacles at home where Fonnie still considered her too fragile to be going with a man, and Ernest too young to be that man. A letter from Ernest waited for her upon her return and she sat down and wrote, "Ernest you darling . . . I am missing you very much—you spoiled me—you are an adorable companion."[17] The lovers wrote each other with intimate immediacy, thousands of pages over the next nine months.

16. Mowrer, Sokoloff tapes, Hemingway Collection, JFK Library.
17. Hadley to EH, Nov. 5, 1920, Hemingway Collection, JFK Library.

One of the stories that Ernest gave to Hadley to read was "The Ash Heel's Tendon," written the year before in Toronto. The story is about an underworld hitman named Hand Evans who is so tough and hard that neither the inebriating effects of alcohol nor the softness of a woman can break him down. A cop in Kansas City discovers that his real name is Guardalabene and suspects that like all Italians he must have a weakness for opera. Whenever Hand returns to Kansas City to do a job he always frequents the same bar and the cop, whose name is Jack Farrell, arranges for the bartender to play "Vesti la Giubba" on the phonograph. Hearing Caruso singing the aria so moves and distracts the killer that Farrell slips easily behind him and slaps handcuffs on his wrists. The story ends as the cop gloats over the supposedly indestructible killer.

In this story, the young author is finding his métier with plot and dialogue, but the spiraling over-descriptive prose—

> Back in the days before cocktails were drunk out of teacups,
> Hand Evans was a gun. Now a gun is a widely divergent character
> from a gunman. A gunman, and present styles seem to tend
> toward the two-gun man, is an individual with chaps, a broad-
> brimmed hat, a southern drawl, a habit of working his jaws so his
> cheek muscles will bulge in the close-ups (the same effect can be
> acquired by chewing gum consistently) and two immense pistols
> in open holsters tied low on his hairy pants"[18]

—was written to titillate readers of popular fiction with a posturing style that Hemingway would learn to discard as he realized the value of the clear, direct sentences he had been taught at the *Kansas City Star*.

In November, Ernest moved in with Bill Horne, sharing small rooms in a third-floor walk-up in a house at 1230 North State Street, just a couple of blocks from Y. K. Smith. Ernest worked on his fiction, writing stories during the day, and stepped out on the town at night, sometimes with Katy Smith. He was looking for work and had little money but

---

18. Peter Griffin, *Along with Youth*, 174.

could eat well and cheaply around the corner at a Greek restaurant that had a Negro cook, filling up on steak and potatoes for sixty cents. He drank cheap wine and took in everything around him, including the crowd at Y. K. Smith's, where he was always welcomed. He missed Hadley. She had let him touch her intimately when they were alone on the roof of the house at 100 East Chicago Avenue. She missed him, too, and planned another visit to Chicago very soon. She knew about the other girls, but that did not discourage her because she knew he probably loved her more than the others, including Katy Smith.

Bill Horne's sales job was in jeopardy—his company was not doing well and called him to the headquarters in Cleveland—but he paid the rent, and Ernest continued to stay at their flat. From a want ad in the *Chicago Tribune* in December, he found a job writing and editing for the *Co-operative Commonwealth*, the monthly publication of the Co-operative Society of America, a trust set up by a man named Harrison Parker to seize upon a resurgence of the agrarian-populist movement that had swept through the country twenty years before under William Jennings Bryan. Through the monthly magazine, Parker urged prospective subscribers to "provide for your old age by investing in the great Co-operative movement," also promising "to cut the cost of living through the elimination of profiteering on the necessities of life."[19] Though the society's assets were mortgaged properties in Muskegon, Michigan, Parker would acquire over eighty-thousand subscribers and receive over ten million dollars of investments that would eventually disappear. Hemingway had suspicions but he needed the work; with a salary starting at forty dollars a week, it was enough to eat and live and enjoy himself even if he didn't trust the organization or the man and wife behind it. He wrote to his mother about it: "I ought not to play the role of the rats deserting the stinking ship yet," and of the possibility of taking a job in New Mexico, "the odor from the ship is just beginning to be perceptible. When it becomes a full blown stench I may chase down there yet. 'Nother words I havena all the confidence in the world

---

19. *Co-operative Commonwealth*, Dec. 1920.

in the [Cooperative] movement."[20] But the steady income would hold him there for almost a year.

Hadley took a train to Chicago in early December. Ernest met her under the pink granite and red brick clock tower of the Dearborn Station. Away from St. Louis, where she had been working with lawyers on her mother's estate, her robust physical nature, so long denied by her mother and sister, came to the fore. Able to keep up with Ernest and his friends as they made their rounds into the night, she was a good drinking companion. These few days were filled with nonstop activity of music and theater and people. Staying with Y. K. and Doodles in a front room with a window above the street, she and Ernest were always together, even if rarely alone. The love they felt for each other deepened. It was hard to part at the train station. On the platform just before she left, she was upset because he would not kiss her. "I tho't maybe you didn't really want to kiss me goodbye," she wrote him. "I was shot to pieces myself cause I certainly didn't want to leave."[21]

Ernest wrote back, "Guess I was thinking too much about how I didn't want you to go . . . Don't you believe I love you? Dunno how I can make you believe."[22] A little later, she told him in one of her letters that she would like for him to be her "Papa."[23] Nearly always apart during their courtship, it was through letters written to each other almost every day that they negotiated the rocky shoals of romance that led to marriage. Hadley was more mature than Ernest, and coming out of her cocoon, had more tolerance and patience. When they were together, she noticed his faults and was understanding. "Ernest always had ideas of grandeur," she remembered. "[People] found him a little bit bossy, but he was very popular."[24] He embarrassed her at a party at Y. K.'s one night when they were stretched along a chesterfield listening to a record on the Victrola, feeling an invasion of their privacy as Ernest announced to everyone "that we were the little prince and princess." Hadley was also

20. EH to GHH, Dec. 22, 1920, *The Letters of Ernest Hemingway, Vol. 1*. / "havena" [*sic*].
21. Hadley to EH, Dec. 21, 1920, Hemingway Collection, JFK Library.
22. EH to Hadley, Dec. 23, 1920, *The Letters of Ernest Hemingway, Vol. 1*.
23. Diliberto, *Hadley*, 69.
24. Mowrer, Sokoloff tapes, Hemingway Collection, JFK Library.

more sophisticated than Ernest, knowing more about the variety and depths of life.

Chicago was a tumultuous city where the year before there had been race riots requiring six-thousand troops of militia to restore order in the bleeding streets. Like all Oak Parkers, whose racism was benign and unconscious, many of them espousing racial equality so long as it didn't happen in Oak Park—where among the population of twenty thousand there were only about one-hundred Negroes, who were likely in subservient positions—Ernest Hemingway went out of his way to appear unprejudiced. Hadley, however, being from St. Louis, where there was a large black community and her family was active in promoting better race relations and improving the living conditions of poor minorities, was less inhibited. Sometimes her language shocked him. When she referred to Negroes as "nigs," Ernest was upset and asked her not to use the word. Though he would use such words commonly enough, women in Oak Park did not. Hadley was amused. She assured him that the finest ladies in St. Louis used no other term, but if it bothered him she would refrain. Like everything about her during their courtship, she revealed herself slowly, including her knowledge of literature, which at this time was probably more than his, and the substantial size of her trust fund. In the bloom of their romance, mostly at a physical distance, the lovers held secrets from each other.

Ernest loved this older nurturing woman. He had refused the opportunity of college, and Hadley, who had spent a year at Bryn Mawr, guessed correctly that he was sensitive about not going. "Ernest I have never taken an attitude of olderness to your youngerness in anything that mattered, have I?" she wrote. "Seems to me you're a wise man and much much beyond me in experience and understanding."[25] She asked him to come to St. Louis for the New Year; he wrote that he didn't have the money, which was probably true because he needed new clothing, and whatever extra he had he had spent on Christmas gifts to his family. He confided to her more about his writing and the literary life he wanted

---

25. Hadley to EH, Nov. 25, 1920, Hemingway Collection, JFK Library.

to lead, and she approved and encouraged him. When they first met she was more steeped in literature, but this was about to change dramatically with the introduction of one of the primary movers of the modern movement into his life. He began to pare down the other girls and concentrate more on Hadley. They declared their love for each other in their letters. Then, in January, in one of his letters to Hadley, Ernest proposed marriage, possibly as early as the coming fall. He also began writing about Italy and what a wonderful place it could be for them. She was open to the idea and began to open up about her trust fund. The idea of leaving for Europe to pursue his writing ambition was a dream that Ernest held close, but how likely could he have done so without the enthusiastic partnership of a mature, understanding woman like Hadley Richardson?

When Bill Horne's rent money ran out, Y. K. Smith came through again and offered a room at a palatial apartment with a marble foyer and winding staircase in an elegant old building he had just moved into at 63 East Division Street. It was referred to as "the club," or the domicile, and was not far from the attic apartment Ernest had been sharing with Bill. With Doodles having gone to New York to study music, Y. K. invited other bachelors to stay there too. Y. K. was an articulate and well-read man with a mature if sometimes errant point of view that established a lenient temper within the house. Hemingway moved in just after Christmas. In most conversations, and in the fraternal horseplay among the free boarders, Ernest was invariably the leader. "He was by far the most colorful of us," Smith would remember, "and very witty."[26]

Don Wright, still in residence at the domicile, remembered Y. K. and Ernest being good friends that year (which was one of the reasons why Ernest became disturbed when Doodles returned and had an affair with Don Wright before everyone's eyes). Hemingway learned many things from his older friend Yeremya Smith, and unlike others in the house, such as Wright, who thought of Ernest as merely competent, Y. K. felt Ernest had a gift. While he may not have known exactly what he wanted to write, he certainly knew what he did not want to write. "He hated the

---

26. Charles Fenton, *The Apprenticeship of Ernest Hemingway*, 100.

idea of a nine-to-five job," Smith remembered. "He wanted his freedom. He had no illusions about journalism, but he'd concluded that it was at least better than anything else he had seen."[27]

At the "club" at the domicile, Ernest's diligence and intensity stood out. When the others were idling in the living room, he was often in his own room working very hard on both the *Co-operative Common-wealth*, which would soon be revealed as the scam operation Ernest had sensed from the beginning of his employment, and on his own stories. His thoughts on writing were already changing. In Toronto, he had read Joseph Conrad and had taken to heart the preface to *The Nigger of the Narcissus*, where Conrad writes "an appeal, to be effective, must be an impression conveyed through the senses." He was under a strong new influence, a new, more solid direction, and was serious about his chosen field of writing. He worked on new methods and ideas, trying to find the right one, and when he read his stories to the group he would ask "Do you think it will sell?"[28] for he was more concerned about practicalities than the "artistic verities" he was hearing from the others. Living with the fellows around Y. K. at the domicile, he couldn't help but be affected by their passionate talk; but while they talked about art like dilettantes, he talked about writer markets, soldiering, and the fighters he watched at the gym when working out. "You've got to see it, feel it, smell it, hear it,"[29] he once declared, thinking about the strong sensations he felt in the gym, getting his hands taped in preparation to train and work out with boxers. And when he got back from the gym, rather than hang around talking to the others, he would go back to his room and write everything down.

He was given this new and more solid direction when Sherwood Anderson, a friend who worked with Y. K. at the Critchfield Agency, was introduced into the group that winter. Hemingway would otherwise never have known anyone like Sherwood Anderson. When they first met in Y. K.'s apartment, he must have taken a long moment to absorb this older and most unusual man, Ernest's warm brown eyes looking

---

27. Fenton, 101.
28. Fenton, 102.
29. Fenton, 103.

quizzical, and then once known, he would have smiled his wonderful smile that was almost impossible for people to resist. Surely he sat down and learned all he could from a warm, generous, turbulent soul—and young Hemingway had an enormous capacity for learning and could learn very quickly too. Despite the differences between the younger and older writers, differences that ranged into style and understanding and intent, they also had much in common.

Sherwood Anderson was writing some of the best short stories then being written in America. A godfather to twentieth-century American Literature and the modernist movement, which would come to be embodied by the style honed by Ernest Hemingway in Paris, he was an open, generous man, attracting many aspiring writers to whom he gave kindness and good advice, which helped them realize their talents. He had been at the center of new thoughts about literature and writing in Chicago where, along with Ring Lardner, he told his stories through characters using a clear, although stylized, vernacular. In his *Memoirs* he called this new movement "a Robin's Egg Renaissance," a small but real birth in the arts that would be lasting. By 1920, most of the eggs had fallen out of the nest; Floyd Dell and Ring Lardner had moved east along with some of the Chicago magazines. Sherwood Anderson was the last of the robins remaining, writing advertising copy alongside Y. K. Smith at the downtown Critchfield Agency. He was living nearby on Division Street with his wife, the sculptress Tennessee Mitchell, and came by the domicile often that winter, where he met and befriended young Ernest Hemingway.

For Sherwood Anderson, it was a time of success and recognition; his collection of tales, *Winesburg, Ohio*, was considered a masterpiece, and he was delighted with Ernest Hemingway. "Thanks for introducing me to that young fellow," he said to Y. K., "I think he's going to go some place."[30] Some of the other fellows at the domicile kidded Anderson affectionately about his flamboyant dress, his extravagant stories, and flights of imagination, but Ernest was always polite to the older man,

---

30. Fenton, 104.

and quiet and attentive in his presence. Even then, as nice as he could be, there was always an edge to Hemingway, especially when it came to advancing his career. His attitude toward Sherwood Anderson was like that of a young apprentice sitting respectfully at the feet of an older and more experienced successful writer, but Y. K. Smith, reflecting years later, thought he saw something else. It was his experience that Ernest handled personal relationships like a good boxer encouraging his opponent to overextend himself, growing more tense and silent as a situation developed, and intrigued by Hemingway's complex personality and attitudes, Y. K. thought, "It probably means a storm's brewing."[31]

Sherwood's visits to the club at the domicile were notable events; Carl Sandberg accompanied him a couple of times. Ernest read aloud some of his work and continued to be polite and respectful, listening quietly, though mostly keeping his thoughts to himself; he did not like Anderson's concept of unconscious art and was once or twice vocally critical. Years later, Anderson wrote, "If others said I showed Hemingway the way, I myself never said so. I thought . . . that he had his own gift, which had nothing particularly to do with me."[32] However, the impact of a famous older writer upon a much younger and aggressive one can be very strong, and this would have been especially true of Sherwood Anderson, who gave everything of himself to people he liked, and whose own life, convoluted and outreaching and unable to escape the truth, needed artistic expression. From humble beginnings, he grew to be a pioneer of the modern movement and helped to change the course of American Literature. Yet, as complicated and erotic as he must have seemed, he, too, was a Midwesterner, having grown up in Ohio.

Success always eluded Sherwood's father, who preferred telling tales of the years he fought in the Civil War more than he did work, and so for years the Andersons moved from town to town throughout western Ohio. When Sherwood was seven, they landed in Clyde, a town of about twenty-five hundred in the north-central part of the state. There, as the fortunes of the boasting, incompetent father further declined, the

---

31. Fenton, 104.
32. Fenton, 105.

Andersons moved from rented house to rented house, slipping farther down the social scale of the great democracy of America. Living on the edge of town with "the cornfields coming down to our kitchen door,"[33] they were among Clyde's poorest families; but, in the small Midwestern towns of the nineteenth century, no one was forgotten. There was always food, and people would take in the poor. Still, the hurt of childhood poverty would never really leave; Sherwood would always remember the discouragement when he and his older brother Karl visited prosperous families at Christmas and saw all the presents under their tree, and this left him with deep and sympathetic perceptions.

There were five other siblings, and as the father drifted away, their mother, Emma, kept the children together. To ease his mother's burden, Sherwood scrambled to get ahead: mowing lawns, sweeping out stores, driving a grocery carriage, working in a bicycle factory. He worked with such intensity that folks called him "Jobby" and encouraged him in all his endeavors, some of the elders advising him "money makes the mare go."[34] Years later, he wrote in his *Memoirs*, "I wanted passionately to rise in the world, to make money. . . . I loved money, loved the feel of it, was hungry for it."[35]

Upon his mother's death, he struck out for Chicago, where, sharing a room with his older brother Karl, he worked in a warehouse making two dollars a day. The great burgeoning city bewildered Sherwood and the venture was brief and unhappy. When the Spanish-American War broke out in the winter of 1896, he eagerly returned home and joined the Guard unit in Clyde. For Anderson, the war was "a glorious national picnic."[36] He fell "in love with the thought of the possibilities of myself combined with others,"[37] and, intoxicated with the physical exhaustion of training, did not have to worry about making a living. When the hometown company finally left for Cuba the armistice had been signed—they never fired a shot nor saw an enemy soldier—and they returned to

33. Kim Townsend, *Sherwood Anderson*, 7.
34. Sherwood Anderson, *Memoirs*, 101.
35. Anderson, 26–27.
36. Anderson, 170.
37. Anderson, 171.

Ohio to adulation and celebration. He remained around Clyde and soon enrolled in the Wittenberg Academy in Springfield, where he excelled in all disciplines and finished an education he had not before been able to obtain. "I had picked the right war,"[38] he wrote years later.

He returned to Chicago in 1900 as an executive in the rising industry of advertising. A good talker, handsome and persuasive, he was a brilliant salesman who knew just how to act with a client. He quickly moved up the ladder of success and soon had an office on Wabash Avenue. "Anderson was both a producer (of everything from layouts to sales policies) and a salesman,"[39] remembered Don Wright, who knew him at the Critchfield Agency. Other agencies offered him jobs. Only in his mid-twenties, he had come very far very fast. "The advertising business is one that lends itself peculiarly to what I wanted to do in life," he wrote years later. "You are an actor given a role to play and you play it."[40] He could make up almost anything to make a business successful.

He built up his wardrobe, walked confidently along Michigan Avenue in the shadows of the new skyscrapers, and went to parties wearing spats and a dinner jacket. "His charm, interest and sympathy made friends and enabled him to draw out more deep down inside thinking and hidden experiences than a father confessor of the Holy Church,"[41] said a friend. Yet even in the flush of success, Anderson felt sorry for the downtrodden or the clown others laughed at; always inside him were divisions and tensions that would increase as time went on. Reading calmed his soul, and at work, producing a steady stream of articles and aphorisms about people or life in general, learning and practicing the art of writing, he discovered that through writing he could also come to terms with these conflicts. When a stronger urge came upon him to write fiction, he would express his thoughts and feelings in a way that had nothing to do with business and advertising.

He soon took a bride—Cornelia Lane from Toledo, Ohio, but their marriage was restless from the start. Visiting clients on the road, Anderson

38. Anderson, *Memoirs*, 172.
39. Walter Rideout, *Sherwood Anderson, A Writer in America* (Vol.1), 182.
40. Anderson, *Memoirs*, 189.
41. Townsend, *Sherwood Anderson*, 46.

had one-night stands. He was disgusted with his behavior but couldn't stop. When a mail-order business offered him the top job, he moved his small family to Cleveland. As president of the United Factories Company, he produced a catalog to sell manufacturers' products. The effort was not successful, but Sherwood remained committed to business and moved his wife and three children to Elyria, Ohio, to become president of a company that sold paint and roofing products. This time, through contagious enthusiasm, good advertising, and selling cheap products in expensive containers, he was successful and made a lot of money.

They lived in a nice house in a quiet part of town and became members of the Elyria Country Club. It seemed they had arrived; Sherwood played golf and Cornelia joined a book club. But Sherwood Anderson always doubted ambition and could never conform to conventional surroundings. He began to bevel off from the life and society he had so eagerly seemed to embrace. "I had been struggling to be what nature did not intend me to be, a man of business," he wrote years later in his *Memoirs*. In the evenings, he fled to a room in his house where, as truthful as he could be—not lying, as he often did with advertising—he tried to write clean metaphors for no one else to read. He began to learn to face himself, and reimagining his own life as a revolt against money-making, wrote a novel called *Windy McPherson's Son*. When he finished that one, he began another, which became *Marching Men*, a book that rejected everything he had achieved since the Spanish-American War. "That's what I'm going to fight," says the main character in *Marching Men*, "the comfortable well-to-do acceptance of a disorderly world." His wife, Cornelia, was infuriated; she did not want an altruistic man of letters for a husband.

Sherwood came to hate his work at the paint company, and as the psychological stress became unbearable, he began walking the streets at night. Finally, on a Thursday morning in late November 1912, he entered his office and sat down to work, and staring out the window at the railroad tracks, told his secretary something about his feet being wet from wading in a river too long, and got up and left and never returned. Four days later, he walked into a drugstore in Cleveland not knowing who he was, looking dazed, with mud splattered on his trousers, and was taken to a hospital. Years later he wrote, "After several days of wandering my mind came into my body." When his secretary came to the hospital, he "sat up in bed ready to cry out, eager to express to her my joy at being back among the living . . . I had begun a new life."[42]

Early the following year, leaving his wife and children behind, he returned to Chicago and again went to work for the Critchfield Agency. His brother Karl had become prominent in the art world of Chicago, and a show of his paintings was reviewed by Margery Currey, who was married to Floyd Dell, who was making a profound impact on American Literature with his original and modern commentary as an editor of Chicago's *Evening Post*. Karl gave Margery a copy of Sherwood's unpublished novel *Windy McPherson's Son*, which she gave to Floyd Dell, who wrote an admiring review in the *Friday Literary Review*. The Dells were living in an old arcade on the South Side, and in the late spring of 1913, they invited Sherwood Anderson to attend one of their Sunday evening salons, which were the beginning of the Modern Age in American Letters.

The old arcade was rows of one-story buildings along 57th Street at Stoney Island Avenue across the street from Jackson Park. Here artists lived and gathered in large single rooms with big storefront windows under peaked facades that had once been a stand of concession shops for the Columbian Exposition of 1893. These rooms were cheap and ideal for the bohemian soul searching for expression in art. In close proximity to the University of Chicago, there had been artists in this neighborhood for many years. A few years earlier, to save money on rent, sculptor Lorado Taft had moved his studio from the Fine Arts Building to a remodeled barn just south of the university. Of the many that followed, most were destined for obscurity; the craftsmen, artists, and lovers of life who provide the needed critical mass for the existence of such bohemian settlements.

The Jackson Park Art Colony reached a critical mass that would open the way for further development in this modernist approach to

---

42. Townsend, 82.

the arts when Floyd Dell and his wife Margery Currey moved into separate but contiguous rooms with back doors opening onto each other in the block of old concessions shops. Their marriage was breaking apart because of Floyd's philandering ways, but they needed each other and were intent on trying to be open and "modern" in their relations. In the corner studio between them lived the soon-to-be Paris-bound post-impressionist painter Bror Nordfeldt, who painted a flattering portrait of Dell as a decadent dandy. The Sunday dinner gatherings were part of their ménage, and among those who came were some of the brightest stars in the American artistic firmament.

They gathered in the evenings to eat and dance and drink wine and read poetry and verse in Dell's studio. With curtains drawn across the windows, a troupe from the Little Theatre in the Fine Arts Building would rehearse a new play. Lucian Cary and Llewellyn Jones, succeeding editors of the *Friday Literary Review*, came often, as did sculptress and piano tuner Tennessee Mitchell, who had once been the mistress of Edgar Lee Masters. A lawyer named Arthur Davison Ficke would chant verse by candlelight, or the poet Eunice Tietjens would go through the motions of a Noh Dance clad in a Japanese robe. A short, squat Russian named Alexander Kaun told stories of life and persecution of the poor in Russian villages as Carl Sandberg and a youthful Ben Hecht sat and listened in silence. Theodore Dreiser, whose realistic novels had helped pave their way, appeared there too. "We were in love with life," Floyd Dell later wrote, "and willing to believe almost any modern theory which gave us a chance to live our lives more fully."[43] On one special evening, Margaret Anderson, who worked in a bookstore in the Fine Arts Building, announced her plans to start the *Little Review*, a magazine that would publish their words for the world to read.

Sherwood Anderson was shy the first time he went to a dinner, but Margery Currey gathered him into their bohemian bosom where he, too, sat and listened "with black eyes shining, taking things in."[44] Handsome and attractive, wearing colorful scarves around his neck, he made an

---

43. Townsend, 88.
44. Margery Currey to Harry Hansen, 1923, Newberry Library (Chicago).

impression. "He didn't talk ideas," remembered Margaret Anderson, "he told stories."[45] No longer the outsider he had always felt himself to be, he was now at the center of a group of people of whom he really wanted to be a part. None of them had any money, but they were all working jobs. "It was a time of a kind of renaissance," remembered Anderson in *Memoirs*. "We are going to write world shaking novels, become intellectual leaders of a nation, paint a picture that will be at once recognized as a masterpiece, sing a song that will reverberate through the hearts of all men."[46]

In Chicago, and across the Midwest, it was a time of literary flowering with Edgar Lee Masters writing *Spoon River Anthology*, Vachel Lindsay composing stirring verses of poetry, the publication of *Sister Carrie* by Theodore Dreiser, and the founding of the magazines *Poetry* and the *Little Review*. There was a seismic shift in the thoughts and ideas of intellectual expression. "We had been brought up on English literature sifted down to us through New England," wrote Anderson. "We wanted to reveal something new."[47] This new school of writing thought that writers both past and present wrote tales too far removed from the actual life that people were living. Sherwood asked himself, "Should I use in my writing words that were not part of my own every day speech?" and answered "No!"[48] Theirs was the language of the streets of American towns and cities, the factories and warehouses, the rooming houses, saloons, and farms. "It is my own language," wrote Sherwood. "I will have to learn to work with it."[49] They would not bear Victorian smugness but recognized sex as the tremendous force that it really is and put this, too, into their arts. "We wanted in our stories and novels to bring it back into its real relation to the life we lived and saw others living."[50] And in their searching, they uncovered vast fields of literature that already existed—novels and plays by the great Russians Turgenev, Dostoevsky, Chekhov, Gogol,

---

45. Townsend, *Sherwood Anderson*, 92.
46. Sherwood Anderson, *Memoirs*, 217–19.
47. Anderson, 341.
48. Anderson, 341.
49. Anderson, 341.
50. Anderson, 343.

and Tolstoy, and a new book called *Three Lives* by a woman named Gertrude Stein—that profoundly influenced their own.

When the Jackson Park Art Colony fell away the following year, Sherwood moved to a room in a boarding house on the near North Side. He spent his days in the advertising office, but in the evenings, he concentrated and worked with his new ideas and talked to the other people in the boarding house and listened with much empathy. "Little Children of the Arts,"[51] he called his neighbors, since they were nearly all young aspiring musicians and actors and painters and writers too. He had the idea to transpose their lives into a small imaginary town like the ones where he had grown up in Ohio. "I was in this house and it was winter. I began suddenly to write short tales."[52] One following the other, he wrote the tales within a few months.

When he completed the first tale, called "Hands," about a misunderstood former schoolteacher who lived in a house by a field just beyond the town and was very expressive with his hands, he knew he had it the way it should be and exactly the way he wanted it; experiencing an emotional ecstasy, he walked the streets long into the night. These stories were printed individually in little magazines across the country and then collected and published as *Winesburg, Ohio*. They were subtle stories of diffused plot and meaning that revealed deep truths about people in the small towns, their yearnings and desires, and why they were the way they were. Breaking the "O. Henry grip" of tricky storytelling, they brought the short story in America into a new relationship with life and placed Anderson, who had finally divorced Cornelia and married Tennessee Mitchell, into the forefront of the new American authors of the emerging modern movement. When he met Ernest Hemingway, his book had been out for over a year and he poured into the ears of this impressive young man all he knew and thought important; Hemingway listened and absorbed every word. Among the thoughts and tales he shared was one about the woman named Gertrude Stein who lived in Paris and used words as if they were active little creatures each containing its own different life.

---

51. Anderson, 347.
52. Anderson, 347.

In the winter of 1921, an education in fine literature, which by his own choice Hemingway had not received in college, was given to him in a personal way by this older distinguished writer. Anderson pointed him away from the popular stories in *Red Book* and the *Saturday Evening Post* by introducing him to a much wider realm of literature and making him aware of the new movements. Through conversations at Y. K.'s, in Anderson's own dwellings on Division Street, and his cottage at Palos Park, in restaurants and bars under the tram line off busy downtown streets, the older man told the younger one about books by great Russians and an Irishman named James Joyce. He gossiped about other literati like Stieglitz, Georgia O'Keefe, Anita Loos, the critic Max Eastman, and H. L. Mencken and Theodore Dreiser, people he personally knew, and brought him up on contemporary American fiction by telling him to read *Moon-Calf* by Floyd Dell, and his own book, *Winesburg, Ohio*—stories that would give young Hemingway a new vision. Sherwood told him about the importance of finding an honest publisher and cultivating magazine editors and book reviewers. He also learned from Anderson that in the modern age one could write about that which had long been forbidden: deviant behavior and sexual congress, covered with a veil by the preceding generation. A writer needs a special room, Anderson told him, where he can work alone with absolutely no interference.

They did not remain close for long; Anderson left for Paris by mid-spring and did not return to Chicago until November. However, after all the rejections—and it was nothing but rejections for his stories—the praise and sponsorship of a successful respected writer such as Sherwood Anderson was of very real value both psychologically and professionally, bolstering Hemingway's confidence, knowing that Anderson believed in his abilities and was achieving recognition with the nearly same kind of material as his own. Anderson read some of his stories, saw the influences of Kipling and O'Henry, and gave his critique. Ernest listened and absorbed and began reading the books and learning and pouring words onto paper. "He was always writing,"[53] remembered Hadley, who had

---

53. Mowrer, Sokoloff tapes, Hemingway Collection, JFK Library.

also met Anderson and read *Winesburg, Ohio*, and encouraged her man in his efforts too. For as early as Chicago, Hemingway regarded writing with much intensity and conviction, and people were either for or against him; there was no compromise or variation. "Absorption in his ideas," Sherwood speculated much later after being satirized by Hemingway in *The Torrents of Spring*, "may have affected his capacity for friendship."[54]

Hemingway kept busy throughout the winter, working on his stories, which kept getting rejected, and with the work he did for pay on the *Co-operative Commonwealth*. Harrison Parker had hired an experienced editor and made the magazine a monthly publication with good layouts and captions and the use of photographs to capture a larger audience and increase the number of investors in his so-called "co-operative movement." Ernest delivered original copy with interviews and human-interest stories, much like he had done in Toronto, along with what he referred to as "thinking and planning editorials," doing much of the work alone in his room in the domicile. "Interviewed Mary Bartelme today and she is the genuwind old darticle," he wrote his mother in January (Mary Bartelme was an early child rights advocate who helped establish the juvenile court in Chicago). "An excellent woman and I fell hard for her and wrote a wonderful story."[55] He worked hard on the magazine, but the writing he put his soul into would always be his fiction. Hemingway could sense Parker's scheme more and more—putting the cash from the subscriptions into his own pockets—but his salary was increased to fifty dollars monthly in January, and needing the money, he took the raise and continued the work. But that such a fraud could be perpetrated upon the public increased his distaste for certain values he thought endemic to America, characteristic of the surface appearance of commercialism, and his determination to avoid bondage to such an employer.

The young artists and advertising men who gathered in the evenings at the domicile of Y. K. Smith were also dissatisfied with conventional values. Both the tenants and their friends had in varying degrees the same attitude of a break with convention as Sherwood Anderson expressed in

54. Fenton, *The Apprenticeship of Ernest Hemingway*, 105.
55. EH to GHH, Jan. 10, 1921, *The Letters of Ernest Hemingway, Vol. 1.* / "genuwind old darticle" [*sic*].

his work and conversation. Without proposing any solutions to the ambiguities of materialistic values, they mocked the situation as it involved
them personally and in the larger terms of the whole system. "We had
much fun after hours," remembered Wright, "telling yarns about the
scheming of the low grade morons who were our bosses in agencies and
magazines."[56] Hemingway was especially entertaining, coming up with
a plan to bottle blood from the stockyards and selling it as "bull gore for
bigger babies."[57] And as his skepticism about the Co-operative Society
of America increased, he began to regale them with stories about the
scheme. Y. K. remembered with cynical delight one story he told about
Harrison Parker's front men declaring that "members got a voice but
not a vote."[58] Even though Hemingway came to realize the scheme was
crooked, he decided to stay on, collect his paychecks, maybe expose it,
but near the end "very much wrought up about it," decided to "just rack
it up as experience and the hell with it."[59] Hemingway would not hold
himself responsible for the milking of innocents' money, nor would the
public when Harrison Parker came to trial within the year.

Soon after Ernest had arrived in Chicago, Y. K. had taken him to
Critchfield's and introduced him to Roy Dickey, the copy chief, who
had no jobs available. Hemingway pretended a lack of concern and told
Dickey he already had a job writing a column for the *Toronto Star*, which
was true because he continued sending them stories that were being
published, and even though he was paid very little it kept alive his single
promising alliance in journalism and through the winter and spring gave
him an outlet from the fraud of the *Co-operative Commonwealth* and
the doctrinaire principles of art expressed at the apartment—principles
he did not trust. The stories he wrote for both the *Toronto Star* and the
Co-operative Commonwealth showed a shrewd instinct for the audience's
taste, and though the *Co-operative Commonwealth* was a consuming job,
it did teach him much about editing and writing copy, skills he would
fall back on again and again.

---

56. Fenton, *The Apprenticeship of Ernest Hemingway*, 105.
57. Fenton, 105.
58. Fenton, 105.
59. Fenton, 105.

In the pieces he sent to the *Toronto Star* that winter and spring, a satiric talent, already revealed in the sketches he did with Bill Smith in Northern Michigan, showed a maturing sophistication. In May, he sent Cranston a column with a humorous theme about American resorts that suggested the best guarantee of living a long, healthy life was to violate the traditional American insistence on annual vacations, an idea that thrilled Canadians' dislike of all things American. He described one fictional resort as "Beautiful Lake flyblow nestled like a plague spot in the heart of the great north woods. All around it rise the majestic hills. Above it towers the majestic sky. On every side of it is the majestic shore. The shore is lined with majestic dead fish dead of loneliness."[60]

Playing further upon Canadian distaste for American insensitivity, in another column he proposed that public entertainers, including politicians and artists, could be traded between nations just as players are traded among professional baseball teams. Describing fictional ceremonies following the purchase of Shakespeare's citizenship by the United States, he wrote, "The little English town of Avon was decked with American flags and all the buildings placarded. We want Bill, and We Got Him, and Yea Bill! You Brought Home the Bacon were the legends on some of the placards."[61] He also thought that Prohibition was a farce. Under the caption "Chicago Never Wetter Than It Is today," he described a "members only" speakeasy by writing "there has never been any record of any one being black balled," and further mocked the entire experiment by reporting, "There are eight federal prohibition enforcement officers in Chicago. Four of them are doing office work, the other four are guarding a warehouse."[62]

Hadley wrote him every day, and every day he wrote to her. As their feelings became stronger and they thought more about marriage, the interests Ernest had in other women no longer mattered so much. It was with Hadley that he shared the most intimate details of his life. Ernest was reading Havelock Ellis's *Psychology of Sex* and wanted Hadley to read

---

60. *Toronto Star Weekly*, May 21, 1921.
61. *Toronto Star Weekly*, Feb. 19, 1921.
62. *Toronto Star Weekly*, July 2, 1921.

it, too, but she wasn't that interested in a book about sex. "Don't know enough about the facts of life but calculate neither did Adam & Eve," she wrote Ernest jokingly. "What the devil's a masochist? . . . I've heard of females like that that love the hurt . . . Think all women get sumpn out of it if a male does it to them—don't you."[63] He wanted to see her again, and she responded, "There aren't any arms in the world I want around me as much as yours you see and there's no heart like yours for me."[64] They held off visiting because of money. Her mother's estate had not yet been settled, and with the intent of returning to Italy, Ernest was spending most of his paycheck buying lira. "Ernest was being very careful of money," she remembered. "Ballet and opera he was mad about."[65] But to save more money he no longer went to the theater.

He had been telling her about Italy and what a wonderful place it would be for them. His enthusiasm increased when he had received a letter from Jim Gamble in December, inviting him to spend five months in Rome. He wrote to Hadley about the proposal: Jim would pay for everything and he could spend his days writing fiction. Hadley knew she couldn't stop him if he really wanted to go. "Rome sounds so wonderful— I would be so envious of you!" she wrote, but she didn't encourage him either; "I would miss you pretty frightfully unless I tho't it was going to be great gain to your work."[66] Ernest admired Jim, who had saved his life when he was wounded in the trench near the village of Fossalta, but he knew the five-month separation could hurt his relationship with Hadley, and he wanted her more than he did the trip to Rome with Gamble. "Jim Gamble is great," he wrote to her before the New Year, "I love him a lot—but not like I love you."[67] He cabled Jim Gamble in Philadelphia: "Rather go to Rome with you than heaven. . . . but am broke,"[68] and did not go. But the idea of Europe stayed with him as something he would share with Hadley when they were married.

---

63. Hadley to EH, Jan. 28, 1921, Hemingway Collection, JFK Library.
64. Hadley to EH, Jan. 30, 1921, Hemingway Collection, JFK Library.
65. Mowrer, Sokoloff tapes, Hemingway Collection, JFK Library.
66. Hadley to EH, Jan. 15, 1921, Hemingway Collection, JFK Library.
67. EH to Hadley, Dec. 23, 1920, *The Letters of Ernest Hemingway, Vol. 1.*
68. EH to JG, cable, Dec. 27, 1921, *Selected Letters*, 45.

In March, he took the train to St. Louis wearing a new Brooks Brothers suit, carrying his Italian officer's cape along with a scrapbook of his articles in the *Toronto Star*. Meeting him at the station, Hadley was shy at first but managed to say "I love you." He slept in the home of Mrs. Charles but spent all his time with Hadley at the house on Cates Avenue where he sat on a stool in the kitchen watching her prepare large meals. Her friends liked him; Helen Breaker thought she had found a wonderful man, but Fonnie and Ernest disliked each other intensely. "She thought he was terrible, this gorgeous, blustering, outlandish young man," recalled Hadley. "But I never wavered in my wish to be married to him when I found out he wanted to be married to me."[69] She had begun to reveal that she had an inheritance that would let them live well almost anywhere they wanted and began sending him sums to invest in Italian lira. In Italy, he said, they could live on three cents a day and he could make extra money boxing as a sparring partner. He was "full of plans for our future," remembered Hadley, "and that was very exciting."[70]

On the following week, Hadley returned the visit, boarding the Midnight Special to Chicago with her friend Ruth Bradfield and taking a room at the Plaza Hotel. Nervous at first about seeing her lover, when he came down the winding marble staircase to greet her in the foyer at the domicile on Division Street he eased all pain with his tender eyes and smile. She spent most of the days and all of the evenings with Ernest, cuddling and petting in private repose and kissing on the streets. One night she put on a black satin dress and went to a dinner party at the Victor House on Grand Avenue with Ernest, Katy Smith, and Bill Horne, filling up on spaghetti and red wine. They were a handsome pair. Years later Ruth Bradfield remembered Ernest as

> a beautiful youth. He was slender and moved well. His face had
> the symmetry of fine bony structure and he had a small elastic
> mouth that stretched from ear to ear when he laughed. He laughed
> aloud a lot from quick humor. . . . His focused attention to the

69. Mowrer, Sokoloff tapes, Hemingway Collection, JFK Library.
70. Mowrer, Sokoloff tapes, Hemingway Collection, JFK Library.

person he was talking with was immensely flattering. . . . He generated excitement because he was so intense about everything, about writing and boxing, about good food and drink. Everything we did took on new importance when he was with us.[71]

On Saturday they went to Oak Park to meet his family at the large house on Kenilworth. Grace took Hadley into the music room where the latter played the piano and Grace sang. Hadley liked Dr. Hemingway, who was "quick talking and acting, anxious to give me the warmest welcome," and Ernest's brother and sisters were nice and had "all the handsome Hemingway features."[72] Ernest's family liked Hadley very much and was thrilled he was going to marry her.

Hadley was not snobbish, but she appreciated nice things. The gift Ernest had given her for Christmas was not at all to her liking, though she loved the sentiment behind it, and in the afternoon of their visit to Oak Park, she found the opportunity to get rid of his present.

He took me out in a canoe on the Des Plaines River. He gave me something very characteristic of the Hemingway family who were always seeking bargains . . . We didn't do that at our house . . . we liked to buy the best we could possibly afford. He had found a bargain, a perfectly beautiful bead purse . . . but here and there were places where the beads were out. I was very much annoyed at this . . . I wasn't a bead worker . . . we were out on the canoe, and he was very proud of it . . . and somehow or other it fell into the river."[73]

Their engagement was like a ship in the night toward an unseen shore. Ernest had been sly about it, telling Hadley to tell no one. Daylight was now breaking; they knew they would land and began planning their wedding. Ernest became more worried about money and wanted a secure,

71. Baker, *Ernest Hemingway: A Life Story*, 103.
72. Mowrer, Sokoloff tapes, Hemingway Collection, JFK Library.
73. Mowrer, Sokoloff tapes, Hemingway Collection, JFK Library.

steady income. Knowing the *Co-operative Commonwealth* had no future, he applied to John Bone for a position with the newspaper. Hemingway wanted a full-time salary of eighty-five dollars a week. John Bone was interested and continued buying some of the stories Hemingway sent to the paper, but he was not yet ready to hire Ernest Hemingway at eighty-five dollars a week. Even when not writing for the *Toronto Star* he told unflattering tales of American inferiority, often talking to his friends at Y. K.'s apartment about his eagerness and determination to leave the Midwest and get back to Europe. He still wrote a lot of hack journalism, his stories were not selling, and the direction he was going was beneath his capabilities. But his friendship with Sherwood Anderson was starting to change his sensibilities and make a profound difference in his life.

Hadley encouraged his writing and approved of the literary life he wanted to live. "You've such a magnificent grip on the form back of the material no matter how strange it is, like the icebergs,"[74] she wrote, an idea about writing she had seen and heard and read in the letters and voice and presence of her betrothed as it evolved in his mind. His attention and compliments made her feel beautiful and cherished and unlocked her from years of unhappiness. When Ernest returned to St. Louis in April, they played tennis at Forest Park. Hadley kept up on the court and gave him a good game. She was at long last restored to her true nature, which was strong and healthy. "The world's a jail and we're gonna break it together," she told him. Her letters were now flowing with joy: "Oh, Mr. Hemingway, how I love you. How exciting you are."[75]

When apart from Hadley, Ernest often suffered. He hated the long hours required at the *Co-operative Commonwealth*, especially the end-of-month push for another new issue that left little time for his fiction, which buoyed and excited him. "Come home from the office," he wrote Bill Smith, "feed, shoot a couple or three rubberoids of bridge with the men and then go to bed, sleep a little while and then wake up and can't sleep for nawthing, so start working and keep going until [I] get sleepy in

---

74. Hadley to EH, Aug. 10, 1921, Hemingway Collection, JFK Library.
75. Hadley to EH, June 4, 1921, Hemingway Collection, JFK Library.

the morning."[76] He was also worried about his father's health—the doctor suffered from angina—and was disheartened to see him sick and tired when he visited Oak Park. Ernest himself was often feeling tired and run down. "Have rated splitting headaches that damn near mort a man."[77] Hadley sensed his feelings and wrote encouraging letters, particularly about his father, but was herself very happy, delighting in spring weather and awakening to robins singing in the trees.

She was working with lawyers probating her mother's estate and to make extra money took in boarders at the house on Cates. She gave weekly piano recitals and sometimes entertained old beaux like Dr. Leo Loeb, a pinched and dour man in his fifties who did cancer research at Washington University and whom she thought "pathetic." She even drove to the country several times to pose nude for a sculptress friend who told her she had a classic body. She was also planning her marriage. Not even Fonnie's meddling and dislike of Ernest bothered Hadley, who finally took her sister aside and shouted "'twas none of your business!"[78] when Fonnie rushed out of the room in tears after Hadley warned her to never speak about Ernest or their marriage plans again. In the middle of June, an engagement party was held in St. Louis with the papers carrying the announcement. Ernest did not attend; his work at the *Co-operative Commonwealth* kept him in Chicago. Hadley, who, like Ernest, disliked duty and formality, but, unlike him, did not like being the center of attention, stood alone in the receiving line greeting old friends and accepting their well-wishes. The doctor and Grace sent a congratulatory telegram that arrived during the party.

Some of his friends were advising him against marriage: Howie Jenkins said that he shouldn't do it, and on a train to Oak Park for a Sunday dinner at his parents' house, Y. K. had told him that being tied to a woman could be bad for a gifted young man. In the spring, Ernest began to miss his bachelor summers in Michigan. Writing to Bill Smith in April, he dreamed about trout fishing in the streams near Walloon Lake:

---

76. EH to BS, April 28, 1921, *The Letters of Ernest Hemingway, Vol. 1.* / "nawthing" [*sic*].
77. EH to BS, April 28, 1921, *The Letters of Ernest Hemingway, Vol. 1.*
78. Diliberto, *Hadley*, 71.

"Wish to hell I was going Nort when you men do. Doubt if I'll get up this summer . . . sometimes get thinking about the Sturgeon and Black during the nocturnal and damn near go cuckoo."[79] But he had made up his mind about Hadley, smooth, luscious, kindly, and beckoning to his deepest needs, and wanted her to be his wife. "Dat's de way tings are," he wrote in the same letter. "Guy loves a couple or three streams all his life and loves 'em better than anything else in the world—falls in love with a girl and the goddam steams can dry up for all he cares."[80]

One night, Ernest stepped out with Katy, Y. K., and a quiet fellow who worked with him at the *Co-operative Commonwealth* named Krebs Friend, to the renown German beer hall Wurz n' Zepps on North Avenue, and a few "other splendid places," eating German food and drinking "beer at 40 cents the stein."[81] It amused him to see Krebs's personality emerge under the influence of alcohol.

By the time Doodles returned from studying music in New York in late May "the club" had switched domiciles, returning to the larger apartment at 100 East Chicago Avenue where Ernest wrote Marcelline about his "wonderful view" from "my front window looking down over the queer angled roofs of the old houses on Rush street down to the big mountain of the Wrigley building, green of the new grass along the street and trees coming out."[82] He continued to inquire about a permanent position with the *Toronto Star,* but John Bone would not commit, and slowly, sensitively, he worked on his fiction. Sending a story titled "The Current" to Hadley, she wrote back that it was "the most wonderfully keen and superbly thing done. . . . I'm completely under its power."[83]

Despite its fluid style, good dialogue, and some proficiency of character and plot, "The Current" is a stilted, narcissistic story written with the mark of a virgin, which, despite the braggadocio of supposed conquests, it was just as likely the author happened to be and would be until the end of the summer when he and Hadley consummated their love in

79. EH to BS, April 28, 1921, *The Letters of Ernest Hemingway, Vol. 1*.
80. EH to BS, April 28, 1921, *The Letters of Ernest Hemingway, Vol. 1.* / "tings" [*sic*].
81. EH to BS, April 28, 1921, *The Letters of Ernest Hemingway, Vol. 1*.
82. EH to MHS, May 20, 1921, *The Letters of Ernest Hemingway, Vol. 1*.
83. Hadley to EH, May 13, 1921, Hemingway Collection, JFK Library.

a hotel room on her last visit to Chicago before their marriage. Hadley's keen enjoyment of the story was probably because she recognized it as a sublime declaration of Ernest's love for her, for the object of the main character's love is a woman named Dorothy Hadley, whose hair "was the raw gold color of old country burnished copper kettles, and it held all the firelight and occasionally flashed a little of it back."[84] The tale is about a very handsome young man named Stuyvesant Byng who is in love with Dorothy Hadley who won't have him because "You've never stuck to anything," but if he would "pick something out and make an absolute, unqualified success of it,"[85] then he can ask her to marry him again. Byng decides to develop his skill as a middleweight boxer, and after a fierce championship match against an ape-like fighter, becomes the world champion and is caressed by Dorothy Hadley as he leaves the ring. The subject matter of love and athletic skill meant much to the author, and the grandiose overtures are kept down with smoother prose, good dialogue, and a proficient use of working knowledge about boxing. But the tale is self-absorbed and doesn't ring true, almost like juvenilia. In Paris, within a year, he would soon learn how to write with greater concentration and truth.

Hadley believed that art gave life shape and meaning, and she was an acute observer of her man and his art. She understood his growing vision to write in a clear, clean, spare prose, a vision he had begun to obtain by listening to Sherwood Anderson and reading the books he recommended, especially Sherwood's *Winesburg, Ohio* and *Moon-Calf* by Floyd Dell; these two books alone could have changed his attitude toward writing, as through them he would have seen a more meaningful purpose to fiction than the stories in popular magazines, and these books were also an introduction to the modernist movement that arose in Chicago just a few years before. When he sent her articles accepted by the *Toronto Star*, Hadley was very proud and wrote that she loved the way he "eliminates everything except what's necessary and strengthening . . . I'm wild over the way you pounce on a strong word and use it

84. Griffin, *Along with Youth*, 201.
85. Griffin, 201.

in the right place without any of this darned 'clever' effect most present day writers have."[86]

As their wedding plans progressed, life with Y. K. and the gang at the domicile was beginning to sour. When Hadley had visited in March during Doodles's absence, the bachelor lifestyle of Ernest and his friends had shocked her. The apartment was like a rowdy fraternity house with drunken people running in and out; one night, Howie Jenkins, Ernest's friend from the ambulance corps in Italy, had shown up with a couple of prostitutes. When Doodles returned from New York, the situation at the domicile became worse, as the marriage between Y. K. and Doodles Smith began to reveal itself as hardly a marriage at all—certainly not in the traditional sense understood by Hadley and Ernest—as Doodles began an affair with Don Wright. Thinking their behavior adulterous and very wrong, and worried about Y. K., Hemingway spoke to Doodles and Wright about it. Wright was infuriated and would no longer speak to him, while Doodles began to speak against him to Y. K. To get away from these disputes, Ernest took to sleeping on the flat roof of the house with "all sorts of shaped chimney pots," sometimes dreaming about "the bay with the moon coming up over a hill . . . and a big rainbow trout making a swirl in the moonlight on the bay."[87]

In the final summer of his bachelorhood, the first summer in his life not spent in Michigan fishing and roaming the countryside with friends, he worked hard to try to make some "seeds" so that he could support himself and his wife. He was also drinking a lot of wine. "Liquor is all that has carried the enditer [Ernest] through the last month," he wrote to a friend. "By Gawd Liquor is a fine thing. Let there never be any throwing off on it. By liquor mean wine of course."[88] Sometimes his emotions dropped like a flag on a windless day. Overworking, excessive drinking and smoking, insomnia, and a chronic sore throat contributed to the strange, unhappy feelings that often came upon him. Describing this condition of himself in his letters to Hadley, she became alarmed and

---

86. Hadley to EH, May 13, 1921, Hemingway Collection, JFK Library.
87. EH to Grace Quinlan, July 1921, *The Letters of Ernest Hemingway, Vol. 1.*
88. Oliver Rowse, "Becket and Hemingway," *Arete Magazine*, Winter 2011.

worried that he might take his own life, a state of mind she had brushed against for many years. "Not so truly low as to crave mortage are you?" she wrote. "Remember it would kill me to all intents and purposes. . . . You gotta live—first for you and then my happiness. I know how it feels cause I have so very many times wanted to go and couldn't on account of the mess it'd leave some other people in."[89]

Hadley visited Ernest again in early July and stayed at the domicile with Y. K. and Doodles, but the couples weren't getting along well because of Doodles's affair with Wright, a violation of the devotion of love that Hadley and Ernest felt strongly for each other; the situation was further exasperated when Wright tried to flirt with Hadley by asking her to let him kiss her. Ernest spent his days at the office while Hadley spent "long hot unoccupied days with Doodles stretched out on my bed watching me."[90] But at night they strolled the streets together, and stopping to eat in a restaurant, Hadley found Ernest's eyes "gleaming and warming and softening at me across a table."[91] For his twenty-second birthday, she bought him a new Corona typewriter.

Late in July, Ernest wrote a letter to his friend Grace Quinlan, giving some thoughts about his upcoming marriage.

> Course I'm too young by the calendar and would seem terribly funny to be married and horrible to be domesticated and settled into a dead rut of seed getting and maybe children having and all that. Chance though that it won't be that way at all—Good chance that it'll be just two people that love each other being able to be together and understand each other and bum together and help each other in their work and take away from each other that sort of loneliness of that's with you even when you're in a crowd of people that are fond of you. Think marriage might be a terrible fine thing you know—anyhow Hash and I are going to have a very fine try at it.[92]

89. Hadley to EH, July 7, 1921, Hemingway Collection, JFK Library.
90. Hadley to EH, July 15, 1921, Hemingway Collection, JFK Library.
91. Hadley to EH, July 13, 1921, Hemingway Collection, JFK Library.
92. EH to GQ, July 1921, *The Letters of Ernest Hemingway, Vol. 1.*

"Things are fouler than ever at the cile," he wrote Bill Smith early in August, "Goddamn I would mort Wright except that it wouldn't do me any good," explaining the situation as he saw it at the domicile. "Wright has conducted an intensive campaign [against Ernest] with Diles [Doodles] on the grounds that the enditer [Ernest] is 'no Gentleman' . . . During part of that time Wright was yencing [fornicating] his nympho-maniac paramour . . . in Diles own cile." Hemingway "spoke honestly to Wright for a few brief phrases he has posed as a martyr in Diles eyes and will not come into the cile as long as I am here." Ernest and Y. K. had not yet broken over it, but "Yen's words to me are 'you can never understand what Don means to Doodles.' Yen is right. I can't."[93]

What Ernest did not understand about the situation, growing up with parents devoted exclusively to each other through all good and bad times, and probably did not care to understand, was that Doodles and Y. K. had an unconventional open marriage—a marriage which may not even have been legal since they had pledged their vows in a private cer-emony written by themselves—in which each could take other lovers if they so desired. Hearing tales from his wife, Y. K. took offense at Ernest's gossip, and Ernest took offense when Y. K. spoke to him about this. Had-ley tried to keep things calm with the Smiths and reminded Ernest that Y. K. and Doodles were letting him stay rent-free and had also invited them to live there after their wedding. "We can't stay there unless we are really friendly," she wrote to Ernest. "You and I have to stop criticizing poor old Doodles—whether Y. K. hears it or not, he feels it—it must hurt like the Dickens too."[94] As long as they were together Hadley would often try to soften Hemingway's "grand animosities," remembering many years later that "he was such a good hater."[95]

The couples, however, were falling away from each other. Y. K.'s younger brother Bill had long been one of Ernest's best friends, and in the same letter as above he had written to him that he "would sooner take his promised bride to the back room of the second floor of a brothel in

93. EH to BS, August 3–5, 1921, *The Letters of Ernest Hemingway, Vol. 1.*
94. Hadley to EH, July 15, 1921, Hemingway Collection, JFK Library.
95. Mowrer, Sokoloff tapes, Hemingway Collection, JFK Library.

Seney, Michigan than to a cile inhabited or even frequented by Donal McCloud Wright."[96] Ernest would remain with Y. K. in the domicile only through the end of August as he prepared for his marriage to Hadley. The breach between them would widen to the point of no return. Although his brother and sister would be in their wedding, Y. K. would not be there, and when Hadley and Ernest returned from Michigan as husband and wife, they found another place to live.

Their wedding was on; they picked out the place and, with Grace's help, began sending the invitations. They did not want the pomp of a big wedding in Chicago or St. Louis and decided on the small country church in Horton Bay, inviting their own families and close friends, many known by the Hemingways from living and summering in the country around Walloon Lake for all the years that had passed. Even Fonnie was now pleased and helped with preparations for her sister's wedding. Hadley spent money on a beautiful wardrobe and wedding gown, packed up her room, and left her life in St. Louis to spend the weeks before her wedding with her friends the Breakers in a resort in northern Wisconsin, but first stopped in Chicago to see Ernest, arriving on August first. Not staying at the "domicile" because of the strained relations, she took a room at the Virginia Hotel a few blocks south, and it was there where she and Ernest made love for the first time, blissfully and truly discovering sexuality, and continued to do so throughout the several last days of their time together before Michigan. On the last night, they ate at a German restaurant—she later wrote how she felt sitting across the table, "I could have kissed you so hard, so easily, at any moment"[97]—and then she caught the train to Land O'Lakes, Wisconsin.

Through the month of August, Ernest worked hard at his job at the *Co-operative Commonwealth*, the slick publication that was much better than the organization it represented, and was lonely and nervous. To Marcelline he wrote, "as yet I do not realize the full horror of marriage . . . if you wish to see me break down at the altar and perhaps have to be carried to the altar in a chair by the crying ushers . . . be on tap for that

96. EH to Bill Smith, August 3–5, 1921, *The Letters of Ernest Hemingway, Vol. 1.*
97. Hadley to EH, Aug. 10, 1921, Hemingway Collection, JFK Library.

date."[98] To keep his head clear he wrote letters and worked out at Silvio Ferretti's Gymnasium, a place where mob tough guys hung around, and sometimes sparred with pro boxers. It may have been during this month that he started work on a story about a seduction on the wooden planks of a dock reaching out to the lake at Horton Bay, a story he would tell from the point of view of the young girl who was harshly seduced. It was not like any of the others he had written because it was not for popular consumption: he was spare in his use of words and trying to capture the feeling of an incident. Not so ironically, by concentrating harder and writing a real story he was using his imagination to a greater degree than ever before. He also looked for an apartment upon their return—not telling his mother the real reason, writing her only that Y. K. was giving up his apartment—and found a walk-up at a house on 1239 North Dearborn "for 75 seeds a month."[99]

Finally, he left for Michigan on the twenty-seventh of August, a Saturday, and arrived on the train at Boyne Falls early Sunday morning, spending a few days fishing on the Sturgeon River with Howie Jenkins and Charlie Hopkins, his old friend on the *Kansas City Star*. When Hadley arrived at Horton Bay a few days later, she stayed with the Charles family on their farm where she was joined with her bridesmaids, one of whom was Katy Smith, who had agreed to be part of the wedding party despite the estrangement between Ernest and Y. K. and her disappointment over losing Ernest. The marriage took place on Saturday, September third, at four o'clock in the afternoon in the white wood framed Methodist Church next to the general store in the village of Horton Bay, Michigan.

The day was bright and hot. Hadley arrived almost late because she had gone swimming in the lake and her thick red hair was slow to dry. Those in attendance were family and a few close friends, among whom were the Connables and some members of the McLallen and Nickey families from Indiana who had summered at Walloon Lake as long as the Hemingways. Ernest and the men in his wedding wore dark blue coats and white trousers; Hadley wore a cream lace wedding dress with

---

98. EH to MHS, Aug. 11, 1921, *The Letters of Ernest Hemingway, Vol. 1.*
99. EH to GHH, mid-August, *The Letters of Ernest Hemingway, Vol 1.*

satin slippers and a veil. After the ceremony, pictures were taken under the trees on the lawn at Pinehurst Cottage across the road. Hadley was tall and smiled happily in her wedding gown, holding her bouquet of baby's breath. Grace and the doctor, wearing light-colored clothes, looked very proud of their son, who stood tall and smiling in his white pants and dark coat, holding his large hands together, surrounded by all the others. After the pictures, the Dilworths called them all in for a fried chicken dinner.

The newlyweds left the party at dusk. A friend drove them four miles in his Model T Ford along the sandy road across the ridge to Grace's cabin at Longfield Farm. Someone had put a JUST MARRIED sign on the bumper, and the doctor attached some tin cans and old shoes on a string to drag behind it. At Longfield, Ernest located the small boat and oars and rowed a mile across the lake to Windemere. (Perhaps Hadley was perched on the stern while they crossed the lake, and watching her husband row, broke into a long tear of laughter as did the lovers escaping into Switzerland in *A Farewell to Arms*). At Windemere, Grace had had the floors varnished, the piano tuned, the porch roof repaired; placed on the music rack was one of her own compositions, "Lovely Walloona," along with a note welcoming the newlywed lovers to the cottage. Ernest dragged the mattresses from his parents' beds and put them together before the hearth. The last days of summer turned cool, and they built a fire and made wine by fermenting raisins in a large kettle.

Grace was at Longfield with her youngest daughter, Carol, and on days when there was no wind and the lake was still the newlyweds could hear the sound of her piano waft across the water. They caught colds, and when they got better Ernest took Hadley into Petoskey and introduced her to Marjorie Bump and Grace Quinlan. Maybe Ernest thought it would make him look good to show his bride these girls "who cannot live without me,"[100] or maybe he was just showing off his bride, but Hadley, thinking it vain and immature, was furious: "I'm sure I acted like a fool because I was in the position of a fool."[101] One day when

---

100. Mowrer, Sokoloff tapes, Hemingway Collection, JFK Library.
101. Mowrer, Sokoloff tapes, Hemingway Collection, JFK Library.

they finally rowed across the lake to have lunch with Grace and Carol, Grace was genuinely hurt that they had not responded to her note and told them so. Upon returning to Windemere, Hadley wrote her mother-in-law apologizing for "my apparent ingratitude for your welcome and your explanation of many material comforts."[102] Grace was deeply fond of her new daughter-in-law, and Hadley, who knew about domineering mothers and the effect they can have on some children, later admitted that Grace had been kind to her and she wished she had given her more attention, but that Ernest hated his mother and "he trained me to dislike her too."[103]

Late in September, they returned to Chicago to a top-floor walk-up apartment in a house on Dearborn Street in a cheap but rundown area on the near North Side. Grace and the doctor were celebrating their twenty-fifth anniversary with a party at their home in Oak Park on Saturday, October 1. Among the many friends invited were Y. K. Smith and Doodles, which gave Ernest, still seething over the Doodles and Don Wright affair, the opportunity to destroy what may have remained of the once close friendship by writing a letter on the very day of the party: "I'm taking a couple of minutes to rescind it [the invitation] personally," further stating that he would come to "collect the residue of my clothes and my probably well-thumbed correspondence," and ending with "Go hang yourself on a Christmas tree."[104] Y. K. immediately replied that Hemingway could collect the items from the Aldis storeroom, adding "You can readily understand that your having written me as you have makes your presence in my house quite impossible, at any time, under any circumstances."[105] Y. K. had done much for his young friend, and Ernest had returned some of the favor by opening himself up to Y. K. and taking him along to Oak Park for Sunday dinners with his parents, but their ending was terrible and complete—and this would not be the only time that Ernest Hemingway would turn against a benefactor for no good reason.

102. Hadley to GHH, Sept. 22, 1921, Hemingway Collection, JFK Library.
103. Mowrer, Sokoloff tapes, Hemingway Collection, JFK Library.
104. EH to Y. K. Smith, Oct. 1, 1921, *The Letters of Ernest Hemingway, Vol. 1.*
105. Y. K. Smith to EH, Oct. 1921, Hemingway Collection, JFK Library.

The rooms of the apartment on Dearborn were small and ugly and some of the furniture was broken. Ernest performed his last editorial duties for the *Commonwealth* magazine as the scam behind Harrison Parker and the *Co-operative Commonwealth* became exposed in the news. The trust went into receivership and the principals were sued. Ernest collected his last monthly paycheck of one hundred and fifty dollars (he was only paid for two of the three weeks of his honeymoon), and the job evaporated. The newlyweds lived off his paycheck and another one-hundred dollars the doctor had given him for a wedding present. Hadley's trust funds, which would total almost fifty-five thousand dollars and yield in dividends and interest of almost three-thousand dollars a year, would not be completely settled until the following year. They planned to leave Chicago and the Midwest and go to Italy. They did not know how or when they would leave, but the momentum built quickly, especially when Sherwood Anderson and Tennessee blew back into town from Paris and had them out to dinner at Palos Park.

Sherwood had never looked better. He spoke effusively about Paris and how wonderful the city was and that it was the perfect place for a young writer to write. Paris was ancient and beautiful, he told them, a city of old cathedrals and lovely stone bridges that stretch with arches across the Seine. Lovers strolled and kissed along the walkways of the banks of the famous river. There were pleasant rooms and good cheap wine. In the public gardens and sidewalk cafes, Anderson said, ideas flowed and you could fill up your notebooks with stories about America. There were bookstores all over, and he said he would write a letter of introduction to an American lady named Sylvia Beach who ran an English bookstore called Shakespeare & Company on rue de l'Odeon where many writers congregated. He told the Hemingways about the literati who lived in Paris: the Irishman James Joyce; a poet named Ezra Pound, who was born in Hailey, Idaho and grew up in Pennsylvania; and more about the remarkable woman from San Francisco, Gertrude Stein, in whose atelier hung the finest and most remarkable collection of modern art anywhere. He would write letters of introduction to them all telling them about this "quite wonderful newspaper man" with "extraordinary talent" who was a "writer instinctively in touch with everything worthwhile" and that he and his wife "were delightful people to know."[106]

Ernest hesitated. He had wanted to return to Italy so very much where he understood and spoke a little of the language. Though Hadley wanted whatever it was that Ernest wanted, she did know French from years of schooling. And then an offer came through from John Bone of the *Toronto Star* for a European correspondent, but the location had to be Paris where the *Star* had their foreign headquarters. Ernest was a perfect fit for what Bone had in mind: a talented, unknown foreign correspondent; so talented and unknown that Bone could have his stories rewritten and, all but unknowingly, sell to other newspapers and keep the money (an unspoken agreement Bone had with the chief who could pay him less because of it). So, he negotiated again with Bone and got a good contract, and so to Paris it would be for the young Hemingways.

One day, Grace came to the apartment house and climbed the flights of stairs, entered the rooms, and took Hadley's hands within her own. Grace had a big florid face, which she covered with white powder to tone down the pinkness. Her purpose in calling, as Hadley remembered, was "to teach me about love"[107] as she talked about the importance of wifely devotion. Hadley thought that Grace was worried "that I didn't love Ernest enough. She wanted to make sure her son had a completely devoted wife,"[108] and without saying so directly, Grace also wanted to know that her son was sexually satisfied. The doctor, too, visited them during the brief time they lived on Dearborn Street. He came in the morning after Ernest had emptied the chamber pot and was starting to work on a story, to complain about the .22 rifle Ernest had given him in exchange for the honeymoon provisions: Ernest had ruined it by trying to shoot out a clog in the bore. The doctor was also upset that the cottage had been left so messy.

Another visitor came bearing much better news. Nick Nerone, who Ernest had met in Italy, worked in the Chicago Italian Consulate. Unlike

---

106. Anderson to Lewis Gallantiere, *Letters of Sherwood Anderson*, 85.
107. Mowrer, Sokoloff tapes, Hemingway Collection, JFK Library.
108. Mowrer, Sokoloff tapes, Hemingway Collection, JFK Library.

Ernest, whose war wound was an accident he had aggrandized into a fortuitous event, Nerone was an authentic hero who had fought with the Italian Army during the retreat of Caporetto and earned four silver crosses on his way to becoming a captain. They drank wine together in the small cafes in Chicago that spring and summer as Ernest listened to Nick's true tales of the fighting during the disastrous retreat to the Piave River. Ernest told Nick some war stories, too, but unlike the stories Ernest heard from Nick, they were probably not true. The two had bonded and were good friends and when Nick came to their apartment it was with the news that General Diaz, who had commanded the Italian forces at the victory of Vittoria Veneto, was coming to Chicago.

Nerone had proposed that the great general himself formally decorate Ernest with the medal he had received in Italy, and he was working on the plans. There would be a parade down Michigan Avenue in honor of the general, followed by a banquet at the Congress Hotel where the general would present the medals. The *Chicago Tribune* ran a spread on the activities with pictures of Diaz, Nerone, and Hemingway, who would be "decorated by General Diaz for bravery while serving with the Italian army."[109] But the general was there to decorate real heroes like Nick Nerone, who was wounded three times in a single battle, not Red Cross volunteers who had placed themselves in the line of fire, even if they told such convincing stories that those who had actually been in the fight would believe them, and Ernest would not be decorated nor even meet the general. The medals didn't matter much to Ernest anyway. It was the tales he heard from Nerone about actual combat that really meant something to him, and over the next few years, he would absorb these tales as if they were his own, so much so that, in time, he would recreate them in a grand tale about the war as perfectly as they had happened. But he still had much to learn about creative writing, and even though he was attempting to write a novel about the war in Italy, he was not yet ready to write such a tale.

Gold dropped from the sky in November when out of the blue Hadley received eight-thousand dollars from the estate of Arthur Wyman, her

---

109. *Chicago Tribune*, Nov. 20, 1921.

mother's younger brother. The Hemingways would be leaving Chicago and the Midwest for Paris, their minds having been changed by the moving descriptions of Sherwood Anderson, whose spirit had been restored by his visit to Paris, and the practicality of a job there. Ernest crunched a few numbers—he was good at personal finance (his parents had taught their children well)—and realized that with the money he could make with the *Toronto Star*, and that which Hadley's trust funds would yield, there would be more than enough for them to live well in Paris. Soon afterward, walking down North Dearborn Street, they passed the office of the Chicago agent for the French Line and stopped and stood together in the cold, looking through the window at the ads for the liners crossing the Atlantic. In late November, they booked passage on the *Leopoldina* leaving from New York to Le Havre on December eighth.

They had to travel light. Several days before the young Hemingways left, the doctor drove into the city to pick up boxes for storage. Among the wedding gifts and kitchenware and clothing, which included Ernest's shredded war uniform, was a box containing the manuscripts of the unpublished short stories Ernest had written before meeting Sherwood Anderson. He had revised his concept of the short story and took with him, instead, the new fiction he had started writing: a few stories set in Italy, a first version of "Up in Michigan," and a novel about the Italian war he had started in the spring. They left Chicago on a cold Wednesday morning at the LaSalle Street Station, boarding their train and waving goodbye to a small crowd of family and friends who gathered to see them off. Hadley's hands were bare and cold in the frozen air, and so Marcelline, her beautiful sister-in-law, took off her gloves and tossed them to her as a farewell present.

As their train traveled east across America, Oak Park took no special notice of the parting of another native son. Ernest Hemingway had never been seen as an extraordinary youth. Years later, his high school English teacher, Fannie Biggs, remembering little about the writing class she had taught him, could recall much more about his mother than she could about Ernest. "Thinking of his mother's exuberant vitality, the rich curves of her every move, the warmth of her vital personality," Miss Biggs said, "I have wondered if Ern would find a wife with the lush mother-hood he knew."[110] At this same time, some Oak Park mothers gathered in the name of common decency to establish the *Friends of American Writers* with the purpose that "all education should be based upon good clean literature." They wanted their books filled with "high ideals and a desire for a higher life,"[111] and among other ideas, they would discuss the detrimental influence of Jazz upon the arts. These ladies were going to be disappointed with the modern age of literature, whose most prominent practitioner would be a native son. Hemingway had little care for what these women thought. His boyhood home had become for him "a village of broad lawns and narrow minds," and though taking much of it with him, he had left Oak Park behind years before. It was the future to which he looked, for waiting for them in Paris through Sherwood's letters of introduction, the Hemingways would soon meet a strident poet who wanted to change the world and the great woman who practically invented the modern age.

---

110. Michael Reynolds, *The Young Hemingway*, 260.
111. Reynolds, 260.

The Water Tower

Hadley in the spring of 1920

Chicago streets

Dearborn Train Station

Sherwood Anderson

Arcade Art Colony

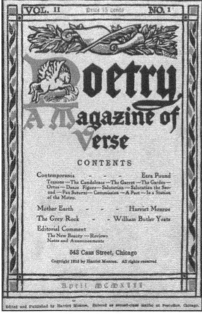

Poetry Magazine

Co-operative Commonwealth

The Little Review

Hadley with Ernest in St. Louis

Wedding day with family

The newlyweds

THE MODERN WORLD
OF PARIS

Paris was where the twentieth century was.
—GERTRUDE STEIN

IKE BALZAC and Gertrude Stein, Ezra Pound was spellbound by the preceding generations of his family. The mercurial career of his grandfather held his imagination the most. His grandfather, Thaddeus Coleman Pound, had been born in a log cabin and made and lost three fortunes before turning to politics. A natural orator, he ran for Congress from Wisconsin and served three consecutive terms in Washington, DC, where he was promised a cabinet position by Garfield, but when his wife left him and he began an affair with a married woman, lesser men disapproved and his political career soon came to an end. There was enough political capital remaining to secure his quiet, placid son a government appointment to establish a land office in Hailey, Idaho, where Ezra was born in October of 1885, the only child of Homer and Isabel Pound. Isabel did not like the rough town of Hailey, where land claims were often settled with guns, so the family moved to Philadelphia in 1889, where Homer became an assistant assayer at the United States Mint.

As a boy, pampered and spoiled by his mother, Ezra had long curls and was called "the Professor"[1] at the Quaker school he went to because he wore glasses and used complex polysyllabic words. At home, his parents wrote letters in verse, and Ezra began writing verse too. The first

---

1. John Tytell, *Ezra Pound: The Solitary Volcano*, 1.

125

poem he wrote was about the populous politician William Jennings Bryan. At a military school, he hated drill and marching but was a prodigious student who loved Greek and Latin, fencing, and playing chess. Entering the University of Pennsylvania at fifteen, carrying a gold cane and walking the campus with a leonine mass of auburn hair under a broad-brimmed hat with a swooping feather, he fought every regulation and professor who tried to make him conform to what they considered the proper path of learning. Stating that he wanted "to write before I die the greatest poems that have ever been written,"[2] he was naïve and bullied and made average grades. His parents encouraged him to transfer to a smaller college, Hamilton College in upstate New York, where he was introduced to the medieval poetry of Dante and the Provençal troubadours of southern France and began translating verse written between the Dark Ages and the Renaissance that had connections to the classical world of the Greeks and Romans. Here, too, at Hamilton College, he began his lifelong pursuit of beautiful women.

Returning to Philadelphia, to graduate school at Penn, young Ezra worked hard and finished his master's degree before turning twenty-one and was awarded a fellowship in Romantics. But he antagonized and bewildered the graduate faculty and, doubting that his own creativity could be sustained in the dryness of academia, left before completing a doctorate. In the fall of 1907, he made the first of his many unusual sojourns to take a job teaching Spanish at tiny Wabash College in Crawfordsville, Indiana. The small-town atmosphere of Crawfordsville, its tree-lined streets, stately homes, and the knell of church bells on Sundays, provoked Ezra into more flamboyance. He dressed in a black velvet coat and soft collared shirt, smoked in his office, visited faculty members with a flask of rum to spike his tea, and was a firebrand in class. "I do not teach! I awake!"[3] was his mantra, telling students that religion was useful only to the extent that it popularized art. Admonished by the school president, with whom he shared a lady friend, he complained that Crawfordsville was the sixth circle of Dante's desolation. Then, when he met

---

2. Tytell, 19.
3. Tytell, 32.

a touring actress and invited her into his room, it caused such a scandal that he moved to other quarters, and when the actress was again found in his room the president dismissed him from the faculty. Traumatized by the Puritan rejection, Pound soon left for Europe, crossing the ocean on a cattle boat, vowing to "break the silence"[4] of social convention and Victorian morals.

In the summer of 1908, he hung around Venice long enough to pay a printer to publish a sheaf of his poems and then left for London to establish his reputation. In London, with little money, he ate little, lived in small rooms, and worked very hard on his poems. He wanted to express the fusion of art and ecstasy, a "sensation of the soul in ascent,"[5] and aware of the past and knowing that Walt Whitman wrote in a vernacular, he knew this was his right direction. To make a little money, he delivered a series of lectures on the development of literature in southern Europe at a polytechnic school near the British Museum and looked up a bookseller named Elkin Matthews who ran a shop in a narrow bent lane off Regent Street. Matthews's shop was a favorite place for writers to gather, and Pound would talk and sip tea there in the late afternoon with his reddish-gold hair brushed back rising from his forehead, his long, lithe appearance and uncompromising demeanor attracting the attention of the literary world of London. Dorothy Shakespear, whose mother, Olivia, was a novelist and sometime lover of William Butler Yeats, was enchanted. "He has a wonderful, beautiful face, a high forehead, prominent over the eyes, a long delicate nose," she wrote, "all your ideas, your knowledge, your bluey eyes, your great loneliness."[6] Pound's life was rich, but his wallet was poor, so he would write to his friend from Pennsylvania, William Carlos Williams. He met Yeats through Olivia Shakespear and became friends with Ford Madox Hueffer, who later Anglicized his last name to Ford.

Ford was tall and blond with a blond mustache and had grown up among painters, musicians, and writers and very early learned the power

---

4. Tytell, 35.
5. Tytell, 40.
6. Peter Ackroyd, *Ezra Pound and his World*, 19.

and importance of words. He was editing the *English Review*, where he published the writings of Thomas Hardy, Henry James, W. H. Hudson, Joseph Conrad, Anatole France, Arnold Bennett, H. G. Wells, and John Galsworthy. He would also publish some of Pound's best poems during these formative years of his writing. Ford wrote that "Ezra would approach with the steps of a dancer, making passes with a cane at an imaginary opponent. He would wear trousers made of green billiard cloth, a pink coat, a blue shirt, a tie hand-painted by a Japanese friend, an immense sombrero, a flaming beard cut to a point and a single large blue ear-ring."[7] Ezra, slim and agile, playing a good game of tennis, found a home among Ford and his writer/artist friends and was soon introduced into a circle of poets with new thoughts called "Imagism" that demanded a direct treatment of the subject composed in the sequence of a musical phrase and using no word that did not contribute to the presentation; thoughts that helped him capture moments in time, like a camera, as a more coherent voice began to emerge in his verse:

> I who have seen you amid the primal things
> Was angry when they spoke your name
> In ordinary places.
> I would that the cool waves might flow over my mind,
> And that the world should dry as a dead leaf,
> Or as a dandelion seed-pod and be swept away,
> So that I might find you again,
> Alone.[8]

Pound was living in a room in Kensington by a church with bells pealing at any hour so loud that the walls vibrated. But still, he produced his art. "Mr. Ezra Pound is that rare thing among modern poets, a scholar. He is not only cultivated, but learned,"[9] wrote a reviewer of his poems. Others noted the beauty of his lines. William Butler Yeats took

---

7. Ackroyd, 21. / "ear-ring" [*sic*].
8. Ezra Pound, "Francesca."
9. Tytell, *Ezra Pound: The Solitary Volcano*, 54.

Ezra seriously as a poet and invited him to his Monday evening salons where Ezra, often nervous and self-conscious, saying the first thing that came to mind, became giddy with stimulation and dominated the room, distributing the older man's cigarettes and wine and laying down the law about poetry. He spent time with D. H. Lawrence, the two men admiring each other, but while Lawrence worshipped the sensual life in his art, Pound worshipped beauty. When Ford paid him £15 for some long poems in the early spring of 1910, he set out for Lake Garda in Northern Italy by the ruins of the villa of Catullus and was soon joined by Olivia and Dorothy Shakespear, who loved the blue beauty of the water too.

Undetermined about his future, Pound returned to America in June 1910, where he was introduced to a wealthy lawyer in New York City named John Quinn who would provide financial support to many of his plans in the coming years. He tried to like New York, moving to Greenwich Village where he reunited with an old flame, Hilda Doolittle, who now had women lovers but still wanted to marry Ezra, and even had a book of his poems and translations published by a publisher he met in the city, but his heart was abroad, and with money from his parents, he returned to London in the New Year (and decided that if he were to marry he would marry Dorothy Shakespear, though her father strongly disapproved because the young poet had no consistent income).

Pound liked to see the places of the people he studied, and in the summer of 1912, he toured the region where medieval troubadours had lived and performed in Southern France, sometimes walking twenty miles in a day. A letter arrived from Harriet Monroe in Chicago, offering the job of foreign correspondent for her new international magazine, *Poetry*. Harriet Monroe liked old and new and had stumbled upon Pound's poetry in London a few years before. Pound was exuberant and immediately wrote her a long, enthusiastic letter enclosing two of his own poems, and in a further effort to sweep out the old and bring in the new, also sent poems by Yeats and a Bengali poet named Rabindranath Tagore.

His staunch peculiarity bearing fruit, every man of letters in England knew of Ezra Pound. An interview in the *Philadelphia Record* noted that he "knew almost everyone worth knowing," and "was one of the kindest men that ever lived."[10] Yeats, too, trusted Pound's criticism, saying that Ezra's medievalism had taught him precision. When Robert Frost came to London in early 1913, he found his way to Pound. Ezra read his work and liked it and sent his poems to Harriet Monroe for publication in *Poetry*. Pound left again to travel on the continent, and in Paris, on the terrace of a restaurant near the Luxembourg Gardens, he was introduced to Skipwith Cannell and his tall, vivacious wife, Kitty. He liked them both very much, and they followed him back to London where he found them rooms in his building on Church Walk. Kitty was a dancer and an excellent mimic. When the Cannells fled London at the outbreak of war, her imitations of Ezra delighted the New York poets.

Spending the summer of 1913 with Yeats at a cottage in the south of England, Pound edited some of Yeats's poems and worked on translating Japanese plays. The older poet wrote to a friend that Pound "helps me to get back to the definite and concrete away from modern abstractions."[11] During these months together, Yeats told Pound about a young Irishman named James Joyce. Pound wrote to Joyce, interested in publishing some of his work in various reviews and wanting his poem, "I hear an army charging," in an anthology he was putting together. Joyce wrote back delighted that someone was interested in publishing his dormant work. Pound sensed the genius in the man and was instrumental in getting Joyce's great prose stories published. Years later in Paris, Joyce would tell Robert McAlmon that "he pulled me out of the gutter."[12]

In April 1914, Ezra Pound and Dorothy Shakespear were married in a small civil ceremony in London. Pound's work was changing too. As Imagism began to split apart, Pound and those around him sought poetry that moved as well as presented, more like cinema than a snapshot. An idea they called "vorticism" was seen as a means of breaking loose from passive and insignificant art: "at the heart of the whirlpool is a great silent place where all energy is concentrated,"[13] stated Wyndham Lewis, Pound's friend and cohort in the movement. The vorticists were

---

10. J. J. Wilhelm, *Ezra Pound in London and Paris*, 106.
11. Noel Stock, *The Life of Ezra Pound*, 130.
12. Wilhelm, *Ezra Pound in London and Paris*, 136.
13. Wilhelm, 146.

trying to do to literature what cubism had done to visual art, to open and free it of pointless strictures. When the magazine *Blast* appeared, heralding the new movement with poems by Pound and praise for Joyce, it represented iconoclasm at its most strident and created a stir, but no money was made with the venture and vorticism faded quickly as World War I broke out and young men began evaporating from the streets. "Artists are the antennae of the race,"[14] Pound once wrote, and since they transmitted a sense of moral value that held civilization together, and he could see that with the outbreak of war artists were scarcely heard, he figured the crumbling of civilization was coming too.

Remaining in London during the war, he had beautiful lovers—never was he faithful to Dorothy—and an extraordinary array of literary activity. He wrote to Harriet Monroe that "Language is made out of concrete things. General expressions in non-concrete terms are a laziness; they are talk, not art, not creation."[15] When a young American named Thomas Stearns Eliot appeared in town on a fellowship studying philosophy at Oxford, he shared tea with Ezra and Dorothy in the triangular room in their small apartment on Holland Place. Pound wore his velveteen jacket and corduroy pants and was outspoken and far-ranging. Eliot was shy and pedantic and gave Pound a copy of "Prufrock" to read: From its first lines,

> Let us go then, you and I,
> when the evening is spread out against the sky
> Like a patient etherized upon a table,

through the end,

> We have lingered in the chambers of the sea
> By sea-girls wreathed with seaweed red and brown
> Till human voices wake us, and we drown,[16]

---

14. Pound, *Literary Essays of Ezra Pound*, 297.
15. Wilhelm, *Ezra Pound in London and Paris*, 174.
16. T. S. Eliot, "The Love Song of J. Alfred Prufrock."

Pound extolled the author and his poem with great enthusiasm to Harriet Monroe until she finally published it in *Poetry*.

In the summer of 1915, Yeats and Pound secured literary grants for Joyce, who had fled to neutral Zurich, Switzerland, to keep him going while he worked on *Ulysses*; Ford accepted a commission with Welsh troops and was sent to France, where he was gassed and suffered a physical and mental breakdown; and Pound began working on a long project he called the *Cantos*, a world epic treating good and bad in history, which was probably first conceived at Hamilton College. Pound was delighted when Margaret Anderson asked him to become foreign editor of the *Little Review*. Margaret Anderson was a fearless and honest editor who would provide the new vanguard of writers with a reliable publishing venue and help launch a new modern era in literature. Weary of the terrible, destructive war and feeling discouraged about humanity, Ezra became politicized and grasped onto an economic theory that bankers were the heart of the problem of economic failure and had to be strictly controlled. When the war ended, James Joyce returned to Trieste, Italy, and continued writing *Ulysses*, sending chapters to Pound for publication in the *Little Review*; Ford and his mistress, Stella Bowen, bought a chicken farm in the country; Yeats would remain in Ireland and soon received the Nobel Prize for literature "for his always inspired poetry"[17]; and Ezra and Dorothy went on a long-ranging tour of southern France, visiting ancient towns where the troubadours had roamed singing and chanting their poems and songs.

In Venice, in April 1920, Ezra Pound and James Joyce finally met each other. On their way back to London, the Pounds stopped in Paris, where Ezra found his way to Sylvia Beach's bookstore, Shakespeare & Company. He offered her free carpentry work. Sylvia was struck by his elongated, feline appearance and his friendliness. Through Pound, Sylvia would meet James Joyce, whom she greatly admired, and despite threats of censorship from government agencies inclined to sniff out obscenity, would publish his masterpiece, *Ulysses*. Ezra persuaded Joyce to gather his

---

17. Citation upon a Nobel Prize for Literature, 1923.

family and move to the magic city of Paris where all true artists belong. At the end of the year, the Pounds left London for good, never to return, and in Paris, on their way to the south of France, Ezra was interviewed by the Paris edition of the *New York Herald*, saying that he "finds the decay of the British Empire too depressing a spectacle to witness at close range."[18] They would spend the cold winter months at St. Raphael on the Côte d'Azur before settling in Paris in spring.

The Great War had devastated France. Almost three million of its young men had been killed or permanently disabled, and millions more had been forced to flee from their homes in areas overrun by Germans. Thousands of buildings were destroyed, livestock herds had been wiped out, and factories had been systematically disassembled and shipped to Germany. The government policy to compensate citizens who had suffered war damage helped create an expanding inflation. Rent controls imposed as a war measure remained in place with the result that landlords refused to install electricity and modern plumbing that many buildings lacked, and investors were loath to put money into the construction of new dwellings. Uncertainty about the nation's economy discouraged farmers from purchasing motorized equipment and caused manufacturers to shy away from producing a cheap car for the masses. There were as many horses on French farms in the post-war years as there had been in 1850 and as many horse-drawn carriages on the streets of French cities and towns as the early 1890s. And though France was in deep economic trouble, from an expatriate point of view, living there was extremely attractive. Horse-drawn carriages were not seen as a technological lag but evocative symbols of Old World charm; and if having to contend with outdated living facilities was bothersome, the problem was made much easier by hiring a maid since an ever-more favorable rate of exchange put servants, as well as many other amenities, within the financial grasp of even the marginally well-off.

Paris became a magnet for foreigners in the twenties, especially for Americans and artists. The dollar stretched enormously due to post-war

---

18. Wilhelm, *Ezra Pound in London and Paris*, 254.

inflation—twelve francs to a dollar and going higher—and there was the perpetual loveliness of the city, a spell cast more easily with the excellence of its wines and cuisine and the personal freedom offered since Napoleon, bestowing not only tolerance but even respect upon historically unconventional people like artists and people of color. Soon after arriving, Ezra wrote John Quinn that his meager amount of money went much further than it ever had in London. In Paris, he moved in the worlds of millionaires, writers, musicians, and painters; worlds with their own constellations that overlapped at the edges. He never moved among the rich for very long; he encountered them in the salons of Natalie Barney, whom he had first met in Paris before the war and became reacquainted on his trip to visit the troubadour sites when she gave him a sheaf of her poetry to read. Almost ten years older than Pound and no longer the dazzling beauty of her youth, Miss Barney was a remarkable woman who had affairs with other extraordinary gay women and wrote books about homosexual life. Admiring Ezra's critical judgment, it didn't bother her much when he said she was "out of touch . . . with the best contemporary work,"[19] for she found Ezra charming and was friendly to his literary friends such as Ford Madox Ford, who printed a couple of her poems in the *Transatlantic Review*; James Joyce; and a young man soon to arrive in Paris named Ernest Hemingway.

Paris was a city of salons, and the salon held by Natalie Barney on Friday evenings was foremost among them. In her sumptuously furnished house, she entertained Paris literati and scandalized even the French with her band of female admirers and discordant rejoinders such as "He who confuses reproduction with love spoils them both with marriage."[20] She came from Ohio, from a family of great wealth that had amassed a fortune building railroad cars. Her father furiously disapproved of her associations with strange homosexual women but upon his death in 1902 left her two-and-a-half million dollars, far more than enough to keep her in wealth throughout her long life and through her many female lovers. She loved Paris—the Napoleonic Code was tolerant of homosexuality—and

---

19. Wilhelm, 262.
20. Tytell, *Ezra Pound: The Solitary Volcano*, 166.

lived in a two-story pavilion in the courtyard of 20 rue Jacob in the St. Germain Quarter of Paris where she held her salons. Tucked in the back of the smaller garden behind the pavilion was a small Greek temple with steps up to a portico supported by Doric columns and a round domed room inside. Her salons were an open house for selected guests and habitués of the Left Bank bohemia and her many women friends who danced gaily together on all sides of the dance floor. Presiding over all, wearing white gowns that accentuated her blonde hair and blue eyes, Natalie mixed with all and mixed all well.

She received her guests downstairs, where a domed stained-glass ceiling arched over Turkish hassocks and opulent couches. Tables along the walls were laden with sandwiches, sweets, champagne, and held vases of white lilies in memory of a female friend, a poet who had died of unrequited passion for another woman. She had been friends with Apollinaire, Proust, and Picasso; James Joyce was reputed to have attended a salon; and she continued to show Pound her poems and elicit his criticism. She also often gave money to his enthusiasms like the *Bel Esprit*, which was to raise enough money to save T. S. Eliot from his job at a bank (though Eliot liked working at a bank), and helped finance the composer George Antheil's efforts to produce music scores to some of Pound's poems. She had been eager to establish her own literary review, but Pound discouraged this idea fearing she would pack it with the work of her women friends and it would be an embarrassment.

When the doctor/poet William Carlos Williams visited Paris in 1924, his old friend Ezra took him to one of Natalie's soirees. "You might think it was something preserved in amber from the time of the Renaissance," he wrote.

> Ezra was full of homage for Natalie Barney, L'Amazone, as she
> was called at one time. But Ezra always paid homage to old
> distinction: it is one of his handsomest traits. So we were to have
> tea with Natalie, a tremendous concession on her part toward
> me, one of the primitives of Ezra's earlier years. She was extremely
> gracious and no fool to be sure, far less so than Ezra under the

circumstances. She could tell a pickle from a clam any day of the week. I admired her and her lovely garden, well kept, her laughing doves, her Japanese servants. There were officers wearing red buttons in their lapels there and women of all descriptions. Out of the corner of my eye I saw a small clique of them sneaking off together into a side room while casting surreptitious glances about them, hoping their exit had not been unnoticed.[21]

When Ezra met the American violinist Olga Rudge at one of Natalie's salons, he began a love affair that would last the rest of his life. Olga moved in the world of aristocrats and millionaires on the Right Bank, while Pound moved in the world of impoverished artists and students on the Left Bank. But her intelligence and musical brilliance captured his heart, and although he never left Dorothy, she became his true paramour. Ezra probably took the Hemingways to at least one of Natalie Barney's parties. Ernest wrote in *A Moveable Feast*, "many American and French women with money enough had salons and I figured very early that they were excellent places for me to stay away from,"[22] which was probably true. During these busy years, Hemingway didn't spend much time in salons, only enough to learn about them, and as with much of what he first learned about Paris and the Left Bank, he learned about them from Ezra. Natalie Barney needed careful explaining to a young married man with the dew of a Midwestern boyhood still upon him, and she must have held his respect; not just because she had a lot of money and was still beautiful—a middle-aged beauty mostly lost upon a young man—but also because she was openly homosexual with other women, caring much less for what others thought about it than how she felt about herself and her true lovers. As his years in Paris and his writings later in life revealed, Ernest Hemingway was fascinated by and often adored homosexual women.

Paris in the early twenties was swirling with thoughts and art and music, and Pound placed himself at the center. Walter Morse Rummell,

---

21. Tytell, 166–67.
22. Ernest Hemingway, *A Moveable Feast*, 111.

the American pianist and grandson of Samuel Morse, who developed the electrical telegraph system, and George Antheil, an experimental orchestral composer, were friends with Ezra, as were Romanian sculptor Constantin Brancusi and French avant-garde painter Francis Picabia. Brancusi piled stones together for a stove to cook steak and chicken and soup served with plenty of wine in a studio where poor Ezra, used to eating only omelets, feasted with much relish. Philosophical movements developed as people sought equilibrium after the renting destruction of war. The nihilistic Dada Movement, part of which branched off into Surrealism, had appeal to Ezra because of its similarity to his Blast philosophy to sweep away current thought, but it had no goal except chaos. Though Pound was ultra-masculine, he would tolerate anyone with a probing mind, and one of his best friends in Paris was the homosexual French poet Jean Cocteau, whom he called the best writer in Europe. But, drawn mostly to those who spoke English, he did not make the big splash in Paris that he had in London. Gertrude Stein did not find him charming. He came into the pavilion at 27 rue de Fleurus, talking and expounding on art, and carelessly leaning and tilting in an expensive fragile chair, he fell backward and damaged the chair. She called him a village explainer: "excellent if you were a village, but if you were not, not,"[23] and did not invite him back. Ezra was disappointed.

The English literary center of Paris was Sylvia Beach's bookstore, Shakespeare & Company. Located near the Luxembourg Gardens, it was across the street from a French bookstore owned by Adrienne Monnier, Sylvia's friend and lover. Born to a preacher in Baltimore in 1887, when her father took his family to Paris at the turn of the century Sylvia fell in love with the French capital and returned during the war. She met Adrienne when she bought a book at her store. Adrienne soon encouraged her to open her own shop. Sylvia's first store was around the corner, but two years later she took over an abandoned laundry across the street from Monnier at 12 rue de l'Odeon. Modeled after Elkin Matthews's establishment in London, Shakespeare & Company began as a lending

---

23. Tytell, *Ezra Pound: The Solitary Volcano*, 186.

library that soon began selling books. There were rooms upstairs, which for a while were rented to George Antheil, who sometimes climbed from the window down to the street. The interior of the shop was two spacious rooms with portraits and pictures of authors on the walls. People stopped by at any time of the day to browse or chat around a large table that served as her desk; it was a homey place that soon acquired a reputation as a center for tourists and expatriates. One person, who admired Miss Beach greatly, had just reached Paris with his wife a few days before Christmas and first dropped by Shakespeare & Company with its warm stove on a cold December 28, 1921. "A customer we liked," Sylvia would later write, "one who gave us no trouble, was that young man you saw almost every morning over there in a corner at Shakespeare and Company, reading the magazines or Captain Marryat or some other book. This was Ernest Hemingway."[24]

The young Hemingways had caught their first glimpse of Spain on their crossing when their ship, the *Leopoldina*, briefly stopped in the western Spanish port of Vigo. Ernest wrote to his family in Oak Park: "In the harbor were great schools of tuna—some jumped 6 and 8 feet out of water chasing sardines." He also dashed off on his typewriter his first overseas article to John Bone, an inspired short report about fishermen in skiffs in the bay of Vigo fighting for six hours to land a big tuna: "It is a back-sickening, sinew-straining, man-sized job even with a rod that looks like a hoe handle."[25] After passing through customs at Cherbourg, Ernest observed the Normandy countryside of "villages with smoking manure piles and long fields and woods with the leaves on the ground and the trees trimmed bare of branches way up their trunks and a roll of country and towers up over the edge"[26] as they rolled along on the train to Paris, where, upon arrival, they took a room at the Hotel Jacob on rue Jacob, a small, inexpensive hotel recommended by Sherwood Anderson on the short narrow street near the Seine in the heart of literary bohemia.

24. Sylvia Beach, *Shakespeare & Company*, 77.
25. *Toronto Star Weekly*, Feb. 18, 1922.
26. EH to the Andersons, Dec. 23, 1921, *Letters of Ernest Hemingway, Vol. 1*.

They marveled at the cost of living, Ernest writing the Andersons, "Think things are even cheaper than when you all were here."[27]

Their first days in Paris were quiet and lonely. They walked "the streets, day and night, arm through arm, peering into courts and stopping in front of little shop windows,"[28] sometimes feeling a little low but easily cheered, filling their time with good meals at a restaurant around the corner called the Pre aux Clercs, writing letters, and reading about Paris. Ernest wrote to Sherwood Anderson that "when it's a cold night in the streets of Paris and we're walking home down the Rue Bonaparte we think of the way the wolves used to slink into the city and Francois Villon and the gallows at Montfaucon."[29] They were together and in love, breaking upon a completely new life adventure and uncertain of the future. They had Hadley's trust fund and Ernest's energy, charm, and vision, but, in the cold days around Christmas when the rains were coming and they warmed themselves before a charcoal-burning brazier drinking rum punch outside the Dome Café on Montparnasse Boulevard, they mostly had each other. Though Hadley spoke French, Ernest, her large-limbed young husband, did not, nor did he know much about Paris and nothing at all about its literary community of English writers. But it was important to him that he appear to be fully integrated and knowledgeable, and so from the very beginning, he listened and studied and read, and the letters he wrote to friends and family and the stories for the *Toronto Star* indicated a full insider knowledge of nearly all there was to know.

When Hemingway first found his way to Shakespeare & Company, Sylvia Beach liked him very much. It was almost impossible to resist young Ernie, for whom humility was an important, if inconsistent, aspect of his personality. He was so handsome and big and nice, with a broad smile that lit up a room, becoming personally involved with people he liked or felt he might need, and he would listen carefully, absorbing all they said, hearing words he later might even use as his own. This was certainly true when he first met Sylvia Beach. "Sylvia had a lively, sharply sculptured

---

27. EH to the Andersons, Dec. 23, 1921, *Letters of Ernest Hemingway, Vol. 1.*
28. EH to the Andersons, Dec. 23, 1921, *Letters of Ernest Hemingway, Vol. 1.*
29. EH to the Andersons, Dec. 23, 1921, *Letters of Ernest Hemingway, Vol. 1.*

face," Hemingway wrote many years later, and "she was delightful and charming and welcoming and behind her, as high as the wall and stretching out into the back room . . . were shelves and shelves of the wealth of the library."[30] He asked her, "When does Joyce come in?" She replied, "usually very late in the afternoon."[31] He didn't have the money on him to join her lending library, but with his promise to return later and pay, she let him take *A Sportsmen Sketches* by Turgenev, the Constance Garnett translation of Tolstoy's *War and Peace*, D. H. Lawrence's *Sons and Lovers*, and *The Gambler and Other Stories* by Dostoyevsky. "No one that I ever knew was ever nicer to me,"[32] he remembered. Hadley returned later in the day and browsed through the store and paid the membership dues for them both.

Their only other friend during their first days in Paris was another they met through Sherwood Anderson's letters, Lewis Galantiere, a small, bespectacled, owlish man a few years older than Ernest, but younger than Hadley by a couple of years. Lewis, the son of Jewish Latvian immigrants, had spent his childhood in Chicago tenements. He spoke fluent French, translated some of Sherwood's books, worked for the International Chamber of Commerce in Paris, and liked the Hemingways very much. He treated them to an expensive dinner at Michaud's and helped them search for a place to live. Ernest did not want to pay much on living quarters; he had other ideas of how to spend their money. He did spend seven-hundred francs for a new wool suit made to measure—an Irish homespun at Alfred Cook, a London tailor and outfitter with a store in Paris—which he wore when needed throughout these years in Paris, especially as a reporter for the *Toronto Star*. Seven-hundred francs was only fifty dollars, which was still a lot of money to young Ernest Hemingway.

The New Year in Paris began chilly and overcast and then turned wet and cold with flurries in the evenings. "There's nawthing[33] much to write," he wrote to Howie Jenkins. "Paris is cold and damp, but crowded, jolly

30. Hemingway, *A Moveable Feast*, 35–36.
31. Hemingway, 35–36.
32. Hemingway, 35–36.
33. "nawthing" [*sic*].

and beautiful."[34] They kept bottles of booze in their room at the Jacob—"Rhum, Asti Spumante and Cinzano Vermouth fill one shelf"[35]—and sometimes got so drunk they vomited. Looking for an apartment early in January, they quickly decided upon a fourth-floor walk-up in the oldest part of the Left Bank at 74 rue du Cardinal Lemoine, a narrow street winding up from the Seine in the working-class neighborhood of Montagne Ste-Genevieve, just off a square by rue Mouffetard called the Place de la Contrescarpe, a rough, down-at-the-heels area away from the crowded cafes on Montparnasse Boulevard. "It was really not very safe to walk down,"[36] remembered Hadley. Their place had neither electricity nor running water but cost only two-hundred-and-fifty francs a month—about twenty dollars.

The building was high and narrow, shouldered between other high and narrow buildings, with a spiral staircase up to their small flat. Hadley remembered, "The apartment was on very strange angles," and it was crowded with "a great deal of very elegant furniture with a lot of brass trimmings." In the bedroom in the rear, "a Napoleonic sort of bed took the room but you could walk around it" and the front room "was almost completely filled with an oaken dining room table."[37] There was a tiny kitchen with a gas burner for cooking, and the closet held a slop jar, bowl, and water pitcher. The actual toilets were primitive commodes shared with the other tenants behind curved doors in the bend of the spiral staircase on each landing. There were rowdy bars in the surrounding streets, drunks often slept in the doorways, and women argued with vendors during the day. "Underneath was music every night until about one o'clock, accordion playing for dancing in a bistro."[38] The noise came from a place on the street below called a Bal Musette, where working men and women danced as the man playing the organ tapped his feet. Their visiting friends thought them poor indeed, a way that Ernest liked at this time in his life because with all his work before him he distrusted

34. EH to HJ, Dec. 26, 1921, *Letters of Ernest Hemingway, Vol. 1.*
35. EH to HJ, Dec. 26, 1921, *Letters of Ernest Hemingway, Vol. 1.*
36. Mowrer, Sokoloff tapes, Hemingway Collection, JFK Library.
37. Mowrer, Sokoloff tapes, Hemingway Collection, JFK Library.
38. Mowrer, Sokoloff tapes, Hemingway Collection, JFK Library.

any semblance of wealth, which would have obscured his growth from the roots.

The Hemingways immediately hired a maid, Marie Rohrbach, a sturdy peasant woman whom they liked very much. Marie worked a few hours each week cooking delicious meals of anything they thought they might like, and cleaning and emptying the pots and carrying up water in buckets. Mme Rohrbach's husband, Ton Ton, was a retired soldier who had fought all over the world, and the Hemingways liked him too. There were nearby points of interest that Hadley and Ernest were keen about: the Jardin des Plantes was barely two blocks east with its botanic gardens, menagerie, and museum; and just to the west on the highest point of the Left Bank was the Pantheon where lay the bones of Voltaire, Rousseau, Victor Hugo, and Emile Zola. In their big bed in the back room, the young couple shared a vigorous and creative sex life, experimenting and often changing roles. Hemingway also wrote in the bed, plying his trade with the *Toronto Star*, dashing off articles on almost anything for his Canadian readers to read under his by-line—"At the present rate of exchange, a Canadian with an income of one thousand dollars a year can live comfortably and enjoyably in Paris"[39]—and being paid and putting money into his bank account. His letters home and to his friends were full of enthusiasms, joy, and not altogether a true reflection of the life he knew around him.

They had hardly settled into their new home when Ernest, who feared death by disease, took to bed with a very sore throat. He had heard about a resort in the mountains in Switzerland and, sensing a bargain and wanting to get away from the damp, cold weather, reserved a room by telegram. Near the middle of the month, they took a night train from the Gare de Lyon and arrived the next morning in Montreux on the eastern edge of Lake Geneva. An electric train took them up the mountain to a small two-story chalet perched on a slope a thousand feet above the lake looking out upon Alpine peaks where for almost three weeks they lived inexpensively, loving the high mountain air and each other, playing and

---

39. *Toronto Star Weekly*, Feb. 4, 1922.

sleeping in a clean white feather bed, out cold almost until eight the next morning when the madam entered to light the fire and heat the room and bring trays of food for breakfast. "Here we are filling our lungs with the cold dry air of the Swiss Alps," wrote Ernest to his family, "and hiking and bobbing all day."[40]

They would take a tram farther up the mountain, and with a bobsled that had a steering wheel and two hand brakes, exhilaratingly careen down the mountain slope for several kilometers on a narrow bending road, leaning in on the turns. "If you want a thrill of the sort that starts at the base of your spine in a shiver and ends with your nearly swallowing your heart, as it leaps with a jump into your mouth, try bobsledding on a mountain road at fifty miles an hour," Ernest wrote under his by-line in the *Daily Star*. "You hang on to the wheel, watch the road and a mountain unreels alongside of you like a movie film. . . . There is a great snow valley on the left with huge saw-toothed bulks of mountains on the other side, but you only get rushing glimpses of it out of the corner of your eye as the bob shrieks around another turn."[41] They would do this several times each day, both of them enjoying this winter activity and learning to do it very well—Hadley again showing her athleticism, which had been tamped down by her sister and mother. From this higher point they looked out upon a rugged range of southern peaks, some rising well over ten-thousand feet. One morning, Ernest dashed off two articles about tourism and winter sports in Switzerland—"watch the sun go down over the great sweep of snow covered country and wonder why people go to Palm Beach or the Riviera in the wintertime"[42]—and sent them to John Bone.

They explored the medieval castle jutting out onto the lake at Montreux, discovering where Byron had carved his name on a pillar in the dungeon, and ate very well throughout the trip. "We rate meals like roast beef, creamed cauliflower, fried potatoes, soup before and blueberries with whipped cream after for two seeds [dollars] a day," wrote Ernest

---

40. EH to family, January 1922, *Letters of Ernest Hemingway, Vol. 1.*
41. *Toronto Daily Star*, Mar. 4, 1922.
42. *Toronto Daily Star*, Mar. 4, 1922.

to Katy Smith late in January. "It is so beautiful here that it hurts in a numb sort of way all the time, only when you're wit somebody you're lovers wit the beauty gets to be jost[43] sort of a tremendous happiness. It's so damn beautiful, Butstein, and we have so damn much fun." But they were also missing Paris. "It's an all day ride to Paris and we're going to take it in day time so we can catch the country. I'm beginning to get a little lonesome for Paris and will be glad to get back . . . this town of Paris bites into a man's blood."[44] Years later Ernest would remember, "When we came back to Paris it was clear and cold and lovely. . . . On the fresh washed gravel paths through the Luxembourg Gardens . . . the winter winds blew across the surface of the ponds and the fountains blew in the bright light. All the distances were short now since we had been in the mountains."[45]

Upon their return, the Hemingways soon met Ezra Pound and Gertrude Stein. Ernest, inherently shy and independent, did not have to use Sherwood's letter to Ezra because they encountered each other in Shakespeare & Company. Ernest, probably intimidated in the presence of Ezra Pound, a recognized leader of the modern movement, spoke little about books and writing but had an earthy immediacy and boyish charm that Pound found irresistible. The older poet invited the young couple to his studio in Montparnasse where, among other objects in the large, art-filled room, a great Gaudier-Brzeska sculpture of Ezra's head stared upon them like a statue on Easter Island as they sipped Dorothy's Chinese tea. Hemingway, keeping his opinions to himself, found the studio gloomy and Pound pompous and strange as he raved on about things literary. Hemingway's values were still those of Oak Park, and they would not sustain him in Paris. Impatient with literary manifestos and "O art O beauty" discussions, and repulsed by Ezra's poetic costume and posturing, the same initial trouble he would have when first meeting James Joyce and Gertrude Stein, he rushed home and composed a scathing satiric poem about this post-Byronic imposter, which Lewis Galantiere wisely

43. "wit" [*sic*], "wit" [*sic*], "jost" [*sic*].
44. EH to KS, Jan. 27, 1922, *Letters of Ernest Hemingway, Vol. 1.*
45. Hemingway, *A Moveable Feast*, 11.

counseled him to destroy. Ernest took the advice, and to his satisfaction, instead gave the poet some of his work to read.

Once Hemingway got past Ezra's esthete street mask, he found a frank, sensible, sexual man who enjoyed the physical life, too, and the literary father he needed most in these early years. Hadley remembered that at their first meeting "Ernest listened at E. P.'s feet as to an oracle, and I believe some of the ideas lasted all through his life. Ezra was kind and helpful to the young, oncoming talents, at least those he liked or believed in."[46] Pound read Hemingway's writing and was impressed by the avoidance of affectation and sentimentality and the economy and lack of superfluous language (this he was learning from newspaper writing, but not altogether). He saw a kind of Imagism in prose and tried to show Hemingway how to make his style even more sparse and unadorned. Pound didn't dismiss theories, but he thought that the art was in the artist and the artist must do his work to best bring it out. He told him to read Joyce and Eliot: reading *The Waste Land* at the elbow of the master must have been good because Pound would have drilled home the advice about cutting, revising, and eliminating the dross, as his own blue pencil had reduced Eliot's original draft by a third. "Use no superfluous words," he preached, "no adjective which does not reveal something . . . Go in fear of abstractions." He also told Hemingway "be influenced by as many great artists as you can, but have the decency either to acknowledge the debt outright, or try to conceal it."[47] These lessons were not easily or quickly absorbed, but their effect would be apparent within a year. It was Pound, claimed Ernest much later, "who had taught me to distrust adjectives."[48]

To encourage his new friend, Pound submitted six of Ernest's poems to Scofield Thayer's *Dial*. They were rejected, but it showed Hemingway that Ezra was truly interested in his work. He had a lot to learn about the business and politics of literature; he also had much to learn from Pound's Imagist theories about writing. Ernest told Galantiere, "he's

46. Mowrer, Sokoloff tapes, Hemingway Collection, JFK Library.
47. Reynolds, *The Paris Years*, 29.
48. Hemingway, *A Moveable Feast*, 134.

teaching me to write and I'm teaching him to box."[49] Ford Madox Ford and Wyndham Lewis saw some of these boxing matches in Pound's studio at 70 bis rue Notre-Dame-des-Champs, which Hemingway clearly controlled, barely breaking into a sweat. Pound boxed with Ernest out of sport, and when that finally paled, they played tennis, where Pound, a good tennis player who loved the game, did much better. Ezra continued to use his influence to push his young protégé's literary career, introducing him to important publishers and eventually getting the rejected poems published by Harriet Monroe in *Poetry*. Hemingway did not share Pound's love of "kulchur," drawing the line with most cathedrals, nor did he like the noise when his poet friend played the bassoon. Ernest, lean and with the back and shoulders of a football player, said, "You go on and learn everything," referring to Pound's continued exploration of myth and history, "I can't, I'm limited, but I'm going to know everything about fucking and fighting and eating and drinking and begging and stealing and living and dying."[50]

Though they could always joke with each other, Hemingway stood in awe of Pound's curiosity toward all new things and bemoaned his own feeble education, particularly in the classics and grammar. Pound would help Hemingway; from his friend's cluttered conversations, Ernest extracted what he needed whenever it floated to the surface. He was instructed in the use of symbols, that they must first be natural objects, their symbolic function not obtruding into the work: at the primary level, a hawk must first and solidly be a hawk before it could function as a symbol. The older man sent him to the ancient authors: Homer, Catullus, Ovid, Dante, Donne (where he read the line "ask not for whom the bell tolls"), and also insisted he read Flaubert and Stendhal. From Flaubert he learned to be detached, ironic, and precise; and from Stendhal, he learned how to deal with panoramic movement as when he would write about the retreat from Caporetto in *A Farewell to Arms*. Pound also sent Hemingway to Henry James, and like James, the terse dialogue in Hemingway's mature writing seldom conveys direct meaning; as in the

---

49. Carlos Baker, *Hemingway: A Life Story*, 114.
50. EH to Ezra Pound, June 4, 1925, *Letters of Ernest Hemingway, Vol.2*.

short story "The Killers," much of what is really said is unspoken between the lines. After this 'inoculation,' Pound thought the younger writer could then be safely exposed to modernity or anything else in literature.

Through conversations and reading his essays, Pound told Hemingway that bad art "was inaccurate art . . . art that makes false reports. Good art bears true witness, I mean the art that is precise."[51] Bearing true witness in Paris in those early years changed Hemingway's idea of his art, allowing him to see how false the fiction he had been writing in Chicago rang to the ear. His war novel now sounded like a schoolboy's tale, and he would never begin his stories with elaborate flourishes again. By the middle of his first year in Paris, Hemingway would return to the basics, the simple declarative sentence, trying to gain control of the first elements first. It was simple yet demanding: let actions speak for themselves; let images convey meaning without telling readers how to respond, what to feel, how to judge. If action is presented truly, precisely, using only its essential elements, then readers, without being told, will respond emotionally as the writer intended. It was a technique that Pound had pioneered in London in early 1912 with the Imagist Manifesto. When Hemingway arrived in Paris, he was already using some of it unconsciously. Pound and Gertrude Stein made him see clearly what he was doing. At first, he responded self-consciously, intimidated by his new knowledge, but he worked hard and perfected the tools of simplicity, understatement, and irony. Pound would say about Hemingway, "The son of a bitch's instincts are right."[52]

The Hemingways did use Sherwood's letter of introduction to Gertrude Stein, sending it soon after returning from Switzerland. She promptly wrote back, "I do like Anderson so much and would like to meet his friends,"[53] and invited them to tea at her studio on rue de Fleurus, where she lived with her companion, Alice B. Toklas. Hadley immediately accepted the invitation, writing, "Sherwood has told us so many nice things that we are glad to come right away to see you."[54] And

51. Reynolds, *Hemingway: The Paris Years*, 30.
52. Wilhelm, *Ezra Pound in London and Paris*, 280.
53. GS to Hadley, February 1922, Hemingway Collection, JFK Library.
54. Hadley to GS, Feb. 7, 1922, Beinecke Library, Yale University.

on Wednesday afternoon, February 8, the path the Hemingways walked from their flat was a short, pleasant westward walk over the cobblestones through the narrow, crooked canyon-like streets, the old buildings pressed together rising four and five stories, and along the wide paths through the open space of the Luxembourg Gardens, past the royal palace and the broad pool of the fountain before it, crossing rue Guynemer to a smaller street and down a block to the courtyard and atelier at 27 rue de Fleurus, where they were warmly welcomed into the room and were made to sit down and attended to separately by the hosts, who had their own different functions within the salon: Gertrude spoke to the geniuses while Alice took care of their wives. From her large chair by the fireplace, Gertrude spoke to Ernest as he sat at her feet and listened and absorbed every word and took in the Renoirs and the Picassos and Cezannes on the walls and the sight of the great woman sitting and talking before him in a way he had never heard before, while at the other end of the room Hadley sat with Alice as Alice knitted and listened and watched and spoke—and keenly watched and listened especially to the conversation at the other end of the room. Both couples quickly became immensely fond of each other and would be very close for a long while.

Alice, a small, dark, bird-like woman with a large hooked nose and the dark trace of a mustache on her upper lip, had a very pleasant voice and was an efficient administrator—unobtrusive but controlling—her presence was an iron fixture structuring every occasion at rue de Fleurus—as she organized their lives around Gertrude and her writing. Alice loved Spain and Spanish dancing and bullfighting; they often went there on long vacations, and she loved to show their pictures of bullfighters and bullfighting. Gertrude was less than two years younger than Ernest's mother and, except for her short height, was very much like Grace in both demeanor and appearance. She was kind and commanding, egotistical and narcissistic, stout with huge breasts, and wore her hair gathered together above her head. But unlike the way he felt toward his mother, Ernest liked Gertrude very much. Years later he wrote, "I always wanted to fuck her and she knew it and it was a good healthy feeling"[55]; and if Stein knew this, as Hemingway claimed, then Alice would have known it, too, and being a jealous, possessive lover, she would have taken the subtle but firm slow action to rid herself and her mate of Hemingway. Stein found Hemingway an extraordinarily handsome young man, was flattered by his attentiveness, and encouraged their relationship. On an evening a few days later, Stein and Toklas paid a reciprocal visit to the Hemingways, making the short walk to 74 rue Cardinal Lemoine and climbing the steep narrow steps of the stairwell to their apartment.

In the *Autobiography of Alice B. Toklas*, Gertrude wrote that "Hemingway had then and has always a very good instinct for finding apartments in strange but pleasing localities and good femme des ménage and good food."[56] They ate dinner with the Hemingways in the small dining room, the meal prepared earlier by Marie, and afterward, Gertrude and Ernest went into the bedroom where she took a position on the mahogany bed and they went over all the writing he had done up to that time. He showed her some poems and the war novel he had started the previous year. She liked the poems, saying they were "direct, Kiplingesque," but the novel she found wanting. "There is a great deal of description in this," she said, "and not particularly good description. Begin over again and concentrate."[57] Ernest knew her criticism was correct. He had arrived at that same conclusion during his repeated attempts to write one true sentence in his blue notebooks. He then found the courage to show her "Up in Michigan," the explicit story about the harsh seduction of a virgin named Liz Coates on a dock on a lake in Northern Michigan. She read it quickly. "It's good," she said. "That's not the question at all. But it is inaccrochable. That means it is like a picture a painter paints and then he cannot hang it when he has a show and no one will buy it because they cannot hang it either."[58] When Hemingway defended his use of explicit words by saying that they were words people would actually use and, therefore, the only words that could make a story come true, Gertrude

---

55. EH to W. G. Rogers, July 29, 1948, *Selected Letters*.
56. Gertrude Stein, *The Autobiography of Alice B. Toklas*, 200–1.
57. Baker, *Hemingway: A Life Story*, 115.
58. Hemingway, *A Moveable Feast*, 15.

replied, "You mustn't write anything that is inaccrochable. There's no point in it. It's wrong and it's silly."[59] Ernest did not listen to his dear friend's advice about "inaccrochable," but he did listen to her closely for many years and read her many manuscripts and learned much from this extraordinary woman who pioneered modern literature.

In the 1840s, Gertrude Stein's grandparents had walked out of an impoverished Central Europe, leaving behind the graves of children and bringing those children still alive to America. By the Civil War, they owned a six-story building in Baltimore manufacturing and selling clothes. Her father, Daniel, with his brother, Solomon Stein, established a branch of the business in the industrialized boom town of Pittsburgh and brought a large house together across the Allegheny River where there were parks and streams of clear, fresh water. Gertrude was born in Allegheny, Pennsylvania on February 3, 1874, the fifth and last child of Daniel and Milly Stein. When the brothers dissolved their partnership, Daniel moved to California, where the children grew up on a ten-acre estate in Oakland. Gertrude was a pretty child with beautiful eyes, small, strong, and enthusiastic, and very close to her sensitive, introverted older brother Leo. Their mother died when Gertrude was fourteen. Their father soon passed away, too, leaving each child a fortune of $60,000 in the good hands of their older brother Michael, who through wise, shrewd investments would make sure that his younger brother and sister were financially sound throughout their lives.

When Leo departed for Harvard University in Cambridge, Massachusetts, Gertrude soon followed, enrolling in the "Harvard Annex," which, became Radcliffe College the following year. The women lived in boarding houses by the Harvard campus and shared the same faculty. Gertrude found Darwin's theories exciting and took to science and research, spending hours in the laboratory. She came under the influence of William James, a much-regarded professor of psychology and the brother of author Henry James. Proud of her Jewish heritage, she enjoyed being different, sometimes wearing a battered sailor hat. People

---

59. Hemingway, 15.

were drawn to her. They all loved a good argument, to which Gertrude brought a remarkably keen intelligence. "She loved a good discussion," remembered one of the girls, "and not infrequently was as willing to talk on one side of a subject as the other."[60] The summer before her senior year she traveled to Europe to be with Leo.

Meeting in Antwerp, delighted to be together again, they strolled the streets arm in arm. Leo was tall and thin with receding hair; Gertrude was short and stout with her hair coiled atop her head. He was interested in museums; she wanted to do everything she saw. Yet they laughed at the same jokes, liked the same people, and spoke the same unpretentious American slang. A friend they encountered thought Gertrude was powerful, had a beautiful head, and was inspired by her deep temperament. She gladly submitted to her older brother's wisdom and let him teach her about the things he knew. Her terrific energy, gusto, and the ease with which she made and kept friends contrasted with his reclusive sensitive and critical manner, and he basked in her grand personal charm. In matters of art Leo was the expert, while Gertrude's domain was the laboratory and her shrewd, commanding presence with people. Upon her return to Cambridge, Gertrude put forth a burst of energy to finish her studies at Radcliffe.

She thrived in the lab, where a series of experiments on automatic writing she and a professor conducted was published in a journal. (Years later critics concluded this experiment explained what lay behind her more hermetic writing like *Tender Buttons*, something which Gertrude would refute.) She spent so much time in the laboratory that people were certain she would become a scientist. Some of her experiments attempted to determine classifications of personalities. On the advice of Professor James, she applied to and was accepted into John Hopkins School of Medicine in Baltimore, where Leo joined her, switching his course of study from literature to science. They rented a row house on East Biddle Street, hired a German housekeeper, and made friends with two sisters,

---

60. Brenda Wineapple, *Sister Brother: Gertrude and Leo Stein*, 72.

Claribel and Etta Cone, who often entertained in their family brown-stone on Saturday nights.

Gertrude excelled in her first two years of medical school, which were geared toward research and experiment, spending hours in the laborato-ries with her microscope, and then she began to falter. She was candid and opinionated, once challenged an instructor's coarse, anti-Semitic attitude, and did not like the resistance to women in the medical field. Sex and sexuality weighed heavy on her: she would not have her sexual-ity defined by simple reproductive terms. In her final year, interested in treating hysteria, particularly in women, she wrote to the chief of neuro-pathology at Massachusetts State Hospital for the Insane about employ-ment. However, some of the faculty at John Hopkins did not like her, and when a committee voted against her degree, she decided to abandon medicine and confront her own sexuality. She was a virgin when she left medical school but began a romance with another woman, a love that profoundly changed her attitude toward life and being a woman. She soon joined Leo in Europe, who had also abandoned his studies.

Leo was picking through junk shops in Florence and found a Titian drawing authenticated by his friend, the art critic Bernhardt Berenson. When Gertrude arrived in the spring of 1902, he took her to meet the Berensons at their Villa in the hills north of Florence. Mary Berenson thought Gertrude was fat and unwieldy "but with a grand monumen-tal head, plenty of brains & immense geniality."[61] That fall, the Steins settled at 20 Bloomsbury Square in London. Gertrude, exhausted by her separation from Hopkins and distressed by a rocky relationship with her lover, felt depleted and depressed. She began spending her time in the nearby British Museum, reading and writing down the names of authors, piloting herself through English Literature in a rough chrono-logical order, and became increasingly surrounded by writers and artists and aesthetic people whom she admired. She knew she had exceptional verbal gifts and believed she had something to say, but the gray win-ter skies of London and the poverty of so many people who lived there

---

61. Wineapple, 168.

bothered her. She returned to America early the next year where, living in a house in New York City with other women, she began to write a story about an upwardly mobile German-Jewish immigrant family in America seeking assimilation and social acceptance in a culture where the congratulatory pride of the self-made older generation chafes against a younger generation born to unearned privileges. "We need only realize our parents, remember our grandparents and know ourselves and our history is complete,"[62] she wrote. Later she would take the same idea and rewrite the book as *The Making of Americans.*

Leo bought a post-impressionist oil painting in London that thrilled him: "One can actually own paintings even if one were not a millionaire,"[63] he wrote, and then crossed the channel to Paris where the young cellist Pablo Casals told him that he should paint. He enrolled in the Academie Julian for lessons and began sketching statues in the Louvre. Needing a place to live, his cousin, Ernest Keyser, suggested rooms on a small street near the Luxembourg Gardens where rents were low with many artists living in the neighborhood. The building at 27 rue de Fleurus had a light stone front with an archway entrance into a small courtyard where to the right was a two-story pavilion adjoining a high-ceiling studio. The apartment Leo rented consisted of four rooms, a kitchen and bath, and the adjoining atelier. Leo loved painting but was much better as a collector. One day, Leo showed a friend from the Academie a portfolio he had bought of twenty exquisite sketches by Degas. His friend was breathless. "Leo was a true art person," remembered the friend, "he liked to talk about it and he liked to theorize and philosophize about it."[64]

Gertrude returned to Europe in the summer, first touring Florence with the Cone sisters and then leaving for Rome with a group of women. One of her friends remarked, "she is very amusing and good-tempered, enjoys life, chuckles a lot, I like her deep voice and laughter."[65] She soon joined Leo in Paris; together again as brother and sister, they

---

62. Wineapple, 184.
63. James R. Mellow, *Charmed Circle: GS & Company*, 5.
64. Wineapple, *Sister Brother: Gertrude and Leo Stein*, 196.
65. Wineapple, 202.

were known by many as those "very queer Americans,"[66]—attired in the costumes of the day, but without the customs that went with them—and remembered as one of the happiest couples on the Left Bank. She read and studied Henry James, the brother of her mentor, and also liked eighteenth-century prose. Leo looked for exciting art to buy. "Do you know Cezanne,"[67] Berenson asked, and told him to visit Vollard's gallery on rue Lafitte, where among the stacks of pictures Leo began his plunge into the world of modern painting. He haunted the shop with Gertrude. They shared their funds and conferred on each purchase, but it was Leo who made the final decision. First, they bought Cezanne's *Landscape with Spring House*, and then they bought Gauguin's *Three Tahitians* and *Sunflowers*, Cezanne's *Bathers* and *Groups of Bathers*, and two Renoirs. Leo was ecstatic. He wanted a large Cezanne, and so they bought *Madame Cezanne with a Fan* and hung it in the atelier. Cezanne, with curving landscapes of peculiar force, forms simplified to geometric essentials, and the extraordinary use of color, would be the cornerstone of the growing collection at 27 rue de Fleurus. In time, as the walls of the atelier began to fill with pictures, the Steins would have more Cezannes than there were in the Musée du Luxembourg.

The atelier was a long room with a long narrow table piled with books and papers that served as a desk. Across from the table was a couch covered with a heavy rug, and nearby was a small claw-footed chest over which hung the portrait of Madame Cezanne. Gertrude worked at the table. Leo did not paint in the room, but his presence was felt and his talk was always heard. He knew his sister struggled with her writing and suggested she read Flaubert's *Three Tales*. This suggestion, and the large Cezanne portrait before her, led her to write *Three Lives*. "Everything I have done has been influenced by Flaubert and Cezanne," she told a friend many years later. "Cezanne conceived the idea that in composition one thing was as important as another thing. Each part is as important as the whole and that impressed me so much that I began to write *Three*

---

66. Wineapple, 206.
67. Wineapple, 210.

Lives under this influence and this idea of composition."[68] *Three Lives* evolved slowly in the first half of 1905. While she worked, Leo bought a Degas drawing, *After the Bath*, and Delacroix's *Perseus and Andromeda*. In the flare of the gaslight was a display of color and image quite fantastic: provocative nudes and splashes of colors that would both jar and distress some visitors.

Three Lives was a departure from anything yet written; the material, style, and tone of the compositions were completely new. Its three novellas are about young women with repressed, unfulfilled desires. In "The Gentle Lena," a young German girl brought to the United States as a maid is so passive and submissive that she dissolves into a spiritual torpor. The character is constructed through her relations to others, who cajole and push and cheer and scold the gentle, inarticulate, and tractable woman. The portrait is rendered through recurrent phrases, repeating rhythms, and a simplified, almost ungrammatical language. "*Melanctha,*" the middle tale, is about a young black woman keen for experience and desiring power; the changes in her emotions are subtle and profound. Melanctha and her lover cannot come together and in the end are abandoned to each other sadly. Stein, who had an empathy with Negroes, seeing them, too, as outsiders, wrote the tale in a stylized vernacular that challenged prevailing notions about language and expression and appropriate subject matter. "*The Good Anna*" tells the tale of a loyal housemaid to rather dull women of means, whose strange nature of dependent relationships is the irreplaceable focal point of her energy, a story that resounds with the echoes of the repetitive rhythms Miss Stein develops in her prose. With *Three Lives*, Gertrude had completed her first great stories and entered a brave new world of modern literature.

The atelier was also a fine room for entertaining and, with Leo pacing and talking about modern art, became as much a public place as it was a studio. Many American artists in Paris were influenced by what they saw there. At the Autumn Salon of 1906, the Steins encountered a painting of a woman ablaze in electric greens, purples, and reds, colors applied

---

68. Wineapple, 221.

feverishly in a fury of seething brushstrokes, peering coquettish and defiant under a huge outlandish hat. People roared with laughter and even scratched at it, but the Steins were mesmerized. It was Henri Matisse's *The Woman with the Hat.* Leo bought the painting for 500 francs. Matisse, married with children and very poor, was a somber, bespectacled man who looked more like a country doctor than a brave new artist. As an artist, he knew exactly what he wanted in a painting, and even if it meant the loss of a sale, he worked relentlessly until he saw it realized. Leo continued to buy his paintings and hang them on the walls at rue de Fleurus. He also began collecting the work of a young Spaniard named Pablo Picasso and bought *Acrobat Family with a Monkey* and some of his blue-toned paintings. When the Steins introduced Picasso to Matisse there was no fusion. Picasso was too chaotic in his creativity compared to the methodical Matisse.

Picasso drew better than Rubens and rarely spoke. He "seemed neither remote nor intimate—just completely there."[69] The Steins went to his studio in Montmartre to meet him: not in, he left a drawing of himself crouching with his pants down. When Gertrude did meet Picasso, he gave her much pleasure. "Something had been coming out of him," she wrote in a word portrait, "certainly it had been coming out of him, certainly it was something, certainly it had been coming out of him and it had a meaning, a charming meaning, a solid meaning, a struggling meaning, a clear meaning."[70] She was charmed when he asked to paint her portrait. His paintings became a big part of the collection at rue de Fleurus and Picasso, too, was fascinated by the Steins. Both of them as far as he could tell didn't care much what others thought and didn't much mind the ridicule they encountered.

The atelier of the Steins was an incubator of modern art. Nowhere else could one see paintings by Cezanne, Gauguin, Toulouse-Lautrec, Renoir, Manet, Manguin, Matisse, and the young Picasso. "Our collection became in time one of the sights of Paris,"[71] remembered Leo

---

69. Wineapple, 240.
70. Stein, *Selected Writings* – "Portraits of Painters," 333.
71. Wineapple, *Sister Brother: Gertrude and Leo Stein*, 242.

cheerfully. So many people clamored for a look that they decided to open their doors on Saturday nights. "The center of attraction was Leo's brilliant conversation on modern French art and the remarkable collection of mostly contemporary paintings which he made at little cost with the aid of his independent and exacting judgment,"[72] remembered a journalist. The Steins themselves were gracious, warm, and unconventional: Leo swathed in a silk Japanese robe, Gertrude in velveteen, and both wearing sandals.

Gertrude was passionate about character. She believed character was knowable and traceable and began trying to sound its depths by careful note of its various modes of expression, studying collections of letters and epistolary novels and also the letters of friends and acquaintances. As she began working on *The Making of Americans*, she began to categorize the characters and their personalities much like one of her lab experiments at Radcliffe and Johns Hopkins. As the novel progressed, Miss Stein was intent upon untangling the knotty subject of character, her own and everyone else's. Her little blue notebooks filled as she read of William Tecumseh Sherman, Abraham Lincoln, and John Adams. Of the many personal letters she read, the ones sent by Alice Toklas to a mutual friend delighted her the most.

Alice Bebette Toklas was a young Jewish woman from San Francisco who decorated her tailored suits for more panache and created a stir, sometimes stopping traffic with her high heels and gold-topped cane. When her mother died of cancer, she took over the household duties and became an efficient manager who stayed in the background among the men in her family. Gertrude's brother Michael Stein and his wife, Sarah, friends of the Toklas family, returning to San Francisco to check on their properties after the earthquake of 1904, whetted her appetite for Paris. A friend named Harriet Levy loaned her the money and they both went to Paris, arriving together in 1907. Awaiting them there was Gertrude Stein. "[Her voice] was unlike anyone else's voice," Alice remembered, "deep, full, velvety, like a great contralto."[73] Something stirred inside them.

72. Mellow, *Charmed Circle: GS & Company*, 16.
73. Wineapple, *Sister Brother: Gertrude and Leo Stein*, 270.

The next time they met in Paris they walked through the Luxembourg Gardens. Gertrude became more and more infatuated with Alice. She soon took Alice and Harriet to meet Picasso at his studio in Montmartre. When the Steins left for Florence in the summer, Alice came along.

Three Lives was being published by the Grafton Press in New York City, and combined with Alice's flirtations, Gertrude was feeling wonderful. (Leo had found love, too; a woman known as Nine of Montparnasse.) It took years for them to get together, but the attraction was mutual and always there. Gertrude continued working on *The Making of Americans*, and as her relationship with Alice grew closer and closer, her book kept getting bigger and bigger. She worked late into the night, telling the story through fictional families. Alice gathered the results and typed them into neat sheets. Alice had a natural gaiety and was constant and gentle; now and then she prepared meals, ran errands, and always offered encouragement. In Gertrude she had found the brilliant personality worthy of her talents, and she would love her with absolute adoration. She was a jealous person, some visitors thought her cynical, but people close to Gertrude accepted her. "Alice was making herself indispensable," remembered Leo, "all the housekeeping, the typing, seeing people who called, and getting rid of the undesirables, answering letters."[74]

When Michael and Sarah Stein returned to San Francisco in the summer of 1910, Harriet Levy went with them, leaving Alice alone in the apartment they had shared. Gertrude asked Alice to move into 27 rue de Fleurus, and so they began their confirmed relationship as lovers and close friends. Leo was fine with Alice living with them and made her feel comfortable, too, but he and Gertrude began drifting imperceptibly apart. As the rivalry between Matisse and Picasso began to grow, so did the conflict between their supporters. Picasso and Georges Braque were working on a conception of art using interlocking planes and stylized geometric reductions in a quest for the essence of form. As a judge at the 1908 Autumn Salon, Matisse dismissed several of Braque's submissions, protesting "they're made of little cubes!"[75] The work of Braque

---

74. Wineapple, 386.
75. Paul Trachtman, "Matisse and Picasso," *Smithsonian Magazine*, Feb. 2003.

and Picasso would thereafter be known as Cubism, and Cubism would among other things become a prism through which Gertrude and Leo would refract their growing disappointment in each other. Gertrude embraced Cubism, while Leo considered it vapid, and, tired of hearing about Cubism and the problems of form and being, he did not always attend the Saturday night salons. Gertrude concluded that she was a success and Leo was an inward-turning failure.

Three Lives was a critical success, and Paris began hearing more about Gertrude as a writer with a novel style. She finished *The Making of Americans* and began experimenting more and more with word portraits of anyone who struck her fancy, and these eventually took on a life and a style and stature of their own, as in her portrait of Matisse:

> One was quite certain that for a long part of his being one being
> living he had been trying to be certain that he was wrong in
> doing what he was doing and then when he could not come to be
> certain that he had been wrong in doing what he had been doing,
> when he had completely convinced himself that he would not
> come to be certain that he had been wrong in doing what he had
> been doing he was really certain then that he was a great one and
> he certainly was a great one. Certainly everyone could be certain
> of this thing that this one is a great one.[76]

The portraits did not accumulate detail, no color of the eye or hem of a skirt, but attempted to reproduce each personality's rhythm using a spare vocabulary with the repetition of gerunds and participial phrases. "It is naturally gayer describing what anyone feels acts and does in relation to any other one than to describe that they just are what they are inside them."[77] She began moving away from telling stories with a beginning, a middle, and an end. She did not want to exist with the feeling of one thing succeeding another thing and she was trying to express this in her writing. She also began to explore the effect of the sound of words making

---

76. Stein, *Selected Writings* – "Portraits of Painters," 329.
77. Stein, *Selected Writings* – "The Making of Americans," 251.

sense on their own beyond the actual meaning: "This is this dress, aider, aider, why aider why whow" if read aloud sounds like "This is distress. Aid her. Aid her, why aid her, why, how."[78] Her output increased with Alice in her life. She made her first independent purchase of a painting when she bought Picasso's cubist painting *The Architect's Table*.

As more of her work became published, she would not compromise any of her effects and cautioned the publishers not to change her punctuation. People began to ask, "Who is Gertrude Stein?" With her funny sorting of words and unknowable phrases, Gertrude was elevated to an object of parody. But notice of any sort pleased her very much except when it was done by Leo, who began to parody her word portraits. The disintegration of their bond could not be seen at 27 rue de Fleurus, where they appeared to be fine with each other. Alice did not make it happen, but she made it happen better and without much rancor. In the summer of 1913, when Gertrude and Alice went to Spain, Leo went to Italy. When he returned to Paris, he told his sister he was leaving. Their gallery would never be seen together again; Gertrude kept the Picassos, Leo took nearly all the Renoirs, and they split the Cezannes; they would never even speak again. Gertrude and Alice thought about leaving 27 rue de Fleurus but renovated instead, installing electricity, painting and wallpapering the rooms of the apartment, and having a fireplace built in the atelier. Gertrude took charge of the Saturday night salons, the sheer force of her personality dazzling and captivating her visitors. She inspired fierce loyalty and protectiveness and many who met her never forgot her.

When *Tender Buttons* was published by a small press in New York City in the summer of 1914, for some it was a harbinger of the future: modern, revolutionary, and bracing; a musical mixture of words and sounds that refreshed the language composed by a most remarkable writer. Others hailed it as nonsense that bamboozled the public and her overzealous friends. For Gertrude Stein, it was about things that fasten lives together as she described common everyday items in allusive, elusive prose poems. "I tried in *Tender Buttons* to get a combination of sound

---

78. Stein, *Selected Writings* – "Tender Buttons," 476.

and picture that would make the effect,"[79] she told Carl Van Vechten. In one called "Nothing Elegant," she wrote: "A charm a single charm is doubtful. If the red is rose and there is a gate surrounding it, if inside is let in and there places change then certainly something is upright. It is earnest."[80]

She and Alice joined the allied effort during the war. With Gertrude driving, they used their Ford to deliver supplies to the front and acted like mothers to many young soldiers. Afterward, they resumed their lives at 27 rue de Fleurus. Sylvia Beach remembered them bantering in her bookstore: "Alice had a great deal more finesse than Gertrude. And she was grown up: Gertrude was a child, something of an infant prodigy."[81] People who met her, who had thought she must be strange from the opaque, indecipherable prose she wrote, found her outward, sensible, and sane. "She was such a dominant and fantastic woman," remembered Janet Flanner, the Paris correspondent for the *New Yorker*.

> She always led the conversation . . . the excitement of her think-
> ing took on this sudden rumble of laughter, it was so warm like a
> stove roar with heat and when she laughed everyone in the room
> laughed . . . it was a kind of contagion of good spirit . . . She
> talked with the greatest sense, coherency, simplicity and preci-
> sion of any woman I think I have ever heard . . . this was always
> phenomenal considering the way she wrote.[82]

In an article in the *New Republic*, Sherwood Anderson placed her in a great literary kitchen "standing there by the table, clean, strong, with red cheeks and sturdy legs, always quietly and smilingly at work." Diligently experimenting with a systematic, single-minded intensity, she spurned the esoteric and ready-made as she continued "laying word against word, relating sound to sound, feeling for the taste, the smell, the rhythm of the

79. Wineapple, *Sister Brother: Gertrude and Leo Stein*, 385.
80. Stein, *Selected Writings* – "Tender Buttons," 464.
81. Beach, *Shakespeare & Company*, 27.
82. Janet Flanner, *Paris in the 1920s*, "The Twentieth Century."

individual word."[83] Writers of a new generation flocked around seeking advice, encouragement, and good company, and in Gertrude they found someone part mother, part mentor.

When Ernest Hemingway first walked into the atelier at 27 rue de Fleurus he did so carefully, concealing his deepest emotions, and knew what he saw was rare and beautiful. "We had loved the big studio with the great paintings," he remembered. "It was like one of the best rooms in the finest museum except there was a big fireplace and it was warm and comfortable and they gave you good things to eat and tea and natural distilled liqueurs made from purple plums, yellow plums or wild raspberries." He was aware of her female fleshiness—"Miss Stein was very big but not tall and was heavily built like a peasant woman,"—and charmed by her appearance—"She had beautiful eyes and a strong German-Jewish face . . . lovely, thick, alive immigrant hair,"[84]—but could talk about her as though she were a man. "Gertrude Stein and me are just like brothers,"[85] he exclaimed soon after they met in a letter to Sherwood Anderson. By accident or not, when Hemingway finished writing for the day, he sometimes met Stein in the Luxembourg Gardens, one of her favorite places in the afternoon. They walked and talked together a lot. She would invite him to her studio to continue their talks and soon he was told he could call at 27 rue de Fleurus whenever he was in the neighborhood.

Their relationship was mostly based on a dedication to the métier of writing, a concept Stein had long adopted and which was taken up by Hemingway. Their conversations were open and honest and intense. He listened very carefully to everything she said, just as she observed and studied him, thinking his manliness was self-conscious. Beyond writing, he did not agree with everything she told him, particularly about homosexuality being fine in women but not with men, but the principles she taught him about writing, in what she said and through her prose that she let him read, he took to heart and as an artist integrated her concepts

---

83. Wineapple, *Sister Brother: Gertrude and Leo Stein*, 397.
84. Hemingway, *A Moveable Feast*, 13–14.
85. EH to SA, Mar. 9, 1922, *Letters of Ernest Hemingway, Vol. 1.*

into his own writing very effectively. He learned much from her about the use of repetition and finding rhythm within the words. Unlike Ezra Pound, who offered specific advice, Gertrude did not correct details but stuck to general principles—the way of seeing what the writer chooses to see, and the relation between that vision and the way it gets down. When the vision is not complete the words are flat; she insisted it was very simple; there could be no mistake about it.

What she had discovered in Cezanne she passed on to Hemingway: as Cezanne had laid one stroke next to another in near-infinite repetition, so, too, could words through reiterative phrases and shifting emphasis lead to an overall composition with each sentence as significant as any other part. In the rue de Fleurus studio and the Musée du Luxembourg, Hemingway carefully studied Cezanne's paintings, discovering, too, that a story could be fully evoked out of this patient bricklaying method. When he read Miss Stein's *Three Lives*, he saw that her continuous present tense and steady repetition of key phrases created meanings larger than the words themselves. He had used this technique in his Chicago journalism for the *Toronto Star*, but for the first time he analyzed what he was doing and saw how his prose worked. And in the early months in Paris, he began his quest for a simple and direct style. "I would write one true sentence, and then go on from there," he remembered years later. "I found that I could cut that scrollwork or ornament out and throw it away and start with the first true simple declarative sentence I had written."[86] It was hard to do, writing was no longer easy, but within two years Ford Madox Ford would declare that the prose of Ernest Hemingway was as natural as pebbles in a clear stream.

Ezra forced him to become self-critical, to make revisions; good advice, especially as he began writing the short, concise sentences, where every word counted, that were so hard to write. Some of Gertrude's advice was almost the opposite and just as helpful: "I have never understood how people could labor over a manuscript, write and rewrite it many times," she said, "for to me if you have something to say the words are

---

86. Hemingway, *A Moveable Feast*, 12.

always there. And they are the exact words and the words that should be used."[87] He made use of it, too, letting words flow through free association, filling the blue notebooks of school children, as a means of preventing critical thoughts interfering with the flow of creativity. One did not need to know where or how a sentence or a story was going to turn out in order to begin. It was a good way to get started when the well of creative juices seemed dry. Soon he was using Gertrude's technique in other ways too: he could capture scenes quickly, writing quickly by ear, letting the words fall on the paper in their right order, and pinpointing elements that gave an event its impact. One day she asked about his newspaper work. Being a reporter for a Canadian newspaper, Ernest was obliged to the Canadian viewpoint. Gertrude asked if he and Hadley had enough money to live quietly. Ernest said they did. Then, she said, they should do so because if he kept on doing newspaper work, he would never see things but only see words and that would not do if he intended to be a writer. Hemingway replied that he definitely intended to be a writer.

---

87. Reynolds, *Hemingway: The Paris Years*, 38.

Paris sidewalk and café

Ezra Pound

Natalie Barney in costume with elf

Dancers in Natalie's garden

T. S. Eliot

Beautiful Paris

Place de la Contrescarpe

Shakespeare & Company at 12 rue de L'Odeon

Hadley and Ernest in Switzerland

Ezra inside Shakespeare & Company

Joyce, Sylvia, and Adrienne Monnier inside Shakespeare & Company

Gaudier Brzeska sculpture of Ezra's head

Leo, Gertrude, and Michael Stein

The big studio with the great paintings

Gertrude and Alice

Pablo Picasso

Alice enters atelier while Gertrude works

FOREIGN CORREJPONDENT

A S A newspaperman who reported abroad for a Canadian paper, Hemingway was expected to write a lot of frothy colorful human-interest stories that entertained readers, but these did not add much to their knowledge of significant developments in the countries from which they were reported. Since first arriving in Paris, Hemingway, while learning the discipline of a true form of writing, had been doing this well and often to put money into his bank account. Sometimes his interpretations of what he saw were written with the cynical slant of the boy still clinging to his Oak Park upbringing. Not yet understanding that the cafes on Montparnasse Boulevard, in addition to all the gossip that took place among the tables, were vital to the Left Bank artists for relaxation and communication, he wrote in an article called "American Bohemians in Paris," printed in the *Toronto Star Weekly* on March 25, 1922,

> It is a strange-acting and strange-looking breed that crowd the tables of the Café Rotonde. They have all striven so hard for a careless individuality of clothing that they have achieved a sort of uniformity of eccentricity. . . . They are nearly all loafers expending the energy that an artist puts into his creative work in talking about what they are going to do and condemning the work of all artists who have gained any degree of recognition.

Within two years, he would be spending as much time in the cafes as unkempt and ill-dressed and listening to gossip as these people who initially repulsed him.

John Bone gave Hemingway his first specific assignment near the end of March, sending him to cover the Conferenza Internazionale Economica that would convene in Genoa, Italy, on the tenth of April. For the first time, the countries that had fought against and with each other in the Great War would sit down at a table together to discuss the post-war economic rebuilding of Europe and to improve relations with the Soviet Union. The erratic flow of post-war money was the sickness at Europe's heart, depressing currencies and creating unemployment. Lloyd George of England had been the primary mover behind the meetings. The Russian Reds were admitted to the conference with thoughts of making efforts to reopen commercial relations between the U.S.S.R. and Western Europe. Germany was also admitted as an equal for the first time since the war. The United States sent observers but no delegates; the rest of the world could save itself as far as America was concerned. In Canada, where there was much interest in the conference, the readers of the *Toronto Star* would read Hemingway's dispatches. He rode the train south with Guy Hickok, Paul Mowrer, and William Bird, older seasoned reporters with whom he was already acquainted from press associations in Paris, and they arrived in Genoa well before most of the rest of the press. Unlike his feature articles, Hemingway's dispatches were used by the *Daily Star*, not the *Star Weekly*, and for the first time he would cable his material rather than send it by mail boat.

Hemingway was politically naïve when first attending this conference, but, at last having the opportunity to take part in the backstage drama he had heard second-hand at Paris press luncheons, he would learn from experienced, savvy reporters and see for himself the ambiguities of diplomacy and the brutality of fascism in a place where foreigners were ringed by an aggrieved and militant nationalism. One of the other correspondents at the conference thought that Hemingway's basic attitude toward his newspaper work was that "he didn't give a damn about it except that it provided some much-needed funds and gave him an association with other writers."[1] In fact, he was more interested in some

---

1. Charles Fenton, *The Apprenticeship of Ernest Hemingway*, 138.

of the other newspapermen than with Lloyd George and Chicherin. But, overall, despite his youth and inexperience, he acquitted himself well his first time on the international stage and during the conference struck up a warm friendship with veteran newsman William Bird, who also lived in Paris.

As delegates from more than thirty European countries assembled amid a fear of the unknown Bolsheviks, one of Hemingway's first articles was not about the political/economical climate of Europe but the rising instability of Italy, identifying that the essential threat to civic peace at the conference came not from the delegation of Russians rallying local communist sympathizers, who were mostly working Italians, as most of the reporters from the wire services and New York newspapers were writing, but from the "young, tough, ardent, intensely patriotic" Fascists. "They are young ex-veterans formed to protect the existing government of Italy against any sort of Bolshevik plot or aggression. In short, they are counterrevolutionists and in 1920 they crushed the Red uprising with bombs, machine guns, knives and the liberal use of kerosene cans," he wrote. "Under the tacit protection of the government . . . they had a taste of unpenalized lawlessness, unpunished murder, and the right to riot when and where they pleased. So now they have become as great a danger to the peace of Italy as the Reds ever were."[2] Though the article had little to do with the conference, it was one of the first realistic reports about post-war Italy.

The day before the conference opened, Hemingway and some others drove down the coast to interview the Russian delegation staying in Rapallo. It was a mass interview in a guarded atmosphere and his report missed much of the irony that the other reporters caught: that the Bolsheviks, a party of the labor class, were staying at a luxury hotel; their head delegate, Chicherin, was a holdover from the Czarist diplomatic corps; and that it was the first interview of a Soviet spokesman by the western press. He did become close to Max Eastman, an influential editor he had heard about from Sherwood. Eastman was thirty-nine, tall, lean,

---

2. *Toronto Daily Star*, April 13, 1922. / "counterrevolutionists" [*sic*].

handsome, prematurely white-haired, and looked to Hemingway like "a big jolly, middle-western college professor."[3] He had been an editor of the *Masses*, a socialist publication shut down by the Wilson Administration in a much-publicized trial under the Espionage Act, and had started up a new socialist monthly, the *Liberator*. Eastman had a distaste for the bohemianism of Greenwich Village and the Left Bank of Paris and may have sensed a similar feeling in Hemingway. He was taken by Hemingway's personal appearance, enthusiasm, and proper attire, noting that he was "gentle and unassuming, dressed in easy-fitting but conventional suits of clothes and distinguished mainly by a winning laugh, a handsome face and the most beautiful row of teeth I ever saw in man, woman or child." Eastman saw Hemingway frequently in Genoa and remembered the younger man modestly telling him "all about how scared he had been in the war."

Ernest showed Eastman some of the early fiction he had labored on in Paris, "descriptions of scenes and incidents" with which he had been experimenting. "They weren't stories," Eastman recalled, "they were just a paragraph or two long,"[4] and later thought that Hemingway's journalistic training had then had a detrimental effect on his literary style. A little later, Eastman and George Slocombe of the *London Daily Herald* returned to Rapallo to meet Max Beerbohm. Hemingway tagged along and sat quietly with them in the cartoonist's presence. When Eastman made notes about the meeting on the ride back to Genoa, Hemingway smiled, and tapping his forehead, said "I have every word of it here."[5] Meanwhile, they attended the opening session held in the Palazzo di San Giorgio, a grand old decorative medieval hall in Genoa.

Hemingway's response to the opening of the conference had a mocking and cynical tone. Reporting from the Canadian point of view, he described the hall as "about half the size of Massey Hall [in Toronto]" and "an enormous chandelier, with globes as big as association footballs" above the tables. Other reporters described the excellent temper of the

---

3. *Toronto Daily Star*, April 24, 1922.
4. James R. Mellow, *Hemingway: A Life Without Consequences*, 181.
5. Fenton, *The Apprenticeship of Ernest Hemingway*, 138.

delegates, but Hemingway, noting instead the stone plaque honoring Machiavelli next to a statue of "the rather pompous marble Columbus," wrote, "Machiavelli, in his day, wrote a book that could be used as a textbook by all conferences, and from all results, is diligently studied." Nor was he impressed with the delegates: "They cannot find their place at the table and stand talking. The rows of camp chairs that are to hold the invited guests begin to be filled with top-hatted white mustached senators and women in Paris hats and wonderful wealth reeking fur coats. The fur coats are the most beautiful things in the hall."[6] He wrote that when Chicherin rose to speak he looked "like a country grocery storekeeper,"[7] and, unlike many other reporters, did stay to the end of his speech.

He remained in Genoa about another week, identifying the Bolsheviks as important players even though many nations did not recognize their sovereignty, writing favorably about Lloyd George, and sending dispatches about the treaty Russia and Germany signed in Rapallo giving themselves "most favored nation" trade status and tacitly allowing Germany to manufacture weapons, which greatly alarmed the other countries. For a little while, hanging around with the older, more experienced men who liked to drink and eat and joke, listening to them talk about politics and play poker in their rooms, Hemingway found the intense and free life he loved and missed from the summer days at Walloon Lake. With the delegates at a stalemate, he left well before the conference ended. In Paris, he would continue his friendship with Bill Bird and introduce him to Ezra Pound.

The Hemingways liked to walk and hike through the countryside, expending their energy and creative thought, and when Ernest returned from Genoa, they took a wonderful hike into the region of Picardy northwest of Paris. "The country outside of Paris and up into Picardy is beautiful," he wrote to his father. "Fields full of big black and white magpies that walk along the plow furrows like crows do. Lots of larks too. There are lots of common birds I don't know, but I go down to the

---

6. *Toronto Daily Star*, April 24, 1922.
7. *Toronto Daily Star*, April 24, 1922.

Zoological gardens that's right near our house and identify them."[8] From Chantilly they walked some forty miles to Compiegne, spending a night in Senlis in a hotel where several years before the German General von Kluck had stopped during the Battle of the Marne. Senlis "is a lovely old town though," he wrote his mother, "with a beautiful cathedral and abbey and old chateau."[9] They walked through the forests nearly all the way, eating the food and drinking the wine, and he wrote to Clarence, "The forests are very wild and free of underbrush and cover all the hills and ridges. . . . They have deer and wild boar and foxes and rabbits. I've eaten wild boar twice and it is very good. They cook it up into a pasty with carrots and onions and mushrooms and a fine brown crust."[10]

They had planned to walk from Compiegne to Soissons and over to see the great old cathedral of Rheims, but rainy weather set in, Ernest got sick, and they returned to Paris. He took to bed with a sore throat and read the papers and wrote in bed with a typewriter, working on sentences pared from newspaper reports, getting them just right with every word adding to a singular meaning:

> I have watched the police charge the crowd with swords as they
> milled back into Paris through the Port Maillot on the first of
> May and seen the frightened proud look on the white beaten-up
> face of the sixteen year old kid who looked like a prep school
> quarterback and had just shot two policemen. . . . I have stood on
> the crowded back platform of a seven o'clock Batignolles bus as it
> lurched along the wet lamp lit street while men who were going
> home to supper never looked up from their newspapers and we
> passed Notre Dame grey and dripping in the rain.[11]

In the homey atmosphere of love provided by Hadley, Ernest worked with the singular joy of writing one true sentence and, finding the exact

---

8. EH to CEH, May 2, 1922, *Letters of Ernest Hemingway, Vol. 1.*
9. EH to GHH, May 2, 1922, *Letters of Ernest Hemingway, Vol. 1.*
10. EH to CEH, May 2, 1922, *Letters of Ernest Hemingway, Vol. 1.*
11. Carlos Baker, *Hemingway: A Life Story,* "Paris sketches 1922," 120.

place for each exact word, produced six of these remarkably concise little vignettes while his wife nursed him through his cold and sore throat.

When the *Star* sent Ernest credentials for a trip to Russia, Ernest wanted to go, but Hadley, having been left alone in a foreign town for three weeks while he was reporting in Genoa, was adamantly against it happening again so soon and they fought a pitched battle of emotions. The doldrums of a sickbed and Hadley's self-conscious, dowdy appearance, for they spent no money on clothing, exasperated their feelings, but their rancor quickly dissolved as another trip to the Swiss mountains became a reality, this time with Chink Dorman-Smith. In the middle of May, Chink took a furlough from military duty on the Rhine and met the Hemingways in the same small chalet in Chamby-Sur-Montreux where they had recently spent three wonderful weeks. "It's great down here . . . we've been trout fishing and mountain climbing," he wrote his father. "Hadley is very healthy and as red and brown as an Indian. She never looked better." He also received a check from Bone for $465 for his work in Genoa that "was quite welcome."[12]

The three friends climbed seven thousand feet to the top of Cape au Moine and coasted down the snowfields by simply sitting down and letting go. Hadley liked the well-groomed, polite, blue-eyed Chink. She and Ernest would bawdily describe their activity in their bed at night to Chink in the mornings. One night after a beer-drinking contest in a nearby village, Ernest and Chink walked through fields in the lower valleys full of narcissus that were silver under the moonlight. During days, while Chink and Hadley read in their rooms, Ernest ventured to a small stream up the Rhone Valley, writing to Clarence, "It is all fly fishing and as the trout have been fished for over two thousand years or so they are fairly shy."[13] Sitting under a pine tree, taking a break from fishing, he gazed off to a distant waterfall plunging silently over the brown face of a cliff. Perhaps inspired by the money from Bone, he wrote a good article about fishing the little stream "that is barely a yard wide, and flows swiftly and still," and added his sense of history as he walked a road to

---

12. EH to CEH, May 24, 1922, *Letters of Ernest Hemingway, Vol. 1.*
13. EH to CEH, May 24, 1922, *Letters of Ernest Hemingway, Vol. 1.*

a nearby town: "the air is warm from the heat the earth absorbed from the sun. The road is white and dusty, and I thought of Napoleon's Grand Army, marching along it through the white dust on the way to the St. Bernard Pass."[14]

The St. Bernard Pass is the lowest pass on the ridge between Mont Blanche and Mont Rosa, the two highest peaks in the Alps. At Chink's suggestion, they sent the bulk of their luggage by train to Milan and crossed the pass into Italy using rucksacks to carry the bare necessities. A small railroad took them across the Rhone Valley to Bourg St. Pierre where they started their hike, climbing over snow from an altitude of five thousand feet to just over eight thousand to the Great St. Bernard hospice established a thousand years ago. Chink wrote, "eventually we saw the gaunt hospice, like barracks in a moonscape."[15] After encountering and soothing a hostile St. Bernard dog, Chink rang the almoner's bell and gained entrance to the monastery, where they spent the night in the barracks and were given breakfast the next morning. "It was a great trek because the pass wasn't open yet and no one had walked up it this year from the Suisse side," wrote Ernest in a humorous letter to Gertrude Stein. "It took the combined efforts of the Captain and Mrs. H. and a shot of cognac every two hundred yards to get me up the last couple of kilometers of snow."[16] Hadley curiously tiptoed down a long stone corridor, all the doors opening silently as she passed; behind each was a tonsured brother in a long black robe—her husband assured her afterward that she had committed the greatest sin in ten centuries. They left on the morning of the first of June, walking twenty miles down the hill to the village of Aosta and planned to continue to the trek, but Hadley's low-cut saddle oxfords had tightened and split from the wet snow and blistered her feet and she could not go on, so they took the train to Milan where Chink, still thinking Ernest's war wound came from leading Arditi storm troops on Mount Grappa, picked up his baggage and returned to his military post.

---

14. *Toronto Daily Star*, June 10, 1922.

15. Michael Reynolds, *Hemingway: The Paris Years*, 53.

16. EH to Stein and Toklas, June 11, 1922, *Letters of Ernest Hemingway, Vol. 1.*

Ernest was at last able to show Hadley the Italy he had known during the war. As they walked around Milan, he showed her the outside of the palace that had been the Red Cross hospital where he had been taken to heal from his wounding—and may have told her more about Agnes von Kurowsky. They dined at Campari's and walked through the Piazza del Duomo with its black-winged pigeons and pink-stoned cathedral, Ernest gladly reprising this part of the past with Hadley on his arm as they strolled through the Galleria under high-vaulted ceilings, stained glass, and mosaics. They spent days at the San Siro racetrack and did well with their betting, Ernest writing to Gertrude and Alice, "Mrs. Hemingway, with about three cocktails and an indelible pencil to aid her, picks winners as easy as cracking peanut shucks."[17]

When he heard that Benito Mussolini was in town, he used his press card for an interview and was received by Il Duce behind the desk in the editor's office of *Popolo D'Italia* fondling the ears of a wolf-hound puppy beside him and speaking slowly in simple Italian. "A big brown faced man with a high forehead, a slow smiling mouth, and large expressive hands," he wrote in his article in the *Star*. With a quarter of a million "black shirts" ready to overthrow any government opposing his fascist movement, Mussolini was sitting on a powder keg of his own making. The question the article so clearly asked was what did he intend to do "with his political party organized as a military force?"[18] It was an excellent bit of reporting, a coup that made John Bone proud, for before the year ended, this newspaper editor interviewed by Hemingway that spring would be proclaimed fascist dictator of Italy.

It had been easy to reprise the past in Milan, this lovely ancient city where he had recuperated and healed, his broken heart long mended, too, because he was happily in love with Hadley, who was with him completely. He wasn't so much thinking about the past as enjoying the present with a presence of mind so complete that he could sharply seize a journalistic opportunity as it happened and was presented before him. The pleasant reprise of Milan, which may have seemed like a reprise but

---

17. EH to Stein and Toklas, June 11, 1922, *Letters of Ernest Hemingway, Vol. 1.*
18. *Toronto Daily Star*, June 24, 1922.

was more like a nice, lovely visit, would not continue when they traveled on to the region of Veneto where he had served as a Red Cross driver during the war and been wounded in the trench by the Piave River. The rubble of battle had been removed from the old front, deadening the reality of combat, with death no longer there to haunt and vivify his imagination.

Ernest still thought of Schio as one of the finest places on earth. He wanted to spend the night with Hadley at the Two Swords Hotel. They could see the mill that had housed the Schio Country Club, the stream where the boys had swum in the heat of the day, and the small trattoria festooned with wisteria where they had drunk beer under a bombing moon. The young couple took a bus from Milan on June 13 under a gray sky with a hint of rain. His nostalgic dream began to dissipate when they came into Schio, which looked like it had shrunk. Their room at the Duo Spada, a small mean inn, had a squeaking bed with light from a bare-hanging, fly-specked bulb. The old wool mill was back in production with a flow of black muck from washing the wool polluting the old swimming hole. The main street was now mundane; even the girl behind the counter in a wine shop where they stopped for a drink seemed not to care that he had been there during the war. The dinner at the inn was poor, and after a sleepless night, they left in a hired car to see his old front, the gray sky now raining. Even the mountains looked rain-furrowed and dull.

They took a roundabout route, arriving at Sirmione on Lake Garda, where by delightful accident they encountered Ezra and Dorothy Pound, the poet relaxing in the holy place of Catullus and wearing saffron sandals. What better guide to the buried world of the old gods than Ezra under the olive trees of Garda, "wherein the sun drifts in on us through the olive trees a liquid glory,"[19] with the blue water in the rock caves and silver light dancing off the water, creating a rare, wonderful moment outside of time for the Hemingways. From the lake, they took the train down to Mestre and hired a car to Fossalta, where the dark landscape

---

19. Reynolds, *Hemingway: The Paris Years*, 55.

Ernest had walked so often in his sleep (Hadley must have felt some misgivings because too often she had held him in the night, fending off Austrians chasing him into no man's land) was unrecognizable. "All the shattered tragic dignity of the wrecked town was gone," he wrote for an article in the *Daily Star*. "In its place was a new smug hideous collection of plaster houses, painted bright blues, red and yellows." When they drove to the bank of the Piave, all the old trenches and dugouts had vanished. Ernest climbed the sunken road and looked at the river. It was clean and blue with the peaceful activity of a barge being slowly towed by horses on the banks. The site of his wounding was now a smooth green slope of grass to the river. Reflecting upon the intensity of discovering his own mortality in combat, he warned his readers, "don't go back to your own front, because the change . . . the supreme, deadly, lonely dullness . . . will . . .make you believe that the places and happenings that had been the really great events to you were only fever dreams or lies you had told to yourself."

Standing ruefully among the rebuilt houses of Fossalta-di-Piave on an afternoon in the middle of June 1922, Ernest Hemingway was discovering that you cannot reprise the past by visiting old sites and sights, but as he progressed in the writing that meant the most to him he would discover that he could recreate the past in fiction. He was already creating a fiction in this article, "A Veteran Visits the Old Front," by describing a wounding as "the blood soaked your puttee and trickled into your boot, so that when you got up you limped with a squidge"[20] that was actually much different and more heroic than his own and by describing the movement of troops during a major offensive in 1916 as though he had then been there too. The truth for Ernest Hemingway was becoming an artful malleable property. "If you make it up instead of describe it you can make it round and whole and solid and give it life. You create it for good and bad. It is made; not described,"[21] he would say, as the past for him became something between dream and reality where distinctions

---

20. *Toronto Daily Star*, July 22, 1922.
21. Mellow, *Hemingway: A Life Without Consequences*, 187.

blurred, and he would become proficient at making it over, manipulating the truth until it was plausible and habitable.

Hemingway was not yet ready to spend his time completely writing fiction. The qualities of precision, uncompromising economy, and deep emotional clarification in the short stories he would be writing in the cafes on Montparnasse Boulevard within two years were never altogether present in his newspaper work, and the more he concentrated on fiction, work he regarded as dignified and worthy, the more he became cynical about journalism. But in his first years in Paris, journalism kept him constantly writing, enlarged his range of experience, and enabled him to provide financial support in addition to the interest and dividends paid by Hadley's trust fund. (The Hemingways lived prudently but were actually rather well off with a combined income of almost five-thousand dollars a year.) This soothed any anxiety Ernest may have felt about living off his wife. Other reporters liked him and respected his talent, but many sensed he was an alien among them, a man with the capacity but not the temperament for newspaper work. "He was an erratic and obviously brilliant young man," remembered a Hearst correspondent who knew him in Paris. Another remembered that he "lived in the Paris Latin Quarter and was among artists."[22] Miss Stein was never optimistic about journalism, feeling it taught writers to report rather than to make and that it weakened them through reliance on a firm, organized system. In the summer of 1922, for a brief while liberating himself from hack work, Hemingway began to build the foundations of his future in the little magazines and in the literary associations of Paris that catered to the modern movement.

Hemingway—buoyed and steadied by Hadley and by his friendships with Ezra Pound and Gertrude Stein, and the deep purpose of working toward a true literary vision—was saved from a lot of emotional turmoil that might otherwise have afflicted him. For surrounded by literate, older, and more experienced college-trained people (Ezra had a master's degree, knew the classics, and was fluent in French and Italian; Dorman-Smith

---

22. Fenton, *The Apprenticeship of Ernest Hemingway*, 143–44.

had graduated from Sandhurst; Gertrude Stein had almost earned a medical degree, pioneered modern literature, and collected modernist painters and their art; the strange learning, arcane knowledge and extraordinary memory of James Joyce was legendary; and Sylvia Beach, largely self-educated, was fluent in French and years ahead in reading), Ernest, only a high school graduate, was not jealous of what others had that he did not but at times felt uneasy and out of his depth. He hated discussions of literary theory and rarely quoted famous authors but learned that in his enthusiasm for prize fights, horse tracks, bike races, and later, Spanish bullfighting, he could mask his spotty background by turning conversations to topics not learned in books. He shadowboxed walking down the streets, fished rivers real and imaginary when writing in the cafes, and there was always the war and his wound to talk about, and often he played the part of a local Parisian.

Upon returning to Paris in June, the Place de la Contrescarpe became noisier and more crowded as the day progressed. Sometimes when people came to visit, the Hemingways would take them downstairs for a whirl in the Bal Musette. The place was dark and narrow with wooden tables and benches along the walls and a small bare space for dancing to the music by the accordionist. The atmosphere, Hadley thought, was "real old workman's France,"[23] with a scattering of sailors and *poules* among the customers. Patrons bought coins for each dance, and anyone could dance with anyone else. Hadley's wealthy cousin, Bates Wyman, was shocked at the roughness of the neighborhood and the rudeness of the clientele, and Hadley, too, was occasionally frightened by the ruffians who asked her to dance, but Ernest reveled in the smoky atmosphere. Spinning around the floor wearing a striped Breton's fisherman's shirt, he might have been mistaken for a native.

All of Paris was noisy and crowded with summer tourists who flocked to and crowded the sidewalks and cafes of the grand boulevards and beyond. Ernest did his serious writing in the morning before the noise of the city rose into a higher crescendo and then worked to make money by

---

23. Baker, *Hemingway: A Life Story*, 125.

writing humorous stories to send to Bone about persistent rug vendors stalking cafes, displaying faux Bengal tiger skins at tables, and a snippet of café gossip concerning Sinclair Lewis riding a horse in London. Some days he spread the sports pages of English papers and read the racing sheets carefully. With the money left over from Italy, they bet on horses at the local tracks, taking the bus to spend time at Enghien and Auteuil with bottles of wine and picnic lunches eaten on the grass.

Ernest did more at the tracks than drink and eat and bet on the races: he watched and listened to the *touts* and the groomsmen in the stables and the jockeys and owners, the people of the track who trained and took care of the horses. He came to know some of the jockeys, and reading the papers ever more carefully, learned specific details about some of the races won and lost. Around the first of July, first jotting down notes on the back of a telegraph form, he started writing a fictional tale about a father and son who live around the track: the father is a jockey who buys a good steeplechaser from money won betting on a fixed race and gets killed taking a jump during a race. The story is about a father's failure, not by love, but by character—reminiscent in a different way of his own father's failure to his son, and even a prescience of Clarence Edmonds Hemingway's death. It is told by the son with the innocence and inside expertise of a Huck Finn type of boy who may not understand his father's shady past, but his knowledge of European racetracks is detailed, specific, and accurate. Working out themes and techniques he would later perfect, "My Old Man" was Hemingway's first good story written in Paris. Ernest was justly proud. Demonstrating an imaginative ability to weave together firsthand observations with secondary information, it is better than any of the track stories written by Sherwood Anderson. He mastered this part of his craft early; no one taught him to do this. He learned it instinctively on his own and would become so good at it that many assumed his fiction was a thinly veiled biography, but rarely was it so. Direct experience, he discovered, was not necessarily the most reliable source of information for a writer. A careful observer, steady and detached, could imagine what an experience felt like: this he had learned in journalism and carried into his fiction.

Hemingway cultivated the underside of sports like horse racing and boxing by developing inside knowledge quickly and in precise detail. There were always two stories: the one on the surface that anybody could see and the one buried beneath the public display. The fixed horse race and the thrown prize fight fascinated Hemingway. You could bet on the fix and win next to nothing because smart money lowered the odds, or you could bet with your heart and lose anyway. It was a metaphor for life because life, as Hemingway saw it, was only a question about dying; how, where, and when was a truth upon which he built some of his best fiction. "All stories, if continued far enough, end in death, and he is no true story teller who would keep that from you,"[24] he once said. Alone in the trench at Piave with two men splattered over him, courage had not been enough to protect him from the roaring blast of the explosion, nor could it protect him from the fear a close encounter with a violent death can produce, and that night in the trench he had known enough fear for a lifetime. How a man behaved under stress, in dangerous situations, or at the point of death, was his life study found early, and he recalibrated his readings at the races, at ringside, bullfights, and on the battlefield, writing about jockeys, soldiers, prizefighters, bullfighters, and prostitutes, people forbidden in the town of Oak Park—and because they were forbidden, they were of great interest to Ernest Hemingway. Instead, he took the modern precept that no material was forbidden to write about, a rule and condition that his parents did not understand and thought was vile. But he would write about them anyway, even if his father would reputedly burn his first published book.

The name "Ernest Hemingway" first appeared as an honest-to-God writer among the magazines of Shakespeare & Company at the end of June during his first summer in Paris. Pieces he had written in Chicago and encouraged by Sherwood Anderson to submit were published in *The Double Dealer*, a review in New Orleans with a modernist bent sold in Sylvia's bookstore. In a wonderful coincidental bit of Americana, Hemingway's poem "Ultimately" was published on the same page of the

---

24. Ernest Hemingway, *Death in the Afternoon*, chapter 11.

June issue as a poem titled "Portrait" by another unknown first-time published writer named William Faulkner. Within the month, dropping the name of Ezra Pound to show that he had connections, Ernest wrote to the editor requesting his promised payment. The editor wrote back that the check would soon be in the mail. Hemingway also wrote Harriet Monroe to thank her for accepting six poems for *Poetry* magazine to be grouped under the title "Wanderings" (satiric parodies about people) and submitted a requested biographical blurb that, in addition to declaring Max Eastman to be a close friend, said he was "at present in Russia as a staff correspondent for the *Toronto Star*."[25] The American poet James Dickey once said that Hemingway couldn't write poetry, and the irony that his first publications in literary reviews would be poems and not stories was not lost on the writer, for he probably knew even then that it would be through prose, and not verse, where he would make his indelible mark. And though something of a fibber, Hemingway was learning the ins and outs of publication quickly and well, and not just through associations with extraordinary men and women, but also because he knew that if what he wrote was good enough to be published then there should be monetary compensation.

The more Ernest and Bill Bird came to know each other the more their friendship grew. Bird, a slim older American with a bachelor's degree from Trinity College in Hartford, Connecticut, had organized his own wire service, the *Consolidated Press,* with offices on the Right Bank at 19 rue D'Antin. As an interesting hobby, he purchased an old Belgian Mathieu hand press and had it assembled at 29 Quai D'Anjou on the Ile Saint Louis, founding the *Three Mountains Press,* so named after the three hills of Paris. The idea for *Three Mountains Press* came to Bird when Hemingway informed him that Pound might let him publish a few of his cantos. Hemingway introduced Bird to Pound, and Pound, ever ready to make use of any resources, soon convinced Bird to publish a series of books that would constitute an inquest into the state of contemporary English writing. Bird made Pound the chief editor in charge of selecting the books for publication, giving Ezra something more to think about

---

25. EH to Harriet Monroe, July 16, 1922, *Letters of Ernest Hemingway, Vol. 1.*

while Bill Bird and Ernest and their wives, along with Lewis Galantiere and his fiancée, gathered for a summer hike through the Black Forest in Germany. Ernest bought two air tickets for ten dollars and tried to convince Bird to make the flight, too, but he preferred a conventional, safe train for the first leg of the trip.

In early August, the Hemingways flew from Paris to Strasbourg in a flimsy canvas-and-wood bi-plane operated by the Franco-Romanian Aero Company to meet their friends near the border. Commercial flight was in its infancy and neither Hadley nor Ernest had flown before. They climbed into a little cabin and stuffed cotton in their ears. "The plane began to move along the ground, bumping like a motorcycle, and then slowly rose into the air," he wrote in the *Toronto Star*. "The ground began to flatten out beneath us. It looked out into brown squares, yellow squares, green squares . . . I began to understand cubist paintings." He kept staring down while Hadley slept.

> Sometimes we went down quite low and could see bicyclists on the road looking like pennies rolling along a narrow white strip. At other times we would lift up and the whole landscape would contract. . . . We went over great forests that looked as soft as velvet . . . in an open field I could see the old trenches zigzagging through a field pocked with shell holes.[26]

Feeling the sensations of flight as they lowered near the ground from three thousand feet to avoid the height of a storm and "followed a canal that we could see below us through the rain," he moved through the landscape taking his reader with him, a practice he would perfect in his fiction. The plane covered the two hundred and forty-five miles in less than three hours, while the others paid more for the train that took almost nine hours.

At Strasbourg, the six hikers gathered and passed through customs and crossed the bridge over the Rhine into Germany where the German mark was in a free fall and they found prices incredibly cheap. The

---

26. *Toronto Daily Star*, Sept. 9, 1922.

best hotel in Kehl served a five-course meal for the equivalent of fifteen cents, a stein of beer costing about two cents. They marveled at their newfound wealth but were less impressed by the open hostility of the many Germans encountered on their hike through the Black Forest, who resented what they took to be exploiting foreigners. In a humorous manner, Ernest wrote about the falling mark in a feature story for the *Star*. "A Swiss hotelkeeper can raise prices with the easy grace of a Pullman car poker shark backing a pat full house, but the mark can fall faster than even a Swiss in good training can hoist the cost of living."[27] Though at the time no one was worried about Germany, which had lately been the military wolf at the door, what Hemingway and many others did not yet understand was that the future of Germany was the future of the world because the economic chaos ruining shopkeepers and wage earners was creating the emotional climate that would bring Hitler to power.

When the others departed for Paris, the Hemingways traveled downriver through the narrow reaches of the Rhine to Coblenz, the river swiftly flowing past vineyards, romantic ruins, and gothic castles perched on upper ledges. Chink Dorman-Smith met them at the pier and filled Ernest's ears with insider information about what was really going on in Germany, as his stories became much better informed of the political situation. "All over Germany conflict goes on between German police and German mobs," he wrote in an article titled "German Riots" for the *Weekly*. "In the north there are riots against the high cost of living that are quelled by the police with machine guns. In the south there are riotous demonstrations in favor of Hindenburg, Ludendorff and a return to the monarchy in Munich at which the police quell the dissenting Republicans with clubs."[28] The Hemingways were still in Germany on August 23 when war erupted in Asia Minor: two hundred thousand Turkish troops commanded by Mustafa Kemal Pasha smashed through the thin Greek front in Asia Minor and, massacring and burning Greek villages as they drove to the sea, pushed west toward the port city of Smyrna at the head of an inlet on the Aegean Sea.

---

27. *Toronto Daily Star*, Sept. 2, 1922.
28. *Toronto Star Weekly*, Sept. 30, 1922.

The old Ottoman Empire that centuries ago had stretched through most of the Mediterranean had teetered and fallen in the first two decades of the twentieth century, committing genocides against Armenians and Greeks, and finally disintegrating with its defeat in World War I. In a rush to fill the vacuum of an empire now vanished, the Allies sanctioned Greek expansion into the Anatolian Peninsula. Under the cover of French and English navies, Greek forces had landed in Smyrna and moved east, capturing large parts of the eastern part of the great peninsula that had large Greek populations. Retaliating Turkish forces, infuriated by atrocities committed against Turks, united and fighting for their ancient homeland, pushed back on the Greek line of defense. By the time the Hemingways departed Coblenz, the Turks had captured two key Greek positions along the Berlin–Baghdad railway and were moving closer to Smyrna. The Turks wanted the Greeks out of Asia Minor before territorial claims could be settled at a conference to be held in Venice that fall. Ernest returned to Paris in early September with a brown brush of hair on his upper lip, a mustache he would keep for the rest of his life, and, the last great war having started on less provocation, read about the escalating war between Turkey and Greece with mixed feelings about what he might do as the situation became more urgent. On the eighth of September, the Greek army abandoned Smyrna. As American destroyers arrived in the harbor to protect and evacuate the Americans remaining onshore, the Turks occupied the town in an orderly fashion with little violence at first and then began burning the Greek and Armenian sectors of the city, killing over one hundred thousand people.

On September 11, Bill Bird asked Ernest to accompany him to interview Georges Clemenceau at his home in St. Vincent du Jard on the west coast of France. Clemenceau, the eighty-year-old former prime minister of France who had negotiated the Treaty of Versailles, was making an American tour to correct false views of post-war France, and Bird wanted more facts. Hemingway asked the old warrior if he was going to visit Canada as well, and the old warrior angrily replied that Canada had not used general conscription to raise troops and had not fully supported the war effort. When Bone read the interview, he thought it was too incendiary for the Canadian public, wondered if Clemenceau was ignorant or had some other purpose in mind, and asked Hemingway to do another, forwarding a check for expenses. Another interview was pointless; the old man was looking backward, not forward, but Bone sent Hemingway another telegram to go to Constantinople. Asia Minor looked like it might veer out of control, and he wanted him to cover it.

After the burning of Smyrna, the Turks moved north, advancing to the barbed wire of the British military posts at the Dardanelles, and threatened to take Constantinople and the neutral zone the Allies had established to protect the straits from the Black Sea on the north to the Dardanelles on the south. Bone wired Hemingway $500 for the initial expenses, and Hemingway reserved a sleeping compartment on the Simplon-Orient Express from the Gare du Lyon for the night of September 25. Hadley did not want her husband going, was determined that he not, and they argued more dreadfully than they had when she successfully opposed his trip to Russia. She did not want to be left alone in Paris for another long month, nor did she want him going into Middle Eastern chaos reinforcing his already terrorizing dream patterns with more armed violence and risking his life for money. She was also angered by an arrangement he had made with the Paris chief of Hearst's International News Service, Frank Mason, to report for them in Constantinople, too, even though he was under an exclusive contract with the *Toronto Star*. They both knew this was wrong, but Hemingway probably also knew that Bone rewrote the lead on some of his stories and sold them to American papers under his own name, and may have also tried to justify his duplicity by thinking that since Hearst wanted spot news and the *Star* wanted features the money he took from both papers was honest. On the days leading up to his leaving, Hadley neither spoke to him nor accompanied him to any of the sporting matches he loved so well. On the night of his departure, he left in a huff, slamming the door on his equally angry wife. At the station, the taxi driver dropped and broke his portable typewriter, the one given by Hadley the year before, and until he got to Constantinople—a long rail journey of four nights and three days of steady rail clicks broken by passport checks and a few stops—he had to write his dispatches by hand.

The British would resist if the Turks tried to capture the Dardanelles, but when the Greek naval fleet left Constantinople and the British forced the Greeks to withdraw behind the Maritza River in Thrace, armistice talks began with Mustapha Kemal in the town of Mudanya on the southern coast of the Sea of Marmara. The war was over by the time Hemingway reached Constantinople at the end of September, though he stayed on, had his typewriter repaired, wrote what he saw and heard, and some of his reports were excellent. In the Hotel du Londres he contracted a fever, and too sick to attend press conferences, dosed himself with aspirin and quinine pills and worked very hard. "Constantinople is noisy, hot, hilly, dirty and beautiful. It is packed with uniforms and rumors,"[29] he wrote in an early dispatch. Describing the squalor of the east:

> I stood on the dusty, rubbish-strewn hillside of Pera . . . and looked down at the harbor, forested with masts and grimy with smoky funnels and across at the dust-colored hills on the other side where the Turkish town sprawled in square mud-colored houses, ramshackle tenements with the dirty white fingers of the minarets rising like gray-white, slim lighthouses out of the muddled houses.[30]

He also caught its beauty: "In the morning when you wake and see a mist over the Golden Horn with the minarets rising out of it slim and clean toward the sun and the muezzin calling the faithful to prayer in a voice that soars and dips like an aria from a Russian opera, you have the magic of the east."[31]

It was the kind of reporting he liked to do in an atmosphere of crucial events. He caught the politics well, too: "the Turkish concentration of troops between the straits and Constantinople have given them a good

---

29. *Toronto Daily Star*, Sept. 30, 1922.
30. *Toronto Daily Star*, Oct. 18, 1922.
31. *Toronto Daily Star*, Oct. 28, 1922.

position to talk from."[32] The streets to his hotel were jammed with trams and honking cars. In Galata, the business and entertainment district, men in suits and fezzes ambled past the shops, saloons, and banks with signs in four languages. Constantinople, he realized immediately, was not the opulent, gleaming white Middle Eastern city he had seen in the movies. His hotel was so ridden with fleas that in the morning his face was marked with bites. At night, the old city was dark and smelly, the streets slippery with refuse, dogs nosed at garbage as rats scuttled out of the way. In the red-light district, the blowsy sex workers propositioning sailors had no appeal to Hemingway. The city was full of White Russians who had fled the Soviets, allies of Kemal, and were now trapped in what had been their sanctuary; many were reduced to selling their jewelry. Ernest bought necklaces of ivory and amber from one who worked as a waiter. With the ominous threat of a repressive regime closing in, Constantinople was a city of fear for those who could not get away.

Hemingway's initial stories were a flurry of unsigned spot news reports, but he quickly picked up a knowledgeable vocabulary and background in Middle East politics, and his stories assumed authority. "The one big aim of the Kemalists," he wrote of the Pasha and his forces, "is the possession of Mesopotamia . . . It is oil that Kemal and company want Mesopotamia for, and it is oil that Great Britain wants to keep Mesopotamia for."[33] He was too sick to join other correspondents for a briefing on a British destroyer but listened to those who had attended, gathering everything they knew, and pared his stories drastically because of censors at the wire service in Constantinople. Even though his information was secondhand, for journalists were excluded from the signing of the treaty at Mudanya that halted the Turks' pursuit of the Greeks into Europe, he speculated well on the outcome of the Allies ceding eastern Thrace to the Turks: "Eliminating the Greeks from Thrace will unite Bulgaria and Turkey, making a dangerous wedge of pro-Soviet countries that thrust into the center of the Balkans."[34]

32. *Toronto Daily Star*, Oct. 25, 1922.
33. *Toronto Daily Star*, Oct. 24, 1922.
34. *Toronto Daily Star*, Oct. 4, 1922.

Bone caught Hemingway's duplicity quickly. Reading the American papers, he saw eight stories by "John Hadley," whom he must have known was Ernest, and telegraphed him on October 6 that his dispatches were duplicating those of the International News Service. Ernest, sick and depressed and worried, wrote Bone two days later suggesting he might like to return to Toronto to work on a salaried basis. Not much else was said between them as Hemingway, though sick, stayed busy writing and sending more very good articles and stories. While in Constantinople he met the adventurer and soldier of fortune Charles Sweeny, who had fought with Madero in the Mexican Revolution and against Gomez in Venezuela, where he was jailed for a time, had joined the French Foreign Legion, was wounded in battle, and became a lieutenant colonel in the American army during the Great War. Except for the man's right-wing politics, Hemingway saw in Sweeny the kind of man he most admired: a tough, battle-scarred man of action following whichever side captured his imagination. Sweeny amazed Hemingway with his grasp of military science and tactics, and he paid close attention to his war stories and battle assessments and made use of them in his reports. Reporting on the war in Asia Minor, and listening to Sweeny and other British officers who had been with the Greeks at the front, deepened Hemingway's understanding of war.

The armistice signed on October 15 gave the Greek army fifteen days to abandon eastern Thrace, and as they left, fleeing along with them were masses of Greek and Armenian refugees. On the sixteenth, Ernest headed for Murali, eighty miles to the west, and then on to Adrianople near the modern Bulgarian border, all day long passing a stream of tired, unshaven soldiers in ill-fitting American uniforms trudging along the roads that led to western Thrace and Macedonia, with wagon trains of baggage carts drawn by mud-flanked water buffalo being goaded forward. He reported that cut telegraph wires dangled from poles like Maypole ribbons, creating an image of communication futility. Traveling by car, horseback, and foot, experiencing an actual close encounter of the war as he witnessed the evacuation of nearly a quarter of a million people in its aftermath, yet he still managed to borrow a shotgun and shoot twenty-two quail: "Nice open country with sort of sage brush and they seemed easy to hit," he wrote in a letter to his father.

Still stricken with malaria and dosing himself with quinine, he slept on a cot in a room in a small hotel in Adrianople crawling with lice. When he and the others complained in the morning to the proprietor, a fat woman called Madame Marie, she spread her hands and replied, "It is better than sleeping in the road." They stepped outside and "it was drizzling. At the end of the muddy side street we were on I could see the eternal procession of humanity moving slowly along the great stone road that runs from Adrianople across the Maritza valley to Karagatch."[35] It was a sight he would never forget. "Thousands of Christians," he wrote in the *Daily Star*, "many hungry and with all their earthly belongings packed on their backs, trudged out of Thrace today as the cross made way for the crescent."[36] In his mind, Hemingway would return to this sight again and again, trying to distill the essence of the experience so that what he made up was truer than what he remembered, and as he did he would one day weave into fiction the retreat from Caporetto in *A Farewell to Arms*, basing it in his imagination upon the flight of the Greeks from Thrace.

Hemingway left Thrace on October 18, boarding a train traveling by way of Sofia and Trieste, and reaching Paris in three days exhausted, sick, and so covered with insect bites that he had his head shaved. Hadley was at the station to meet him. Feeling guilty over their angry parting, she had written him letters the whole time he was away. His clothes were baggy from loss of weight, and he bore gifts from the East for her: the necklaces of amber and ivory he had bought from the Russian nobleman waiting tables in Constantinople. Hadley was glad to have him back as their little Parisian apartment again became a love nest. Ernest, eating and sleeping and putting on lost weight, caught up on his correspondence. To Gertrude Stein vacationing with Alice in the south of France, he wrote, "Why don't you come back and cheer up this town? I've given

---

35. *Toronto Daily Star*, Nov. 14, 1922.
36. *Toronto Daily Star*, Oct. 16, 1922.

up my other pursuits and sleep all day."[37] Hadley also wrote to Gertrude and Alice thanking them for a large candied Casaba melon that Alice had picked out and Gertrude had sent.

In a letter to John Bone he meticulously detailed his expenses, and to make amends for his duplicity in Asia Minor enclosed a check for three-hundred francs—the difference from the advance which he knew he could have kept, and offered a concocted explanation for his double dealings: stranded with a great story "in Adrianople with all the wires cut,"[38] he wrote that he found an Italian policeman who promised his colonel would wire it to Frank Mason in Paris, who, despite instructions to send it to Bone, stole and rewrote the story. His boss probably didn't believe him, but, to Ernest's relief, in a letter responding to his query about working in Toronto, Bone asked for a definite date for his return. Journalism frustrated Ernest, even though it paid well, because it took time away from what he considered his serious writing, but with the offer to return to Toronto ensured, he and Hadley would have to think about whether or not they should stay in Paris. They made their decision over the wine at her birthday dinner at an expensive restaurant and drank to another year in Paris and the upcoming Christmas at Chamby, this time again with Chink. Ernie wrote Bone that they planned to return to Toronto in the fall of 1923. That would give him one more year to prove himself as a writer of fiction, and it would have to be a year of much more progress than the one soon coming to an end.

Sometimes he felt good about his writing, sure that he was getting better; at other times he felt futility and a moody depression would set in. Resting in his bed in Paris and getting over his eastern fever, good news came on the literary front. The literary scout for the Hearst line of magazines, Frasier Hunt, wrote that "My Old Man" was a great story and that he had sent it to the editor of *Cosmopolitan* hoping he would buy it. Hunt also advised Hemingway to increase his marketability by writing "nice love stories with youth and beauty and spring."[39] The praise was

---

37. EH to GS, Nov. 3, 1922, *Letters of Ernest Hemingway, Vol. 1.*
38. EH to JB, Oct. 27, 1922, *Letters of Ernest Hemingway, Vol. 1.*
39. Reynolds, *Hemingway: The Paris Years,* 78.

welcome, but, having tried the popular fiction formula in Chicago, the advice was discarded. He felt that "My Old Man" and "Up in Michigan," a story he hadn't shown much since Gertrude Stein called it inaccrochable, were his best fiction so far. After ten months in Paris, he had taught himself to write as well as Sherwood Anderson but knew that wasn't good enough. He wanted to write as well as Joyce, with whom he shared a close friend in Sylvia Beach, and probably had *Dubliners* in mind as an effort to achieve.

Ernest received $400 in back pay from Bone and his spirits were running high. At Ezra's studio, he met a portrait painter named Henry Strater, a recent graduate of Princeton who also liked to box. Strater was about the same size as Ernest (6 feet, 200 pounds) and they fought a few stiff, evenly matched rounds at Henry's abode on the west side of Paris near the Bois de Boulogne where he lived with his wife and child. Afterward, Ernest took a bath in the tin bathtub and stayed for lunch. Strater urged him to sit for a portrait, full face, downward grazing, wearing a gray sweatshirt. Known as *The Boxer Portrait*, it was the first portrait of Hemingway painted and the first likeness to show the new mustache. He also met at Ezra's a tubercular young man named Ernest Walsh, who with a pale face and burning eyes posed as a young man marked for early death. Hemingway composed a satirical sketch of Walsh, who created a social manner both dark and intense, and also one of Ford Madox Ford, who was pointed out in one of the cafes. Ernest could hardly believe this arrogant fat man with the walrus mustache was the famous friend and collaborator of Joseph Conrad.

There came further bracing news when the name Ernest Hemingway was listed with William Carlos Williams, B. M. G. Adams, Ford Madox Ford, Wyndham Lewis, and T. S. Eliot in the prospectus of a series of books by authors Pound had lined up for "an inquest into the state of contemporary English Prose" to be published by the Three Mountains Press. Pound, certain something would develop, but not knowing what Ernest would submit, put "Blank" after Hemingway's name. Thrilled to be included in such company, Ernest mailed the notice to friends and relatives. Pound soon received letters from Oak Park requesting the book: "I am the father of Ernest M. Hemingway and want to thank you for all you have done to encourage my son. I hereby subscribe for five (5) volumes of the new book 'Blank' by Ernest M. H. and will remit upon subscription."[40] There was also a request for books from Grace. Ernest did not know what he would put in his book, but, dropping names, wrote a gossipy letter to Harriet Monroe: "Gertrude Stein is down in St. Remy in Provence . . . Lewis Galantiere . . . has just undergone a very trying love affair with a girl from Evanston, Ill. . . . Joyce is sick at Nice . . . T. S. Eliot's new quarterly The Criterion seems to have inspired the Dial;"[41] and asked for permission to use the poems she planned to publish in *Poetry*.

It may have been at this time that Ernest accompanied Ezra to 20 rue du Jacob to the salon of Natalie Barney, and if he did he would have seen the Temple of Amity, the small Greek temple in her back garden, which he certainly knew about. For Natalie Barney subscribed to Ezra Pound's *Bel Esprit* program that collected money to subsidize the work of writers and artists, specifically on this occasion in November, to allow T. S. Eliot (who had suffered a nervous breakdown and spent a couple of months in a sanitarium) to quit his job at Lloyd's bank in London. Ezra asked Hemingway to bring friends visiting from St. Louis around to his studio so he could make his pitch for money to them. Hemingway, his head still closely cropped, was amused by Pound's gesture and thought that Eliot quite possibly was doing very well working in the bank.

The Greco-Turkish war had cracked Asia Minor wide open and was attracting an array of international opportunists. A conference was scheduled for late November in Lausanne, Switzerland to reach a diplomatic settlement in the region. At stake were the vast oil reserves of the Arabian Peninsula, and though the United States would not participate, Standard Oil of America sent unofficial representatives. Hemingway's press mates—Lincoln Steffens, Bill Bird, Guy Hickok—were packing their bags getting ready to go, but not Hemingway because there was no wire from Bone. Then, just before the conference opened, Frank Mason asked

---

40. Reynolds, 80.
41. EH to HM, Nov. 16, 1922, *Letters of Ernest Hemingway, Vol. 1.*

him to cover the wire service releases for I.N.S, and Charles Bertelli soon asked the same for Universal News Service, another Hearst organization. The money was too tempting. He asked Hadley to come along and stay at the hotel, a first-rate one, shop a bit and take side trips to Chamby by train. It would be like a paid vacation. There was no duplicity this time since Bone would pay only for features Ernest might write exclusively for the *Star*. Hadley agreed but came down with a terrible cold. Ernest stayed with her in Paris, missing the opening of the conference, then left for Lausanne without her.

In Lausanne, the English and French tried to control the conference with closed meetings, secret dinners, and bland news releases. Ernest walked down the hill to the conference site and up the hill to his hotel, filing his stories early in the morning to late at night. It quickly became apparent that the fair settlement the conference had promised applied only to England and her allies, who rejected Turkish claims to the conquered territory in Thrace, agreed to give Bulgaria an outlet to the Aegean Sea, and through a subcommittee was ready to recommend the complete disarmament of Turkey. Ernest had underestimated the amount of work and expenses and wired Mason for more money to keep the wire service open. Lord Curzon of Great Britain wanted the Dardanelles and all access to Mesopotamian oil open to England and, really, no one else. The Turks were furious; they controlled Thrace and didn't need England telling them how to run their country. Hemingway sent out bulletins under the name John Hadley, and on November 27 headlines announced: "Conference at Lausanne Breaks Down." Hearst had scooped other American papers on Curzon's promise-breaking policy statements. Mason wired Hemingway that New York was pleased with his efforts and asked him to interview any Standard Oil men that might be at the conference. The world soon knew that the United States, though not officially involved in the conference, had its fingers in the pie because American interests (Standard Oil) wanted the oil lands as open to America as Britain. But Ernest was unhappy with his press arrangements: he was being paid much less than he had with the *Star* and doing a lot more work.

Despite being overworked, Hemingway still found the time to drink and fraternize with other reporters. He made a strong impression on Lincoln Steffens, the great muckraker journalist from San Francisco whom he had already befriended in Paris. Ernest showed Lincoln "My Old Man," the only fiction he had with him in Lausanne. Lincoln wanted to see everything he had written and thought he was the "surest future" among the young writers and artists that he met in Europe. "He was gay, he was sentimental, but always at work,"[42] recalled Steffens. Ernest also spent evenings with the South African journalist William Bolitho Ryall, drinking brandy and discussing politics. Ryall was full of insight and as sharp as a surgeon's blade and made an indelible mark on the younger Hemingway with his view on "the malady of power:" he thought the symptoms were recognizable: it began with a suspicion of one's associates and ended with the absolute conviction of one's own indispensability. Ryall was also disdainful of journalism and this further cast dissatisfaction upon the profession for Hemingway. He encouraged young colleagues like Hemingway to quit before they became burnt-out reporters too long at the trade "cadging drinks and dead-dog assignments" from more successful friends—views that reinforced the advice given by Gertrude Stein. Several years later, under the name William Bolitho, Ryall would write the classic book *Twelve Against the Gods* about twelve great and famous men who made their mark on history in a spectacular fashion only to succumb to hubris or circumstances. Hemingway would acknowledge that Ryall gave him "the beginning of whatever education I received in international politics."[43]

As talks broke down in Lausanne, six ministers in Greece held responsible for the debacle in Turkey were condemned to death and shot. As the whole sickening story came out, broken men huddled in the rain facing rifles they once commanded, Ernest Hemingway read about it hurriedly as he worked the conference in Switzerland. He remembered one of the ministers, Gounaris, from Genoa and tried to imagine that dark face standing against the wall facing death. He thought about the

42. Mellow, *Hemingway: A Life Without Consequences*, 206.
43. Mellow, 203–4.

firing squad, as interesting a means of execution as the guillotine, and how men act in the face of death. He would return to these thoughts, intensely study the news bulletins, and recreate the scene vividly and use it as a vignette for *in our time*, the name he would give to the "blank" book in Bill Bird's series. Although the Greek execution stuck with him, at the time he was too busy to think much about it. "Each country was anxious to present its version of what happened," Hemingway later explained. "Press conferences followed in rapid succession and you had to step very fast to get them all in."[44] He normally filed his last dispatch around three in the morning—work for which Mason was paying so little that it made Ernest angry.

Hadley thought Ernest's passionate dislikes were an outward expression of deep-seated anger toward himself, and she felt that his great kindness, "just about as far in the other direction,"[45] made up for his cruelties. Ernest respected his wife. She was honest and steadfast in a way he never was and could hold his cruel streak somewhat in check. Ernest missed Hadley and wanted her warm body in his bed. Keeping track of her menstrual periods, he wrote, "we haven't lost so much time on the time of the month because you've probably been too sick. I do so hate for you to miss what is the most comfortable and jolly time for mums;"[46] her comfortable time being the supposedly infertile period at the beginning of the monthly cycle when they had unprotected intercourse during the days she was least likely to become pregnant. She reminded him in a letter that he had been out of town during the safest times of the month. Perhaps abandoning caution in his strong desire to have her, he wrote that she shouldn't worry and wired her from Lausanne to join him as soon as possible. "I was thrilled," remembered Hadley, who felt "awfully lonesome to be there alone in the squalid neighborhood."[47] She was also eager to have a baby, but Ernest, desperate to make it as a writer, believed a baby would hinder his work.

---

44. Fenton, *The Apprenticeship of Ernest Hemingway*, 190.
45. Hadley Mowrer, Sokoloff tapes, Hemingway Collection, JFK Library.
46. EH to Hadley, Nov. 28, 1922, *Letters of Ernest Hemingway, Vol. 1*.
47. Mowrer, Sokoloff tapes, Hemingway Collection, JFK Library.

Hadley packed for the trip to join her husband. She was looking forward to the time they would spend in Chamby and packed ski clothes, for this time they would try skiing down the mountain slopes. They planned to be away for a long time to avoid the wet, cold weather of Paris winters. "He had met a man [Lincoln Steffens] . . . very much interested in him . . . an older man . . . and he wanted me to meet him. I put the idea of the manuscripts into my head that he would like to show them to this man," Hadley recalled years later. "I had this brilliant idea that it would give him great pleasure."[48] She knew, too, he would want to work on his fiction when he finished his work in Lausanne. She put the clothes in a large suitcase and then went to the cupboard in the dining room, the first room upon entering, where Ernest kept his work in three folders and gathered them all, the handwritten originals, the typescripts, and the carbon copies of the typescripts, and put them into a smaller valise with toiletries and medicines. "I packed them all . . . even some that was unfinished. . . . Nobody knew about my going. The train was in the Gare de Lyon."[49] On the evening of December 2, crossing the Seine on the Austerlitz Bridge, she took a taxi to the glass-domed Gare de Lyon, where a porter escorted her to her compartment on the Paris–Lausanne express. The train was nearly empty, and she found a comfortable seat. The porter put the big suitcase on a high luggage rack and the small valise lower where she could reach it. "There was a lot of time, so I went out and walked up and down." She walked outside the station to buy a newspaper and a bottle of Evian water from a pushcart vendor on the quay and then strolled around, talking casually to a few other travelers, until she heard the conductor call "All Aboard!" Hurrying to her compartment, she sat down and glanced at the luggage rack. The valise was gone. She panicked and couldn't stop crying. A conductor called a policeman, who was of little help. "It was ghastly . . . I spent a horrible night . . . so worried about Tatie . . . that I had to tell him such a thing." When the train pulled into the station at Lausanne, she saw

48. Mowrer, Sokoloff tapes, Hemingway Collection, JFK Library.
49. Mowrer, Sokoloff tapes, Hemingway Collection, JFK Library.

Ernest with Lincoln Steffens standing on the platform. "So he was there and [with] this nice man." She was so upset and crying that she had trouble explaining what had happened. "I had to tell him so I told him. He was very brave about it but his heart was broken." It was thoughtful of her to take her husband's manuscripts, but careless to put them in the care of a porter and leaving them alone in her compartment. "It was terrible to have been responsible."[50] Lincoln Steffens said Ernest was calm and handled the situation fairly well; Hadley, he thought, suffered more.

Hemingway could hardly believe it and thought that surely the carbons were still in the drawer in the hope that she hadn't taken them too. He quickly hired someone to cover for him at the conference and took the train to Paris, crossing the border at Vallorbe where he had his passport stamped, maybe catching snatches of sleep. Arriving in Paris on Sunday morning, he walked across the Seine on the Austerlitz Bridge and past the Jardin du Plantes to rue Mouffetard and up the hill to their small apartment. It was true. Nearly all of his work was gone, some of it written in Michigan in the summers after the war, and would be forever lost. He did find a copy of "Up in Michigan" shoved back in a drawer and kept separate since Gertrude Stein's disparagement even though he knew the story was right. He spent a hard night in Paris. The next day, Monday, he returned to the conference to go back to work. The courage he sought in life that he knew was necessary he found on the train ride back to Lausanne, helped along with a bottle of wine, and as the train clicked along, he started composing a poem about the conference, venting some of his anger and frustration on the Lausanne diplomats.

All of the Turks are gentlemen and Ismet Pasha is a little deaf.
But the Armenians. How about the Armenians? Well the
    Armenians.
Lord Curzon likes young boys. So does Chicherin.
So does Mustapha Kemal. He is good looking too.

---

50. Mowrer, Sokoloff tapes, Hemingway Collection, JFK Library.

His eyes are too close together but he makes war. That is the way
he is.
Lord Curzon does not love Chicherin. Not at all.
His beard trickles and his hands are cold. He thinks all the time.
Lord Curzon thinks too. But he is much taller and goes to St.
Moritz.
Mr. Child does not[51]

Although it hurt a lot, Ernest Hemingway was not inconsolable
about the loss of his manuscripts. When Lincoln Steffens and Bill Bird
returned to Paris a few days later, they searched through the lost and
found area of the train station and came up with nothing. Bird suggested
that Ernest place an ad in the papers offering a reward, but the amount
Ernest was willing to offer was hardly enough to buy taxi fare to return
the stolen articles, and there is no record of a reward offered in any of
the papers. His story "My Old Man" was not lost because he had had it
with him in Lausanne, and there were the six poems being published by
Harriet Monroe in Chicago. A long story he was working on about fishing on a stream in Northern Michigan was among the lost manuscripts,
but even part of that was recoverable since he had sent the first chapter
to Greg Clark in Toronto. The novel about the war he had started in
Chicago, which Gertrude Stein had read and did not like, was gone, but
he knew Gertrude had been right and that it wasn't very good. The six
true sentences written about Paris that he had labored to write perfectly
were among the loss, but Ezra told him he could recover them by rewrit-
ing because they were in his mind, and this he would do (they may also
have been found in a notebook that had been overlooked). There were
also some sketches and stories he had been working on, but if they were
any good he could rewrite them too. All of it was beginnings that would
have been discarded or rewritten. Ernest Hemingway knew that such
losses could be overcome. He would recover from this heartbreaking loss.
His confidence would quickly recover too. The most damaging effect was

---

51. Hemingway, *88 Poems*, 63.

to his marriage. His trust and faith in Hadley were not destroyed, but it would never be so certain and sure as before. Hadley would feel the pain of losing the manuscripts for the rest of her long life.

There was not much time for self-pity in Lausanne. He had to keep the wire service open and file his bulletins morning, noon, and night. He kept his anger toward Hadley in check. They even took a day off at Mason's expense and took a train to Montreux and the funicular to Chamby where they bobsledded down a snow-covered road in the rose light of a sunset. He did explode on Mason when, following a dispute of his expenses—Mason requesting receipts—Ernest flashed back a wire: Request You Upstick Your Books Assward—Hemingway. The next day, he sent a letter explaining his anger. Mason, not knowing about the lost work, was probably puzzled by the disproportion of Ernest's angry response. There would be no treaty signed at Lausanne until February of the following year. Though his work was unfinished, Hemingway shut down the I.N.S. wire service on Saturday, December 16, and checked out of the hotel with Hadley. They met Chink Dorman-Smith at the station, rode the short rail ride to Montreux, and then went up the mountain to Chamby where they relaxed and ate and drank hot rum punch. The time in Lausanne with Hadley had been more expensive than he liked: the hotel where they stayed cost three times a month's rent in Paris, and nights on the town dancing with Hadley to help her get over the loss, too, added to the costs. But a new chapter would begin in his life as he was closer than he may have known to becoming the writer that he wanted to be.

Young and resilient, Ernest's spirits were high during the holidays luxuriating in the cold, clear air of the snow-covered mountains of Switzerland with Hadley and Chink and friends who came visiting. Together, Chink and Ernest and Hadley drank and roistered like a comedy act, each playing off each other's lines. Chink remembered Ernest singing a bawdy song at a party at the hotel in Les Avants at Christmas that in Ernest's words "displeased the more respectable members of the audience."[52]

52. Reynolds, *Hemingway: The Paris Years*, 93.

Each day, they rode the electric tram winding up through the woods and snow-covered fields to Les Avants, where they took the cable railway to the ski and bobsled runs on the Col de Sonloup. The O'Neil family, Hadley's wealthy friends from St. Louis, staying at the hotel in Les Avants, was there to celebrate with them. Christmas Day came cold and clear with powder snow over a deep base, plenty of wood for the evening fire, and hot rums all around. Laughing and joking through the clear, cold days into the starry nights, Chamby was as good as Lake Walloon had been in the summer. Ernest, wearing a shapeless black hat, often went bobsledding with seventeen-year-old George O'Neil, who became a close companion during their time together. (The other O'Neil child, a teenage daughter named Barbara, became an actress who played the role of Scarlett O'Hara's mother in *Gone with the Wind*.)

After the New Year, when Chink's leave ended, Isabelle Simmons, an old friend from Oak Park, arrived to take his place. They went out skiing every day, sweeping down the saddle of the Dent de Jaman and coming home at dusk along a road so icy that someone slipped every twenty yards. "We both became quite good [at skiing]," remembered Hadley. "I started jumping even [though] my uterus objected."[53] Within a few days Izzy, Hadley, Barbara O'Neil (the mother), and a lovely young woman named Janet Phelan began calling themselves "Hemingway's harem."[54] Growing up in a house full of sisters who left their imprint on his memory, Ernest had been accustomed to their worship and was always fond of rooms filled with women. Hadley understood his need for female presence, and as they sipped drinks by the fire, she shared him with the others in high humor. Ernest could not be feminine, not even in the role reversal games he played with Hadley, but he was interested in feminine sensibilities. His first mature story, "Up in Michigan," took a young girl's point of view. To write with sensitivity, a man must cultivate the feminine side of himself, and in "Up in Michigan" the girl and her seducer were both himself, both coming out of his imagination and experience. Women's hair stimulated his erotic imagination: his sisters drying their hair in the summer sun;

---

53. Mowrer, Sokoloff tapes, Hemingway Collection, JFK Library.
54. Mowrer, Sokoloff tapes, Hemingway Collection, JFK Library.

the long flowing hair, as in pre-Raphaelite portraits, of his mother or Gertrude Stein; the short, mannishly styled female hair so popular in the twenties. At Chamby, Ernest began letting his hair grow to reach the bobbed length of Hadley's so they could be the same person, man and woman blending into one sexual union. But it suddenly became difficult to maintain an idyllic shared oneness because, despite the precautions they took during her fertile period, while they were vacationing Hadley became pregnant.

In the early morning, as they laughed and joked through the first weeks of the New Year, Ernest worked on his Paris sentences and there appeared in his writing a terse new form of putting words together that extended the emotionally detached sentences into paragraphs. The first jerky, broken-off attempt he called "Romance:"

> In the moonlight the long alley of trees
> in the Luxembourg gardens were sharp and black. The boy
> and girl stood against the iron fence looking
> hungrily in at the shadows[55]

He was beginning something, he did not know what; it had never been this way before, but it was going somewhere. Late in January he wrote to Ezra, "I suppose you heard about the loss of my Juvenilia? I went up to Paris last week to see what was left and found that Hadley made the job complete . . . Am now working on some new stuff."[56] Pound called the loss "an act of Gawd," telling Ernest that "no one is known to have lost anything by suppression of early work."[57] The lost manuscripts were not a permanent wound. The wellspring of his writing, a source which he feared to analyze, was fulfilling itself anew.

Ezra and Dorothy Pound were spending the winter in Rapallo. He wrote to Ernest, urging him to join them. Mike and Maggie Strater were there. Ernest could box with Mike and they could all play tennis doubles

---

55. Reynolds, *Hemingway: The Paris Years*, "Romance," 97.
56. EH to EP, Jan.23, 1923, *Letters of Ernest Hemingway, Vol. 2*.
57. Reynolds, *Hemingway: The Paris Years*, 95.

together, and he and Hadley could accompany the Pounds on a tour of the Romagna region walking in the footsteps of Sigismondo Malatesta, a medieval poet and soldier about whom Ezra was writing cantos. "As I was very vague as to who Sigismondo was," remembered Ernest, "and had no wish to eat bad food and sleep in poor inns in Italy in February following the trail of a historic personage, . . . I put off going as long as possible."[58] But when the snows of Chamby began melting to slush, and Hadley announced a coming birth and thought her first pregnancy would do better in the warm sun by the Mediterranean, they packed their bags and took an express train from Montreux to Milan, where they celebrated with a dinner at Campari's so good that Ernest called it the best restaurant in Europe. The next morning, they boarded a train that carried them past the flat fields and vineyards to Genoa and down to the coast, where hidden in an amphitheater of hills coming down to the water was the old fishing village of Rapallo. They found the Hotel Riviera Splendide on the beach road behind tall palm trees and from their upper-story room could look down upon the promenade with the statue of Columbus at the far end.

Mike and Maggie had just had a baby, making Hadley feel better, but Mike sprained an ankle and Ezra and Dorothy soon left for Rome so there wasn't much boxing or tennis. After weeks in the clear, bracing mountain air, Ernest was dissatisfied with the muggy seaside days. One day he looked out the window and saw two cats playing in the rain on a green table in the garden. "The sea is weak and dull here," he wrote Gertrude Stein. "When the surf breaks it sounds like someone pouring a bucket of ashes over the side of a scowl. The place ain't much."[59] When the breeze died, the air smelled of dead fish. He was also having a hard time working on his new style of writing: the clear, sharp sentences that became clear, sharp paragraphs when he wrote in the mornings at Chamby. "It was a very bad time," he wrote of Rapallo in retrospect. "I did not think I could write any more."[60] He tried to write by free association as Gertrude Stein

58. Baker, *Hemingway: A Life Story*, 138.
59. EH to GS, Feb. 18, 1923, *The Letters of Ernest Hemingway, Vol. 2*.
60. Baker, *Hemingway: A Life Story*, 139.

had shown him—"I've thought a lot about the things you said about working and am starting that way at the beginning"—also asking, "If you think of anything else I wish you'd write it to me."[61] Besides talent and much hard work, a man needed confidence and timing to succeed, and though it didn't seem so at first, Hemingway's timing at Rapallo was perfect. Hadley remembered "Rapallo was beautiful," and she found the Straters "congenial."[62] The town was quaint, with open-air markets and excellent food. The garlicky pesto clinging to linguini bathed in sweet walnut sauce was outstanding.

Mike Strater's sprained ankle kept him in his hotel room during the Hemingways' first week there, which gave the men the opportunity to quietly discuss the similarities between their arts while Mike painted Ernest's portrait. Modern painting bore little resemblance to narrative fiction, for Picasso and Braque and Matisse and Magritte had abandoned storytelling to bring out another way of looking and thinking by emphasizing the flatness of the canvas and exposing their illusions as fake. Hemingway was a modern in technique and material, but even as experimental as he had become, he wrote to tell a story and would never abandon that reason. Sitting in the light by the window with Mike on a stool concentrating and looking and resting his ankle, Ernest would walk over and peer at himself forming on the canvas. The first painting had a gray background and he thought he looked too much like H. G. Wells, so Mike painted another with a red background and made his face tougher like a boxer. If a painter could change the light, move the lines, shift the color, and alter the reality until it suited his purpose, Ernest realized that a writer could too. Reality was not art: if the light needed to change or the images to shift to make his point, then, like the painter, he could change what he knew and what he saw and heard to meet the necessity of the purpose of his story. The artist or writer did not put everything into a painting or story, and what was left out was still invisibly present if he did it right. As Ezra had said, fiction and painting were both based

---

61. EH to GS, Feb. 18, 1923, *The Letters of Ernest Hemingway, Vol. 2.*
62. Reynolds, *Hemingway: The Paris Years*, 102.

on selection. The second painting Hadley liked; she thought that his long hair made him look like Balzac.

As Mike's ankle improved, they began playing tennis, and Ernest came to know a visiting editor who wanted to publish his short story. Ezra had introduced him to Edward O'Brien, who was boarding at a monastery in the hills above Rapallo. O'Brien was a shy and gentle man from Boston who had written a volume of poetry and each year since the war had edited a volume of the best short stories. He was gathering material for a new anthology, *The Best Short Stories of 1923*. Hemingway visited him in the mountains, and they talked and drank. Edward asked to see Ernest's fiction. Ernest gave him a crumpled typescript of "My Old Man," which O'Brien read in the monastery and thought was a splendid piece of work. He wanted it for his next anthology. Usually, he selected stories that had already appeared in magazines but would make an exception with "My Old Man." Ernest would, at last, have one of his works between hard covers. This sent his spirit soaring. In an unpublished piece called "Rapallo," Hemingway wrote that he and Hadley were "happy sometimes," but "happiest in bed,"—that there were "no problems in bed"[63]—words that were not the words of a man hurt and dissatisfied with his wife. He proposed to John Bone a feature tour of Germany's Ruhr industrial area, which the French had occupied the month before to squeeze out war reparation payments, and began to write steadily again, working on his own terse sentences, trying to perfect his métier, crafting his unwritten stories into finely chiseled paragraphs.

There had soon appeared in Rapallo another friend of Ezra's, a strange, creative man named Robert Menzies McAlmon, who quickly met both the Hemingways and Straters when he arrived at the Splendide Hotel. McAlmon was short and lithe like an acrobat, had tight, thin lips under a sharp nose, blue eyes that often held a hard expression, and was attractive to both men and women. T. S. Eliot said he was "a very charming man of lively intelligence and amiable personality."[64] Riding a wave of social success in Paris, he knew the bookstores and all the joints

---

63. Reynolds, 104.
64. Mary Dearborn, *Ernest Hemingway*, 143.

on all the boulevards. "He was certainly the most popular member of 'the Crowd,' as he called it," remembered Sylvia Beach. "Somehow he dominated whatever group he was in. Whatever café or bar McAlmon patronized at the moment was the one where you saw everybody."[65] McAlmon had met nearly everyone in Paris, from Constantin Brancusi to Nancy Cunard, and knew hell's own amount of gossip—something which at first endeared him to Hemingway, who soon wrote to Ezra, "McAlmon has given us the dirt on everybody. It is all most enjoyable."[66] McAlmon warmed to Mike, who was, he wrote, "a Southerner, not only unpretentious, but actually modest," but felt uneasy with Hemingway: "He was a type outside my experience," he remembered; there were "suspicions lurking in his peering analytical glances at the person with whom he was talking."[67] James Joyce, who knew both McAlmon and Hemingway well, once remarked to Sylvia Beach, "that he thought it was a mistake, Hemingway's thinking himself such a tough fellow and McAlmon trying to pass himself off as the sensitive type. It was the other way around."[68]

Robert McAlmon had come to Rapallo for the sea breeze and to talk to Ezra, who was not there. He would come and go at a moment's notice but was an industrious writer who was a modern to the core and had recently founded the Contact Press in Paris to publish his own work and that of others. Hemingway was impressed by this fellow Midwesterner when they met that winter (McAlmon was born in Kansas to a Presbyterian minister) but recognized his sexual ambiguity as soon as he read some of his stories. He wrote Ezra, "He has done the village [Greenwich in New York], the coke head, Berlin night life and the homo . . . but three of the stories are the best short stories ever written."[69] Ezra tempered Hemingway's enthusiastic discovery. "I dare say the price is still a bit long," he wrote regarding Ernest's tip to "put a small bet on McAlmon."[70] Nor was Ezra impressed when Hemingway reported that

---

65. Sylvia Beach, *Shakespeare & Company*, 25.
66. EH to EP, Mar. 10, 1923, *The Letters of Ernest Hemingway, Vol. 2*.
67. Robert McAlmon, *Being Geniuses Together*, 157.
68. Beach, *Shakespeare & Company*, 78.
69. EH to EP, Feb.–Mar. 1923, *The Letters of Ernest Hemingway, Vol. 2*.
70. Mellow, *Hemingway: A Life Without Consequences*, 227.

McAlmon "has written 8 or 10 short stories while he has been here," replying, "7–9 stories in a week is a little too much, even for the young." Pound had avuncular relationships with both men and was glad they had met, but of the two it was Hemingway, not McAlmon, whom he chose to be included in Bill Bird's Inquest into the State of English Prose.

McAlmon was a bisexual who delighted in experiencing whatever action there was on the decadent fringes of society. But he was cool, he did not flaunt his sexuality, and Hemingway did not draw back from this man, who, in addition to his generosity, had a cynical turn of mind and a sharp and malicious tongue, and for a while they were friends. Hemingway probably tolerated him for as long as he did because McAlmon was so wonderfully connected to the literary scene. In New York, he was part of the *Contact* and *Little Review* circles; William Carlos Williams, Djuna Barnes, and Hilda Doolittle all knew McAlmon. But after marrying Winifred Ellerman, the daughter of a wealthy shipping magnate, he found himself a husband in name only, for Winifred, a lesbian writer who called herself Bryher, only wanted a husband to escape from the protective clutches of her strict parents and left for Italy to live with Hilda Doolittle, leaving McAlmon in Paris. Robert had genuine affection for his wife and was disappointed, but the arrangement produced a generous flow of cash from the Ellermans that allowed him to go into publishing and kept him independent, paying for his own keep and the bar bills of others, and enabling his support of needy friends like James Joyce, with whom he was close; in fact, McAlmon had typed and edited some of the handwritten pages of Joyce's *Ulysses* that were too cryptic for others to understand. Hard, shrewd, and sometimes bitchy, he was not without feelings and immediately recognized an edge in Hemingway created by verve, originality, and concentration, all modernist attributes, and wanted to publish his work.

McAlmon had written novels and poems and short stories with a hard-bitten sense of reality and at the age of twenty-six was thought by some to be the best of his generation. Ernest Walsh, the tubercular co-editor of *This Quarter*, called him "the most honest and authentically American of our writers, and the only man writing who can seriously

compete with Joseph Conrad and James Joyce."[71] His publishing venture got off to a memorable start, printing the poetry of William Carlos
Williams, Mina Loy, Marsden Hartley, two collections of his own short
stories, and a thinly disguised autobiographical novel by Bryher about a
lonely child who blooms into an artist. He was a discerning publisher who
esteemed his authors, and knowing he was taking a chance on an unpublished writer, that winter he decided to publish a book by Hemingway.
He read the few stories and poems Ernest had on hand in Rapallo and
thought "My Old Man" to be strongly influenced by Sherwood Anderson, but felt that "Up in Michigan" and, later, "Out of Season" were
"fresh and without derivation so far as I could detect."[72] McAlmon had
made some bad calls, but he was right about Ernest Hemingway when he
said he was "going places . . . a natural talent for the public eye . . . just
you watch him . . . Wherever the limelight is, you'll find Ernest with his
big loveable boyish grin, making hay."[73] Hemingway accepted the offer
with gratitude. Before he and Hadley left Rapallo, he wrote a satirical
poem about six women poets based on McAlmon's all-knowing gossip.
The poem suggested Ernest was an authority on the literary scene and
privy to inside information, though he really knew no more about Amy
Lowell or Edna St. Vincent Millay than what McAlmon had told him.
He enclosed the poem, "The Lady Poets with Footnotes," in a letter to
Pound, whom they were about to join on a three-day hike. His own terse
new form, which he was calling "unwritten stories," was starting to shape
up very well.

Near the first of March, the Hemingways joined the Pounds for a
three-day walk with rucksacks through the Malatesta sites, not in Mon-
tagna but among the hills and towns on the Italian coast, ending about
two-hundred miles south of Rapallo in the ancient Etruscan settlement
of Orbetello. "We had an awfully good time on that walking trip,"
remembered Hadley. "He [Pound] was ideal to go with because he knew
everything about every town and we picnicked every day on the side of

---

71. Kenneth Lynn, *Hemingway*, 195.
72. McAlmon, *Being Geniuses Together*, 158.
73. Dearborn, *Ernest Hemingway*, 144.

the hill somewhere with fresh Italian bread and figs and wine. Sometimes we would pick up a sausage. We just walked the whole time."[74] As Ezra provided historical background, Ernest imagined and tried to explain the siege and battles as they happened. Hemingway may have been amused by all the time Ezra spent studying his subject in dusty old libraries, but it was a lesson reinforced, for books were the ammunition for writing, because in fiction historical facts and accurate terrain are important. Though often underestimated as he shadowboxed down the street his first years in Paris, even as a young man Hemingway was contemplative. People didn't know how carefully he listened and that his mind caught and held voices almost as accurately as a tape recorder. They remembered him in the cafes on the boulevards but never saw him writing in his rented rooms; he is well remembered on the ski slopes of Switzerland, but at night he was reading Turgenev and Tolstoy. It was hard to see the whole man then; only a few knew how determined he was to master his craft and how quickly he learned from others.

He was already intentionally separating himself from the crowd by a review he wrote for Gertrude Stein of her newly published *Geography and Plays* that ran in the *Paris Tribune* that March. He had written to Gertrude from Rapallo, "Enclosed is the review . . . You can cut out any or all of it and if you don't like it I'll do another one."[75] The review is admiring, "Gertrude Stein is probably the most first rate intelligence employed in writing today," and points toward previous work, "the Melanctha story in Three Lives is one of the three best short stories in English,"[76] but the focus is really more on the reviewer and his growing insight and knowledge than on the author of *Geography and Plays*, of which he actually tells nothing except that by reading it a reader will probably think less of Sinclair Lewis, H. L. Mencken, and *The Saturday Evening Post*. He also taints D. H. Lawrence, H. G. Wells, the *Dial* magazine, and even Sherwood Anderson, suggesting they're the past and that Gertrude is the future. And since he is aligned with Stein, he is the future too. For, since arriving

---

74. Mowrer, Sokoloff tapes, Hemingway Collection, JFK Library.

75. EH to GS, Feb. 18, 1922, *The Letters of Ernest Hemingway, Vol. 2.*

76. EH review: "Geography and Plays," *Paris Tribune*, Mar. 5, 1923.

in Paris, Hemingway had met and read the works of Joyce, Pound, and Stein and had abandoned his goals and techniques of the years before. In this piece, he declares his independence from his earlier models, which were stories in the *Saturday Evening Post*, and readers might take him to be the most current voice in the literary world. The audience for this review was the Left Bank literary crowd whose allegiance for or against Gertrude Stein was already fixed.

Most of this crowd knew of Hemingway, had seen him in the cafes and heard that he was a disciple of Pound and Stein, but until this review, he had not yet had anything published to show his true skills. The review displayed that he was learning the simple lesson to believe in yourself or no one else will. He got this message from Pound, who was always willing to pontificate on others if it reflected well on himself. He saw it in Joyce, whose reputation as a genius flowered from his careful watering of the soil and the crop it produced. And he heard it from Stein, who with a straight face could say, "nobody has done anything to develop the English language since Shakespeare, except myself, and Henry James perhaps a little."[77]

In Italy, the Hemingways soon separated from the Pounds and in the second week of March traveled to Cortina in the Italian Dolomites for more skiing. Jane Heap, co-editor of the *Little Review*, asked Ernest to contribute to the spring "Exiles" issue of the magazine. He wanted to work on the sharp, clear sentences that were developing into paragraphs and send them to her in the mail. There were six of these short fictions, and all but one were the product of hearsay: three about the war in France, two of which came from Chink; one about bullfighting from listening to Mike Strater; one about the killing of the Greek ministers responsible for the Anatolia disaster, which he lifted from newspaper reports; and one from his own experiences—the refugees retreating from Thrace. He worked to get them perfectly right, taking out dead and unspecific words, paring away details until only the hard essence remained. They were written in a detached voice describing tightly focused events that were small pieces of modern times. Unlike most young writers, Hemingway hardly

---

77. Reynolds, *Hemingway: The Paris Years*, 111.

used his own life as material for his very early fiction. But he so carefully provided his readers with his own special perspective that they thought he was writing out of firsthand experience. From his newspaper work, he had developed great confidence in his ability to create fiction from secondary sources, to write about what he had not experienced. That first year, however, his greatest difficulty was learning how to use his own experience in his writing.

In the small mountain village of Cortina, the cool spring air hung over broad fields of snow where the valley widened and enormous rocky peaks appeared to draw back to let in the sun during the daylight hours. The Hemingways relaxed and skied, and inspired by the mountains and cool, crisp air, Ernest continued to refine his six short pieces until they were like miniatures in motion that would detonate like grenades inside the reader's head. The hotels were mostly empty—another Hemingway off-season bargain. Isabelle Simmons joined them at the Bellevue where they also met a gifted pianist named Renata Borgatta, who was one of the lovers of painter Romaine Brooks and a regular at Natalie Barney's salon. Renata and Hadley went walking and shopping along the short, slanted street in blue berets and sturdy mountain boots. Ernest viewed Renata as one of the guys; she, in turn, was convinced that he was a young man who would definitely make his mark. In chummy discussions Renata told them about the lesbian loves of Natalie Barney and how currently there wasn't much of it, gossip that Hemingway wickedly passed on to Gertrude and Alice, eventually informing them in a letter that Barney "never gets any sexual satisfaction . . . because she no longer has any attraction and she has to be attractive, so she takes it out in polar bearskins and polar bear pajamas and . . . her mind . . . has all the charming quality of a dog's in heat."[78] How the misses Stein and Toklas received the information is not really known, but they may have thought less of the bearer.

For three months, since the Lausanne Conference, Hemingway's only work had been on his fiction. On March 18, his literary labors were interrupted by the cable from John Bone approving of Ernest's proposal

_____
78. EH to GS, Aug. 28, 1924, *The Letters of Ernest Hemingway, Vol. 2.*

for a series of articles on the troubled French occupation of the Ruhr in retaliation for Germany's failure to meet reparation payments. Bone suggested a series of eight to ten articles over four weeks on a salary and expense basis. Hemingway did not want to leave Hadley, whose pregnancy was now definite, nor the fiction that was going so well, but work was important if they were to return to Toronto in the fall, so instead of spending a month on the Ruhr he would do it quickly and return to Cortina in a couple of weeks. He caught the train and was in Paris by Friday, March 23, where he gave Jane Heap the miniatures, which were grouped together in the April issue under "*in our time*" to reflect the current years in Europe, and he started working again as a foreign correspondent for the *Star*, gathering material for his assignment.

Ernest claimed that he was a writer not interested in being called an artist, at least not the kind who talked about their art, its theory, and how it related to the grand scheme of literary flow. Everyone on the Left Bank was an artist, sitting around in the cafes talking and not working. He was always working. Writers wrote stories, not art, and did not pontificate about their work. (Yet Ezra and Gertrude talked about art and their work and he did, however, admire them.) But he would not be an artist; the Latin Quarter housed too many poseurs for him to feel easy with that identity. Yet he was growing his hair down to his collar and his fiction was beginning to appear in arty little magazines and amateur Left Bank publications. The emotional dichotomy he felt toward himself was that of a sensitive, ambitious young man who did not want to be a journalist either, though that was how he was also known to those who knew of him in Paris. But his work as a reporter was maturing, especially when he was engaged with the subject, and the political analysis and exposition of the articles he wrote about the Ruhr were outstanding and beautifully written.

His first report began with a short paragraph: "To write about Germany you must begin by writing about France. There is a magic in the name France. It is a magic like the smell of the sea or the sight of blue hills or of soldiers marching by. It is a very old magic." And the next paragraph went further: "France is a broad and lovely country. The loveliest country that I know. It is impossible to write impartially about a country when you love it. But it is possible to write impartially about the government of that country." He followed these beautiful, logical lines with a sharp, insightful exposition on the politics that led France into the mistake of occupying the Industrial region of the Ruhr. "France refused in 1917 to make a peace without victory. Now she finds that she has a victory without peace. To understand why this is so we must take a look at the French government."[79] In his interviews with politicians, he had discovered an undercurrent of opposition. He delineated in the articles the makeup and balance of the political parties in the Chamber of Deputies that created an unwanted military occupation that was costing much more than it could ever produce and the corruption of the French press by the threat of government subsidies withdrawn if the news was not to its liking. The first three articles were written in Paris, followed by seven from the Ruhr.

The articles he wrote from Germany were written more colorfully on situations and personalities with good descriptions of the places, "From Offenburg to Ortenburg . . . I rode in a motortruck. . . . We crossed a wide, swift, clearly pebbled stream with a flock of geese resting on a graveled island. . . . in the distance were the blue Schwarzwald hills,"[80] and reported on the bitter attitude of Germans and the unseen poverty caused by the extreme inflation of the German mark. His account of the French takeover of the rail lines at Offenburg and the refusal of the German mining companies to ship coal to France, his scathing remarks about German industrialists who sold on the market for pounds and dollars but paid the workers in useless marks, and his reporting on the economic hardships of the German people made it clear that his sympathies lay with the victims of the political and economic manipulation that was a consequence of the Versailles treaty. He gave a reasoned account of the French failure in the Ruhr, citing the huge cost of maintaining a standing army and hired laborers in Germany.

---

79. *Toronto Daily Star*, April 14, 1923.
80. *Toronto Daily Star*, April 25, 1923.

His managing editor, John Bone, was delighted with the effort and urged his readers in the *Star* to follow "these intensely interesting articles" that were written by "Ernest Hemingway, Who Is Taking the Lid Off Europe,"[81] giving the stories front page illustrated coverage. "An important addition even to the Lloyd George articles," one of the blurbs announced, "are those by Hemingway, who is well known to thousands of *Daily Star* readers."[82] His reporting also demonstrated that, unlike the heady, confusing sense of exoticism of many American treatments of the expatriate experience, Hemingway understood and identified with a country not his own and displayed a calm utilization of the European background. Writing to his father, who had complimented him on the series, Hemingway said with some modesty, "Lord knows I worked hard on them . . . They handle the show pretty well, at least make it an actual thing to people instead of simply a name on the map."[83]

While in Paris waiting for his visas to go to Germany, he had gone by 27 rue de Fleurus and shown Gertrude his new form of almost-stories before giving them to Jane Heap in time for the "Exiles" issue of the *Little Review*. Both women were impressed. Hemingway did not know how his creative process worked and worried that any intrusion, such as Bone's request for reporting, would stop the well from flowing. If he knew that fiction and non-fiction flow from the same source, he might have worried less. When he rejoined Hadley in Cortina the snow was gone but the atmosphere was still heady. His creative energy flowed anew, and he wrote "Out of Season," the first full-length story since the loss of his manuscripts. He lifted the events from an aborted fishing expedition that happened to himself and Hadley in Cortina after a morning argument. The story is about a young married couple and a down-at-the-heel villager named Perduzzi who takes them fishing out of season. While writing the story, Hemingway discovered the infinite possibilities of a new narrative technique that consisted of simultaneously developing two intrinsically related truths, such as a good poet does

81. Fenton, *The Apprenticeship of Ernest Hemingway*, 205.
82. Fenton, 222.
83. EH to CEH, June 20, 1923, *The Letters of Ernest Hemingway, Vol. 2*.

with a metaphor that really works. The "out of season" theme applied with equal force to the young man's relations with his wife, Tiny, and the officious insistence by the guide that the young man fish for trout in defiance of the local laws. The confluence of the emotional atmospheres was successful. It was a foremost aesthetic discovery that Hemingway would improve upon throughout his career as he would repeatedly display his gift as a prose poet.

Foreign correspondent with *Toronto Star*

Le Rotonde

Palazzo di San Giorgio interior

William Bird

Benito Mussolini

Georges Clemenceau

Luxembourg Gardens

Constantinople

Greek flight in Thrace

The Boxer portrait by Strater

Gare de Lyon

Hemingway and Steffens

Bobsledding

Rapallo

Robert McAlmon

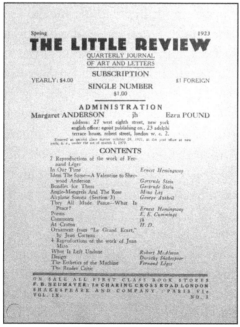

Little Review Exiles number

LA PASIÓN DE LA CORRIDA
DE TOROS

ETURNING TO Paris early in May after months in the cold,
clear mountain air, the heat and humidity were a struggle, but
the franc was lower, reducing the real cost of their small musty apartment to seventeen dollars a month. Since coming to Europe with Hadley, Ernest had spent most of his time away from Paris, on vacations
and assignments, and had written ninety-five feature articles for the *Star*.
Another wire soon came from Bone asking him to go to Russia, where
England was threatening to break fragile diplomatic relations with the
Bolshevik government and tight censorship kept the world from knowing if Lenin had recovered from a reported stroke. Ernest declined and
wired Bone on May 11: "Russia unfeasible for me at present." He could
not leave Hadley alone for another month and needed time to work on
the book of vignettes he was writing for Ezra's "Inquest" series.

He gave McAlmon the typescript of the book they had decided to
call *Three Stories & Ten Poems*, which included "Out of Season," and in
the cool of the morning, he continued to work on his new fiction with
Hadley pregnant and a new puppy in the room. The ideas kept coming,
the writing went smoothly, and he soon finished eleven small fictions that
were mostly about violence and crime. One was about a wounded young
soldier in love with a nurse in a hospital in Milan who returns to Chicago
with a promise of marriage that was soon discarded and catches gonor-
rhea from a salesgirl while riding in a taxi through Lincoln Park. This
vignette was truly a short story, which Hemingway would later rewrite

and title "A Very Short Story." He knew the vignettes were good but he still needed more of them and thought he could get new ideas in Spain.

Hemingway heard about bullfights from Gertrude and Alice and had read a poem that Gertrude wrote about the matador Juan Belmonte with flashes of color during a *corrida de toros* and the aficionados' gossip in the cafes. In Rapallo, he had so carefully listened to Mike Strater talk about bullfights that he was able to construct a fine vignette about matadors struggling against bulls in the ring that appeared in the "Exiles" issue of the *Little Review*. He hungered to go to Spain and see real bullfights. "The only place that you could see life and death, i.e. violent death now that the wars were over, was in the bull ring," he wrote years later, "and I wanted very much to go to Spain where I could study it. I was trying to learn to write, commencing with the simplest things and one of the simplest things of all and the most fundamental is violent death."[1] With Hadley pregnant and a return to Toronto imminent, his prudent nature stopped him from spending the money, but an opportunity came to go to Spain with Robert McAlmon. According to McAlmon, when he mentioned he was planning a trip to Spain, Hadley responded, "Oh Hem would like to go there too. He does want to see a bullfight,"[2] and became so persistent that out of sheer exasperation he suggested Hemingway join him. McAlmon would pay the bills and Bill Bird would join them later. They left for Madrid early in June. Both men were heavy drinkers used to dominating conversations and got on the train well lubricated with whiskey.

Hemingway and McAlmon did not make an easy pair. Robert McAlmon was far from a saint but could display an even temper and behaved better to Hemingway in Spain than Hemingway behaved toward him. The conflict between them rose early in the trip and it came from Ernest when their train stopped at a rail yard next to a flatcar with the maggot-eaten corpse of a dog. McAlmon looked away, but Hemingway stared and "gave a dissertation on facing reality," advising "a detached and scientific attitude." Remembering the war and all the dead, he

---

1. Ernest Hemingway, *Death in the Afternoon*, 91.
2. James R. Mellow, *Hemingway: A Life without Consequences*, 234.

"tenderly explained that we of our generation must inure ourselves to the sight of grim reality." Unmoved, McAlmon recalled Ezra speaking of Hemingway's "self-hardening process." Finally, Hemingway asked, "Hell, Mac, you write like a realist. Are you going to go romantic on us?"[3] With the stench of the dog in his nostrils, Bob cursed and went to the dining car for a whiskey where Ernest soon joined him. But Hemingway's self-hardening process was not as absurd as it appeared, for like the reporter he was, Hemingway made notes on everything, including the sight of the dead dog outside the window. "Death in the sun," he wrote in his note-book, "black—shiny and tar like, lumpy, sun glints, maggots squirm:" observations that would resurface in "A Natural History of the Dead," where he would write that dead "flesh comes to resemble coal-tar . . . it has quite a visible tarlike iridescence."[4]

When Ernest Hemingway saw his first bullfight, he immediately understood the spectacle of la corrida de toros as a metaphor for the bru-tality and ultimate death in life—and that the best a person could do is to have the courage of a brave matador when he faces the deadly rush of the charging bull—and his admiration for Spain, the country and people whose culture could create such an event so extraordinary and meaning-ful, remained an unbounded emotion for the rest of his life. Neither had seen a bullfight before, and before the first one in Madrid they had a few drinks and kept a bottle of whiskey between them to calm their nerves if shocked. "Hemingway became at once an *aficionado*," wrote McAlmon, "that is, a passionate bullfight fan or enthusiast, intent upon learning all about the art."[5] Hemingway jotted down notes on everything: hats worn in Seville, late-hour dining in Madrid, the different sugar on the tables. Mostly he wrote about the bullfights; the expression on the face of the picador, the half-formed dung in the trailing entrails of a gored horse. He carefully watched how the matador behaved and the reactions of the crowd. On a postcard to Gertrude Stein he wrote, "Tomorrow six bulls of Martinez with Villalta . . . Boxing looks paler and paler."[6] They attended

3. Robert McAlmon, *Being Geniuses Together*, 160.
4. Michael Reynolds, *Hemingway: The Paris Years*, 130–31.
5. McAlmon, *Being Geniuses Together*, 161.
6. EH to GS, June 9, 1923, *The Letters of Ernest Hemingway, Vol. 2*.

several corridas and stayed at the inexpensive Pension Aguilar on Calle
San Jeronimo, recommended by Mike Strater, where the bullfighters
stayed. Strater had also recommended a fine old restaurant, probably
Botin's, where they baked suckling pigs on oak planks and served excellent wine. When Bill Bird joined them, he thought Hemingway "was
already behaving like a new initiate in a secret society"[7] and had become
possessive about bullfighting, listening carefully to the toreadors in the
hotel and learning their technical language. He also noticed that Ernest
snarled when he spoke to McAlmon.

Since leaving Paris as seemingly good friends, the tension between
Hemingway and McAlmon had steadily grown. There lurked within
Ernest a mean, bullying streak, which some people brought to the
surface without even trying, and as McAlmon could be unreasonably
bitchy ("I deplored New England and New Englanders," he wrote in his
autobiography as he also "deplored Germany . . . France and her police,
her provincials, and her virtual lack of imagination . . . the taste of Italian red wine"[8]) this would have grated against the son of Dr. and Mrs.
Hemingway and the idealism of Oak Park that, try as he might, Hemingway could never entirely discard. Also, McAlmon, being bisexual, may
have approached or teased other homosexuals in the streets, and while
Ernest was not a man to unduly rage against homosexuals, it would have
triggered his anger. When Bird arrived, Ernest was needling and baiting
Robert with unnecessary spite. Caught in the middle of their barbed
remarks, Bill Bird, kind and sensitive, quieted the friction, but as the tour
of corridas moved from Madrid through Seville, Ronda, and Grenada
their relationship still grew progressively sour. Hemingway kept badger-
ing and insulting McAlmon. At a flamenco performance that Robert
liked in Seville, Ernest growled, "Oh, for Christ's sake, more flamingos!"[9]
McAlmon maintained a stoic reserve. When he paid for a black lace
mantilla for Hadley that Hemingway said he couldn't afford, Bird took
McAlmon aside and informed him that Ernest had more money than he

7. Reynolds, *Hemingway: The Paris Years*, 129.
8. McAlmon, *Being Geniuses Together*, 134–35.
9. Carlos Baker, *Hemingway: A Life Story*, 145.

pretended to have. Bill complained to Hemingway, too, reminding him that McAlmon was paying the bills; Hemingway laughed a bitter laugh and said, "You know, I'll take anything from you,"[10] as an assurance he wasn't angry at Bill.

When they returned to Paris, Hemingway and McAlmon remained nominal friends with no longer any joy between them. Ernest complained to Sylvia Beach that McAlmon had kept him from serious observation and work in Spain by wanting to stay out all night. But, as McAlmon caustically observed, when they visited the nightspots, Hemingway could have left at any time. However, McAlmon still wanted to publish Hemingway and Hemingway became gracious again, inviting him along as part of the gang to the boxing match, a strange, small crowd of friends that included Mike Strater and Hadley, Ezra with his wild hair and velvet jacket, and the mannish Jane Heap in a man's haircut, white shirt, and tie and smoking a cigar. McAlmon soon announced his plans to publish *Three Stories & Ten Poems*, and Bill Bird was going to publish *in our time* on his old hand press on the Ile Saint Louis, which would take much longer than the printing services used by McAlmon in Dijon. Ernest set to writing more miniatures to add to the ones he had given to Jane Heap, prose that Bill had liked very much. He also wanted to return to Spain, as his enthusiasm for bullfighting was very strong. Alice Toklas had told him of a primitive fiesta in Pamplona at the foothills of the Pyrenees that attracted the bravest bulls and the best matadors and where in July some of the very best bullfighting in Spain took place. Hadley was eager to go too. They could escape the confinement of the flat with the perpetual droning music of the Bal Musette below them, and they decided it would be a stalwart influence for the baby inside her.

After his first trip to Spain, Ernest had returned to Paris to find Hadley in her sixth month of pregnancy, swollen and happy; "I discovered what I had been born for and I was exuberant," remembered Hadley. "It was very good for my ego."[11] Her face glowed, her red hair shined in the sun, and she was very much with Ernest. "She was more beautiful than

---

10. Kenneth Lynn, *Hemingway*, 208.
11. Hadley Mowrer, Sokoloff tapes, Hemingway Collection, JFK Library.

ever," Ernest wrote to Bill Horne, "and we loved each other very much and went everywhere together."[12] She listened to her husband's childlike enthusiasm for Spain. The country was too big, too open to take all in at first, he told her, and the meals were heavy with too many courses. There was the language barrier, but once the bullfights started none of that mattered for you didn't need to know Spanish to understand the drama on the sand. They visited Alice and Gertrude, where Ernest talked avidly about bullfights, demonstrating veronicas, and going to Pamplona. It was not a sport, he said, but a tragedy with the bull's death fated from the start. Alice, talking with Hadley and pouring tea, watched and listened carefully. Already wary of Ernest and how he made Gertrude's face light up, she was not enthusiastic about the Hemingways and their trip to Navarre. She and Gertrude had discovered Pamplona, and Alice, not one to share gratuitously with handsome young men, had misgauged Ernest's enthusiasm. Very much in the room, too, was Hadley, radiant in her pregnancy, reminding the lesbian couple of their forsaken biology. An evening of bulls and babies was uncommon talk in the studio at rue de Fleurus.

On a morning in early July, the Hemingways boarded a train in Paris that arrived in San Sebastian that night, and they took a bus the next day to the walled town of Pamplona where the Fiesta of San Fermin in the Basque country of Spain had just begun. They got off the bus with their bags and moved through the crowds in the streets to find their hotel room taken. With luck and belligerence—Ernest had both—they were given a nice room in a private house with a balcony looking down onto the dancing in the streets. "Dancing all day and all night," he wrote to Bill Horne, "wonderful music—drums, reed pipes, fifes." In the crowd there were "faces of Velasquez's drinkers, Goya and Greco faces, all men in blue shirts and red handkerchiefs—circling, lifting, floating dance. We are the only foreigners at the damn fair."[13] They arose every morning to watch a crowd of boys and young men, with red kerchiefs around their necks, rushing ahead of the charging bulls, channeled by wooden

---

12. EH to BH, July 17, 1923, *The Letters of Ernest Hemingway, Vol. 2.*
13. EH to BH, July 18, 1923, *The Letters of Ernest Hemingway, Vol. 2.*

barricades through the cobblestoned streets packed six deep at the edges, into the brilliant sunlight of the arena for the afternoon spectacles. The days and nights ran together with fireworks and music, parades of Riau-Riau dancers and papier-mâché giants, the crowded, noisy cafes on the square. They had never known anything like it. Hadley thrived in the chaos; Ernest took notes on everything, carefully recording details.

In the afternoons under the arcade along the square, they waited their turn, grabbed a sidewalk table, and sipped brandy, poured exactly to the etched line of the glass, until the bullfights began in the stadium. The first three days of bullfights were splendid, hot, dusty afternoons in the Plaza de Toros. Ernest warned Hadley about the gored horses, and when the time came she turned her face and concentrated on knitting baby clothes. She was not shocked or horrified but enjoyed the bullfights, observing and learning with her husband the styles and skills of each matador, coming to appreciate the nuances of a corrida, which Ernest was absorbing at an amazing rate. When the bull and matador began their dance, it was like watching a war from a ringside seat. "The tragedy is the death of the bull," he wrote Greg Clark, "the terrible almost prehistoric bull that runs with a soft run, can whirl like a cat . . . and is stupid and brave as the people of any country and altogether wonderful and horrifying. You never imagined any such power."[14]

Five of eight matadors were gored or tossed during those days, then earthquakes hit the region followed by a rainstorm, and the corridas were canceled for two days. When they resumed, the sandy arena was soggy and the matadors' capes were damp and heavy, but the matadors who fought had great names and gave brilliant performances. The Hemingways so liked Nicanor Villalta that if their child was a boy they agreed to name him Nicanor. On the Friday finale, Algabeno took over and killed five bulls. It was life imitating art, for Ernest's bullfight vignette based on Mike Strater's experience had described an afternoon when a young matador killed the last five bulls on the program. When they left Pamplona, Hemingway could talk of little else but bullfighting.

---

14. EH to GC, mid-July 1923, The *Letters of Ernest Hemingway, Vol.2.*

The Bastille Day celebrations in Paris paled after the fiesta in Pamplona. Friends were fascinated by descriptions of bulls and bullfights and some signed on for future tours. McAlmon observed that Ernest, who used to "prance about sparring at shadows, his lips moving, calling his imaginary opponent's bluff," had "substituted shadow-bull-fighting for shadow-boxing"[15] with an imaginary cape and brandishing sword thrusts into the shoulders of an imaginary bull. Though it was hot in the city, Hadley had a cold from all the joyful, restless activity in Spain. Ernest could not write at first because she was sick, and he could not sleep in the heat, he was doing all the housework, there were visitors, and the streets outside were noisy. He would start to write, but something would always interrupt the flow. In the mornings he bought rolls, made coffee, emptied the slop pails, cleaned the kitchen, and, at last, if he were lucky, found an hour to write before lunchtime. He lay awake at night worrying about writing. Hadley had a craving for waffles and muskmelons, so he rolled over and made coffee and became angry and frustrated because the sketch forming in his head was lost. But he had to finish the vignettes that had started in Chamby, and when the heatwave lifted on July 17 and the proofs of *Three Stories & Ten Poems* arrived, it pulled him out of his doldrums and into a productive cycle. He began writing letters, first a long one to Bill Horne about his first eighteen months in Paris, as a warmup to serious work. Ernest had kinder thoughts about fatherhood: "We're both crazy about having this young feller,"[16] he wrote in the letter to Bill. The weather continued to cool with halting rain, Hadley improved, and the words began to form and take shape. During the last ten days of July, he wrote five bullfight vignettes. The bullfight vignettes were vivid and fresh, always happening now, capturing the drama and violence of the ring.

When Hemingway showed Ezra his vignettes, Pound was enthusiastic but had him go back and rewrite the one about Maera's death because he didn't like it ending in a hospital. Ernest rewrote it, concentrating and not straying from how he truly felt it should be, and had him die

---

15. McAlmon, *Being Geniuses Together*, 161.
16. EH to BH, July 18, 1923, *The Letters of Ernest Hemingway, Vol. 2.*

after being taken from the ring: "Maera felt everything getting larger and larger and then smaller and smaller. Then it got larger and larger and larger and then smaller and smaller. Then everything commenced to run faster and faster as when they speed up a cinematograph film. Then he was dead."[17] Ezra questioned the arrangement of the vignettes too, asking if the experiment had a controlling logic. Ernest had not seemed to write with a larger plan but now he was forced to arrange a sequence. Nor did Ezra like the titles ("too cute") that Ernest gave each vignette. He also thought there needed to be more frozen moments for the book to feel right. Ernest came up with two more vignettes: the hanging of an Italian gangster in Chicago and an interview with the deposed king of Greece and his wife in a rose garden they were confined to, which was based on an anecdote he had heard in Thrace.

Pound, ever the editor, especially on his own conceived "Inquest Series," was right about the ordering and taking out the ironic titles. Ernest changed the titles to numbers "headed Chapter 1, Chapter 2, etc.," and worked on the logic to make it clear.

> When they are read altogether they all hook up. . . . The bulls start, then reappear and then finish off. The war starts clear and noble just like it did . . . gets close and blurred and finished with the feller who goes home and gets the clap. The refugees leave Thrace, due to the Greek ministers, who are shot. The whole thing closes with the talk with the King of Greece and his Queen in their garden.[18]

He wrote the last ones in his room on Cardinal Lemoine, recreating them as if he were there. In all, there would be eighteen sketches for Bird's upcoming volume *in our time*, which would not be released until the following year because of the time it took for Bill to hand print each volume on his old press. The page proofs of the book produced by McAlmon came, and Ernest showed it to Bill Bird and Gertrude Stein,

---

17. Hemingway, *in our time*, Three Mountains Press, Paris, 1924.
18. EH to EP, Aug. 5, 1923, *The Letters of Ernest Hemingway, Vol. 2.*

asking for advice on typeface and layout. In a letter to McAlmon, he enclosed a new cover design that Bird suggested and Stein approved, using a type less squatty and darker than that in the proofs. The result was plain, bold, and professional.

On August 13, the first copies of his slim grayish-blue book appeared in the windows of Sylvia Beach's bookstore. Ernest and Hadley looked at it a long time in the window before going inside, where Sylvia presented him with four author copies charged to McAlmon's account. *Three Stories & Ten Poems* was dedicated to Hadley, and they were both proud of the effort and results. Before leaving for Toronto, they said goodbye to Sylvia, who loaned them $100 to get them through until his first paycheck in Toronto. They packed up, crated their small paintings by Masson, Kumar, and Dorothy Pound, gave their mongrel puppy to Bill Bird for safekeeping, and said they would return in a year. Hadley was glad to abandon their tiny apartment. When they called on the Pounds, Ezra gave her a velvet brocade smoking jacket (which she would wear for years as a bathrobe) and took her aside to say, "Never try to change Hem. Most wives try to change their husbands. With him it would be a terrible mistake. When you come back from Canada with a baby you won't be the same."[19] Hadley had not really much liked Ezra because of his attitude toward women, whom he thought were inferior to men, but she never forgot those words.

They were ready to leave for Cherbourg when it was announced their ship's departure was delayed for nine days, an inconvenience during which their time was not recorded. Finally, it was August 26 when they departed for Toronto. Hemingway was glum about returning to Canada. "Christ," he wrote Isabel Simmons, "I hate to leave Paris for Toronto the city of churches."[20] But he had accomplished much in his years abroad thus far, and during those two years the fact that he was a foreign correspondent for a large Canadian newspaper had given him professional credence. Now, as the author of two books and soon to be a father, he was beginning to cast a shadow upon the world he knew.

---

19. Baker, *Hemingway: A Life Story*, 149.
20. EH to IS, June 24, 1923, *The Letters of Ernest Hemingway, Vol. 2*.

Hemingway and McAlmon in a bullring in Spain

Jane Heap

Margaret Anderson

The passion of the ring

Alice and Gertrude in the atelier

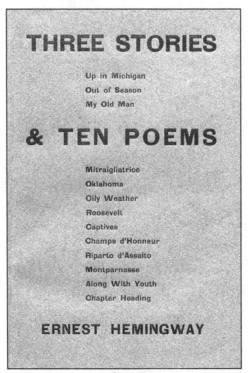

THREE STORIES

Up in Michigan
Out of Season
My Old Man

& TEN POEMS

Mitraigliatrice
Oklahoma
Oily Weather
Roosevelt
Captives
Champs d'Honneur
Riparto d'Assalto
Montparnasse
Along With Youth
Chapter Heading

ERNEST HEMINGWAY

Hemingway's first published book

SELECTED BIBLIOGRAPHY

Ackroyd, Peter. *Ezra Pound and His World*. New York: Charles Scribner's Sons, 1980.

Anderson, Sherwood. *Winesburg, Ohio*. New York: Huebsch, 1919.

———. *Triumph of the Egg*. New York: Huebsch, 1921.

———. *A Story Teller's Story*. New York: Huebsch, 1924.

———. *Death in the Woods & Other Stories*. New York: W.W. Norton & Co., 1933.

Baker, Carlos. *Ernest Hemingway: A Life Story*. New York: Charles Scribner's Sons, 1969.

———. "The Wastelanders." In *Hemingway: The Writer as Artist*. Princeton University Press, 1980.

Beach, Sylvia. *Shakespeare & Company*. Lincoln, Nebraska: University of Nebraska Press, 1956.

Berg, A. Scott. *Max Perkins: Editor of Genius*. New York: Riverhead Books, 1978.

Bloom, Harold. *Bloom's BioCritiques: Ernest Hemingway*. Philadelphia: Chelsea House Publishers, 2002.

———, ed. *Modern Critical Interpretations: Ernest Hemingway's* The Sun Also Rises. Philadelphia: Chelsea House Publishers, 1987.

Blume, Leslie M. M. *Everybody Behaves Badly: The True Story Behind Hemingway's Masterpiece* The Sun Also Rises. New York: Houghton Mifflin Harcourt Publishing, 2016.

Burrill, William. *Hemingway: The Toronto Years*. Toronto: Doubleday Canada Ltd., 1994.

Cowley, Malcolm. *Exile's Return: A Literary Odyssey of the 1920s*. New York: Penguin Books, 1994.

Curnutt, Kirk. *Ernest Hemingway and the Expatriate Modernist Movement*. Farmington Hills, Michigan: Gale Group, 2000.

Dearborn, Mary V. *Ernest Hemingway*. New York: Alfred A. Knopf, 2017.

Dell, Floyd. *Moon-Calf*. New York: Alfred A. Knopf, 1921.

Diliberto, Gioia. *Hadley, a Life of Hadley Richardson Hemingway*. London: Bloomsbury Publishing, 1992.

Donaldson, Scott. *Hemingway vs. Fitzgerald*. Woodstock, New York: Overlook Press, 1999.

———. "Hemingway's Morality of Compensation." In *American Literature* 43, no. 3 (November 1971).

Dos Passos, John Roderigo. *The Best Times: An Informal Memoir*. New York: Harper-Collins, 1968.

Duffey, Bernard. *The Chicago Renaissance in American Letters*. East Lansing: Michigan State University Press, 1956.

Fenton, Charles A. *Apprenticeship of Ernest Hemingway*. New York: Viking Press, 1954.

Griffin, Peter. *Along With Youth: Hemingway, The Early Years*. New York: Oxford University Press, 1985.

Hemingway, Ernest. *The Complete Short Stories of Ernest Hemingway*. New York: Scribner Paperback Fiction, 1987.

———. *A Moveable Feast*. New York: Charles Scribner's Sons, 1964.

———. *The Torrents of Spring*. New York: Charles Scribner's Sons, 1926.

———. *The Sun Also Rises*. New York: Charles Scribner's Sons, 1926.

———. *A Farewell to Arms*. New York: Charles Scribner's Sons, 1929.

———. *The Green Hills of Africa*. New York: Charles Scribner's Sons, 1935.

———. *Dateline: Toronto*. New York: Charles Scribner's Sons, 1985.

Hemingway, Leicester. *My Brother, Ernest Hemingway*. Greenwich, Connecticut: Fawcett Publications, 1963.

Hinkle, James. "What's Funny in *The Sun Also Rises*." In *Hemingway Review* 4, no. 2 (Spring 1985).

Josephs, Allen. "*Toreo*: The Moral Axis of *The Sun Also Rises*." In *Hemingway Review* 6, no. 1 (Fall 1986).

Joyce, James. *Dubliners*. New York: Viking Press, 1968.

Kennedy, J. Gerald and Jackson R. Bryer, eds., "*French Connections: Fitzgerald and Hemingway Abroad*. New York: Harper & Row, 1998.

Knopf, Josephine Z. "Meyer Wolfsheim and Robert Cohn: A study of Jewish Type and Stereotype." In *Tradition: A Journal of Orthodox Jewish Thought* 10, no. 3 (Spring 1969).

Lurie, Mark. *Galantiere, The Lost Generation's Forgotten Man*. West Palm Beach, Florida: Overlook Press, Inc., 2017.

Lynn, Kenneth S. *Hemingway*. New York: Simon & Schuster, Inc., 1987.

McAlmon, Robert. *Being Geniuses Together 1920–1930*. San Francisco: North Point Press, 1984.

Mellow, James R. *Hemingway, A Life Without Consequences*. Reading, Massachusetts: Addison-Wesley Publishing, 1992.

———. *Charmed Circle: Gertrude Stein & Company*. New York: Praeger Publishing, 1974.

———. *Invented Lives: F. Scott and Zelda Fitzgerald*. New York: Houghton Mifflin, 1984.

Meyer, Jeffrey. *Hemingway, A Biography*. New York: Harper & Row, 1985.

Milford, Nancy. *Zelda, A Biography*. New York: Harper & Row, 1970.

Miller, Madelaine Hemingway. *Ernie: Hemingway's Sister "Sunny" Remembers*. New York: Crown Publishers, 1975.

Mowrer, Hadley Richardson Hemingway. Letters to Ernest Hemingway, 1920-21. Hemingway Collection, JFK Library, Boston, Massachusetts.

Reynolds, Michael. *The Young Hemingway*. New York: W. W. Norton & Company, 1986.

———. "False Dawn: *The Sun Also Rises* Manuscript." In *A Fair Day in the Affections: Literary Essays in Honor of Robert B. White, Jr.*, 159-169. Edited by Jack D. Durant and M. Thomas Hester. Raleigh, North Carolina: Winston Press, 1980.

———. *The Paris Years*. New York: W. W. Norton & Company, 1989.

———. *The Homecoming*. New York: W. W. Norton & Company, 1992.

Rideout, Walter B. *Sherwood Anderson, A Writer in America*. Madison: University of Wisconsin Press, 2006.

Rodriguez, Suzanne. *Wild Heart: A Life: Natalie Clifford Barney*. New York: HarperCollins Publishers, Inc., 2002.

Sanderson, Rena, Sandra Spanier, & Robert W. Trogdon, eds. *The Letters of Ernest Hemingway, Volumes 1, 2, & 3*. New York: Cambridge University Press, 2015.

Sanford, Marcelline Hemingway. *At the Hemingways*. London: Putnam, 1963.

Sarason, Bertram D. *Hemingway and the Sun Set*. Washington, DC: NCR/Microcard Editions, 1972.

Sokoloff, Alice Hunt. *Hadley, The First Mrs. Hemingway*. New York: Dodd Mead & Company, 1973.

———. edited tapes of conversations with Hadley Mowrer, 1972.

———. Hadley Richardson Hemingway interview, 1972. Hemingway Collection, JFK Library, Boston, Massachusetts.

Spilka, Mark. "The Death of Love in *The Sun Also Rises*." In *Twelve Original Essays on Great American Novels*. Edited by Charles Shapiro. Detroit: Wayne State University Press, 1958.

Stein, Gertrude. *The Autobiography of Alice B. Toklas*. New York: Harcourt, 1933.

———. *Three Lives*. New York: Grafton Press, 1909.

Stephens, Robert O. "Ernest Hemingway and the Rhetoric of Escape." In *The Twenties, Poetry and Prose: Twenty Critical Essays*. Edited by Richard E. Langford and William E. Taylor. Everett Edwards Press, Inc., 1966.

Tompkins, Calvin. *Living Well is the Best Revenge*. London: Andre Deutsch, 1972.

———. "Living Well is the Best Revenge." *New Yorker*. July 20, 1962.

Townsend, Kim. *Sherwood Anderson*. Boston: Houghton Mifflin Company, 1987.

Tytell, John. *Ezra Pound: The Solitary Volcano*. Chicago: Ivan R. Dee, 1987.

Vance, William L. "Implications of Form in *The Sun Also Rises*." In *The Twenties, Poetry and Prose: Twenty Critical Essays*. Edited by Richard E. Langford and William E. Taylor. Everett Edwards Press, Inc., 1966.

Vopat, Carole Gottlieb. "*The End of The Sun Also Rises*: A New Beginning." In *Fitzgerald/Hemingway Annual, 1972*. Edited by Matthew J. Bruccoli and C. E. Frazer Clark Jr. Dayton, Ohio: National Cash Register Company, 1973.

Wagner, Linda W. "*The Sun Also Rises*: One Debt to Imagism." In *Journal of Narrative Technique* 2, no. 2 (May 1972).

White, Ray Lewis. *Sherwood Anderson's Memoirs*. Chapel Hill: University of North Carolina Press, 1969.

Wickes, George. "A Natalie Barney Garland." In *Paris Review/letters and essays*, Issue 61 (Spring 1975).

Wineapple, Brenda. *Sister Brother: Gertrude and Leo Stein*. New York: G. P. Putnam & Sons, 1996.

Wilhelm, J. J. *Ezra Pound in London and Paris: 1908–1925*. University Park: Pennsylvania State University Press, 1990.

Williams, William Carlos. *The Autobiography of William Carlos Williams*. New York: New Directions, 1967.

INDEX

ABOUT THE AUTHOR

WYLIE MCLALLEN grew up in Memphis, Tennessee where his family has deep historical roots. At the University of Tennessee, while obtaining a degree in History and English, he studied Fiction and Composition under a distinguished man of Southern Letters, Professor Robert Drake: Dr. Drake was a close friend of author Flannery O'Conner and was able to personally introduce his students to the poet and novelist James Dickey. Wylie worked as a programmer analyst at Malone & Hyde Inc., a wholesale grocery distributor in Memphis, and later owned a small business services center. He currently resides with his wife, Nickey Bayne, in Vancouver, British Columbia, where they have raised two grown children. He continues to write both history and fiction and is the author of *Tigers by the River*, a true story about the early years of professional football in America published by Sunbury Press, and soon-to-be released by Sunbury Press, a two-volume history of the early years of modern literature, *Hemingway and the Rise of Modern Literature*.

CPSIA information can be obtained
at www.ICGtesting.com
Printed in the USA
BVHW041238160423
662429BV00010B/13